A History of the Workplace

Interest in the history of the workplace is on the rise. Recent work in this area has combined traditional methods and theories of social history with new approaches and new questions. It constitutes a 'topical contact zone', a particularly dynamic field of research at the junction of social history, history of occupational health and safety, history of technology and the industrial environment. This book focuses on the new approaches in this important and growing area and their possible range of influence. These new attempts to rewrite a history of the workplace are multiple – and in some cases disparate – but share many key characteristics. They are turning away from the assumption that class and class conflict is the prime mover in social history, abandoning the traditional binomial 'workers vs. entrepreneurs' perspective which had long sustained the historical perspective on labour. Moreover, as this collections outlines, these new attempts concentrate on the analysis of complex social networks of actors that defined and configured industrial workplaces, suggesting a broadening of possible social actors.

This book was originally published as a special issue of the *European Review of History—Revue européenne d'histoire*.

Lars Bluma is a senior researcher at the German Mining Museum in Bochum, Germany. He is adjunct professor at the Historical Institute of the Ruhr University Bochum, Germany.

Judith Rainhorn is an associate professor at the Université of Lille-Nord de France, Valenciennes, France, a member of Esopp, EHESS-Sciences Po, Paris, France, and an alumna of the Ecole Normale Supérieure.

A History of the Workplace

Environment and Health at Stake

Edited by
Lars Bluma and Judith Rainhorn

Routledge
Taylor & Francis Group

LONDON AND NEW YORK

First published 2015 by Routledge

2 Park Square, Milton Park, Abingdon, Oxon, OX14 4RN
605 Third Avenue, New York, NY 10017

Routledge is an imprint of the Taylor & Francis Group, an informa business

First issued in paperback 2020

British Library Cataloguing in Publication Data
A catalogue record for this book is available from the British Library

ISBN 13: 978-1-138-80110-3 (hbk)
ISBN 13: 978-0-367-73982-9 (pbk)

Typeset in Times New Roman
by RefineCatch Limited, Bungay, Suffolk

Publisher's Note
The publisher accepts responsibility for any inconsistencies that may have
arisen during the conversion of this book from journal articles to book chapters,
namely the possible inclusion of journal terminology.

Disclaimer
Every effort has been made to contact copyright holders for their permission to
reprint material in this book. The publishers would be grateful to hear from any
copyright holder who is not here acknowledged and will undertake to rectify
any errors or omissions in future editions of this book.

Contents

Contents

Citation Information

The chapters in this book were originally published in the *European Review of History —Revue européenne d'histoire*, volume 20, issue 2 (April 2013). When citing this material, please use the original page numbering for each article, as follows:

Chapter 1
History of the workplace: Environment and health at stake – An introduction
Judith Rainhorn and Lars Bluma
European Review of History—Revue européenne d'histoire, volume 20, issue 2 (April 2013) pp. 171–176

Chapter 2
The hygienic movement and German mining 1890–1914
Lars Bluma
European Review of History—Revue européenne d'histoire, volume 20, issue 2 (April 2013) pp. 177–196

Chapter 3
The banning of white lead: French and American experiences in a comparative perspective (early twentieth century)
Judith Rainhorn
European Review of History—Revue européenne d'histoire, volume 20, issue 2 (April 2013) pp. 197–216

Chapter 4
Aluminium in health and food: a gradual global approach
Florence Hachez-Leroy
European Review of History—Revue européenne d'histoire, volume 20, issue 2 (April 2013) pp. 217–236

Chapter 5
Fiddling, drinking and stealing: moral code in the Soviet Estonian mining industry
Eeva Kesküla
European Review of History—Revue européenne d'histoire, volume 20, issue 2 (April 2013) pp. 237–254

Chapter 6
Hygienists, workers' bodies and machines in nineteenth-century France
Thomas Le Roux
European Review of History—Revue européenne d'histoire, volume 20, issue 2 (April 2013) pp. 255–270

Chapter 7
The factory as environment: social engineering and the ecology of industrial workplaces in inter-war Germany
Timo Luks
European Review of History—Revue européenne d'histoire, volume 20, issue 2 (April 2013) pp. 271–286

Chapter 8
The ideal of Lebensraum *and the spatial order of power at German factories, 1900–45*
Karsten Uhl
European Review of History—Revue européenne d'histoire, volume 20, issue 2 (April 2013) pp. 287–307

Please direct any queries you may have about the citations to
clsuk.permissions@cengage.com

Notes on Contributors

Lars Bluma is a senior researcher at the German Mining Museum in Bochum, Germany. He is adjunct professor at the Historical Institute of the Ruhr University Bochum, Germany. He obtained his PhD in 2004 from Ruhr University Bochum, Germany with a thesis on Norbert Wiener and the origin of cybernetics. After several years as a research fellow at the Ruhr University, Germany he was involved in a three-year research project (2007–9) dealing with the history of the miners' mutual-benefit society in Germany (Knappschaft). Within this research project, which was supported by the Leibniz-Gemeinschaft, he finished a study about health-care policy in German mining. His last research project on industrialisation and the miner's body has been supported by the German Research Foundation (DFG). His primary research interests are mining history and history of technology and science.

Florence Hachez-Leroy is an associate professor at the Faculté d'histoire et géographie of the Université Lille-Nord de France (Artois, France), and junior member of the Institut Universitaire de France. She is an associate researcher in the Centre de Recherches Historiques (EHESS/CNRS), in Paris. She obtained her doctoral degree in 1995 from the Université Paris IV-Sorbonne, France. Under the supervision of François Caron, she wrote a dissertation on the role played by a French cartel, L'Aluminium Français, to develop the market in France, from 1911 to the 1960s, and inside the different international aluminium cartels, to control the global market. Since then, she has been involved in numerous projects relating to the history of aluminium in Europe and North America, and has participated in many conferences on economic history and the history of technology. She carried out a research programme on aluminium in food packaging (*'Emballage et conditionnement alimentaires'*) with the support of the French National Research Agency (ANR). She is now in charge of the scientific part of a new ANR research programme on aluminium entitled 'Crealu: Creation and Aluminium – invention, innovation, markets (XIX–XXIth centuries)'.

Eeva Keskÿla received her PhD in Anthropology from Goldsmiths, University of London, UK, in 2012. Her thesis focused on the changing life and work practices, class and labour politics among Russian speaking miners in Estonia. She is currently working at the Max Planck Institute for Social Anthropology as a postdoctoral research fellow, in a research project entitled 'Industry and Inequality in Eurasia'. Her current project is about miners in Kazakhstan and Estonia. Her research interests include anthropology of industrial work and labour, class formation processes in post-socialism, historical anthropology.

Thomas Le Roux is a researcher at the CNRS (French National Center for Scientific Research) and is currently at the Maison Française d'Oxford. His work deals with the impact of early industrialisation on the environment from 1700 to 1850. His PhD dissertation (University of Sorbonne, Paris) focused on industrial nuisances in Paris (end of the eighteenth century and early nineteenth century). More recently, Le Roux has worked on a comparison between Paris and London, as well as occupational health and industrial accidents. He is running a collective research programme in the history of industrial accidents in France and Great Britain (seventeenth to nineteenth centuries), as well as a research seminar in Environmental History at Maison Française d'Oxford, involving French and British colleagues. His publications include *Laboratoire des pollutions industrielles. Paris, 1770–1830* (Paris, 2011).

Timo Luks (PhD) is an assistant professor at the Institute of European History (TU Chemnitz). His research interests include industrial history, the history of 'modernity' and, recently, police history.

Judith Rainhorn is an associate professor at the Université of Lille-Nord de France (Valenciennes, France), an alumna of the Ecole Normale Supérieure and a junior member of the Institut universitaire de France. She is also a member of ESOPP research cluster (Sciences Po/EHESS, Paris) on population and public policies. She has written her doctoral dissertation on Italian immigrants in France and the United States in a comparative perspective during the mass-migration era, published as *Paris – New York: des migrants italiens, années 1880 – années 1930* (Paris, 2005). Since then, she has been involved in numerous research projects which recently focus on health and environment in the workplace in an industrial context. She is now conducting research on the acknowledgment of occupational diseases, focusing on lead poisoning and white-lead paint in Europe in the twentieth century. In 2013, *Santé et travail á la mine, 19e–21e siécles* was published under her direction (Presses universitaires du Septentrion).

Karsten Uhl teaches History at the Darmstadt University of Technology, Germany. In 2012 he finished a research project on 'Humane Rationalisation? Factories' Spatial Order in a Fordist Century' which was accepted as *Habilitationsschrift* by TU Darmstadt, Germany. He has published a number of articles on the history of industrial labour, Nazi concentration camps, and the history of criminology. Along with Lars Bluma he edited the book *Kontrollierte Arbeit – DisziplinierteKörper? Zur Sozial- und Kulturgeschichte der Industriearbeitim 19. und 20. Jahrhundert* (transcript, 2012).

History of the workplace: Environment and health at stake – An introduction

Judith Rainhorn[a] and Lars Bluma[b]

[a]Université Lille Nord de France (Valenciennes), Institut Universitaire de France, Esopp-EHESS, France; [b]German Mining Museum, Bochum, Germany

The history of workplaces and especially industrial workplaces is a well-established field within the social history of labour, labour movement and industrialisation. In some ways, it is a classical field of historical investigation; founded in the social turn of historical science in the 1960s and 1970s, it lost its momentum in the 1980s. Coming along with the concurrent debate about the death of labour history, research on the history of workplaces was then widely neglected.[1] Since the establishment of social history as the dominant concept in historiography, the discussion on industrial workplaces took place within this methodological framework for the next two or three decades. A special challenge for the history of workplaces arose with the establishment of 'everyday history' in the 1980s and 1990s. Nevertheless, industrial-workplace conditions were still not considered as structural elements as important as wages, working hours or the rate of labour unionisation. It remained a place where class struggle became visible but was not a locomotive force of modernisation nor a specific focus for historians.

However, for a decade or two, there appears to be a new interest in historical workplace studies, which in part proceeds with traditional methods and theories of social history mostly applying new approaches and asking new questions. It constitutes a 'topical contact zone'[2], a particularly dynamic field of research at the junction of social history, history of occupational health and safety, history of technology and the industrial environment. The main target of this introduction to this growing field is neither to give a detailed overview about the social history of work in the last six decades nor to formulate a definite theory. We want to focus here on some new approaches and their possible range of influence. After this we will briefly introduce the articles of this special issue of *European Review of History* dealing with environment and health issues in the history of the industrial workplace in nineteenth- and twentieth-century Europe.

These new attempts to rewrite a history of the workplace are multiple – and in some cases disparate – but share many key characteristics. First, all of them are turning away from an approach consisting of assumptions that class and class conflicts are the prime movers in social history, abandoning the traditional binomial 'workers versus entrepreneurs' perspective, which had long sustained the historical perspective on labour. Moreover, these new attempts concentrate on the analysis of complex social networks of actors that defined and configured industrial workplaces, suggesting a broadening of possible social actors, which cannot be reduced to a simple dualistic class conflict between labour and enterprise. Overlapping interests and day-to-day conflicts beyond class affiliation seem to be the common case and also apply to social history in general. In particular, the traditional focus on institutional histories of organised labour was vanishing, making it necessary to reassess the ambiguous role of labour unions and associations in the workplace and in the main social issues of industrial work.[3] In this broad perspective, comparison between national cases definitely has a heuristic role to play, following Sellers' recent invitation to write a 'cross-nationalising history'[4] of workplace health and safety.

The national framework of labour history as a history of organised interest groups was called into question, and international organisations, networks and associations and their influence on national regimes of work and labour were now more and more often the focus of historians.[5] Beyond a comparative approach between national experiences, the recently theorised 'transnational turn' allows one to reassess the role of international movements and associations, as well as the circulation of ideas and concepts among industrial societies, institutions and states within the industrial world since the nineteenth century. As recent scholars have emphasised, we definitely think that the issues of the industrial workplace and of social policy gain from being assessed both in a comparative and transnational perspective.[6]

Secondly, at a lower scale, works which deal with the workplace in a historical perspective focus more and more on the mutual interaction of the workers' body and its workplace environment. As a consequence of this, these often deal with the problem of work-related diseases caused by this industrial environment. This renaissance of occupational health and safety as an important subject of history (and not only of the sub-discipline – history of medicine – where this topic was usually positioned) deals especially with the hazards of work processes. These include: the culture of work and risk; the influence of gender on occupational health; and the role of complex networks, including a wide range of players such as workers, medical experts, scientists, insurance entities, the government, managers and entrepreneurs. It also deals with the regulation of the work environment through a variety of techniques as well as with the interaction between the workplace and the workers' body.[7] In this context the regulation of industrial workplaces is seen as a way to achieve social control of workers and their bodies. This means that – for example – the spatial order of a factory or the health and safety instructions in mining around 1900 are manifestations of a specific social order or, in other words, are a significant part of the Western project of modernity. Consequently this approach overcomes a perspective which concentrates only on discipline and punishment in favour of a sophisticated view of multiple power relations manifested at the workplace. Therefore Karsten Uhl and Lars Bluma have recently advocated for a historical analysis of industrial workplaces on the basis of Foucault's concept of '*gouvernementalité*', which includes problems of human resource management in general.[8] Techniques of control using constraint and rigid regulations as well as managerial strategies of independent and autonomous work are in this perspective two sides of the same coin. Furthermore, using Foucault's concept of '*gouvernementalité*' makes it possible to connect the real actions taken in the workplace with the discourse and entanglements associated with power and knowledge. With this methodical concept, a historical reconstruction of industrial work is possible: one which describes labour as a form of political technology in which economic programmes and practices, discourses on rationalisation and modernity, as well as moral norms and discipline of the individuals were developed and linked with scientific knowledge – one produced by psychology, medicine, hygiene and physiology – all taken to define the worker's body in view of his productivity and vulnerability.

Finally, it seems that the European political framework plays a role in the emergence of these new perspectives, particularly in the growing sensibility of populations at risk, in whatever form (social, environmental, health or otherwise). Thus, this shift in labour history towards postmodern theories, post- and anti-Marxist thinking and the inclusion of gender concepts is best expressed by the conceptual reassessment of the Society for the Study of Labour History and its series of books (titled 'Studies in Labour History' published beginning in 1998.[9] As shown in recent research, the recently updated French historiography[10] has made the workplace one of the cores of the historical perspective on social movements, social policies and public health. The German debate on this new perspective in labour history is presented in a volume edited by Jürgen Kocka bringing together articles on the visions and discourse on work, on global dimensions of labour, on gender in work in a comparative perspective, and so on.[11] Kocka's statement that 'it is not yet clear what the leading questions and viewpoints structuring the history of work as a general field of research might be'[12] shows a great change for a well-established field of research to renew its perspectives, methods and theoretical framework to establish more connectivity to the leading debates in historiography in general.

The articles in this special volume of the *European Review of History* present different aspects of the industrial workplace in a historical perspective. They mainly focus on Germany and France in the nineteenth and twentieth centuries, with a look at Soviet-ruled Estonia and a comparative perspective with the United States. Beyond these historical experiences, this special issue intends to enlighten processes, stakeholders and specific timeframes which help us understand how working conditions – and especially the human body in the workplace – became an important subject of interest during the industrial era.

The articles presented here address three main historical themes. First, the vision of the workplace as a social environment subject to theoretical debates and practical implementations: Karsten Uhl and Timo Luks illuminate this. Karsten Uhl shows the linkage between the spatial order of fabrics and ways of exercising power at the workplace. His thesis is that at the beginning of the twentieth century, a debate about the so-called 'factory problem' was started that led to new governmental power over workers. Using Foucault's concept of '*gouvernementalité*' he reconstructs the debate of different actors such as architects, sociologists and engineers in the first half of the twentieth century dealing with the humanisation of work. This included concepts of workplaces in factories as a human habitat (*Lebensraum*) and as an environment which promotes the efficiency of workers not by external discipline, surveillance and punishment, but by self-discipline and by utilising the individuality of workers. Producing a humanised, beautiful and also efficient workplace was seen as a technique to increase the potential of the human factor in factory work.

That the spatial order of factories was at the centre of discussions about modernity in Germany shows in Timo Luks' article. Between 1920 and 1960, the fabric was addressed by sociologists, welfare workers and engineers as a spatial and social environment based on an all-embracing order of modernity. The rise of social engineering as a mode of rethinking modern societies to overcome social disintegration and fragmentation caused by industrialisation was a reaction of this discursive linkage of industrial work, environmental concepts of the factory and modernity. Luks' approach uses Foucault's idea of 'problematisation' as a totality of discursive and non-discursive practices that produces a particular problem as an object of mind, and the factory was such a 'problematisation'. Just as Karsten Uhl did, Luks emphasises the importance of the idea that the factory is a social environment.

The control and regulation of workers' behaviour in the workplace is still an important and central topic of on-going discussions within the historical field concerning the workplace. The rise of several control regimes at work depends not only on the spatial and social order within the fabric; it was also driven by the general conditions and requirements of an economic system. Eeva Keskula's article deals with a specific practice in Soviet Estonian oil-shale mining – namely cheating – including misbehaviour like fiddling with output numbers, drinking and stealing. Such misbehaviour in the workplace was part of a general moral economy of the Soviet regime and followed a certain logic, but also caused individual moral dilemmas. Using an oral-history approach, Keskula shows that workers as well as engineers and managers shared the same workplace experience in Estonian mining. Managerial misbehaviour like manipulating statistics to hide injuries and to show higher production numbers, as well as worker misconduct like absenteeism and alcohol abuse were not only part of the everyday workplace culture of Estonian mining: they were also a central element of the overall Soviet economic system. In fact, cheating and misbehaviour were acceptable practices in the workplace and lessened the social distance between engineers and workers bound together by a specific moral economy.

Lars Bluma shows that the environmental concept of industrial workplaces was driven in German mining around 1900 by the influential hygiene movement. The working bodies of the miners were being examined in relation to their work environment; thereafter hygienic and medical regulation of the mining workplace took place. The hookworm epidemic serves in this article as a case study. It illustrates the intense process of medicalisation of the miners and the on-going hygienic intervention in the configuration of underground workplaces, which had become a new field of investigation for medical and hygiene experts. Moreover, miners' mutual health insurance, the so-called *Knappschaft*, became a major stakeholder in this process. The founding of specialised hospitals and the extension of medical services for miners in the Ruhr is presented by Bluma as a manifestation of modern biopolitics which was centred around the miner's body, his productivity and health.

Bluma's article makes the transition to the second issue addressed by articles which present occupational health as a major issue in the historical debates on the industrial workplace. Tackling the early industrialisation period in France in the first half of the nineteenth century, Thomas Le Roux shows how the new machines introduced by new processes made unknown risks at work appear. Scrutinising the ever-growing hygienist literature on industrialisation and faith in economic progress, the author enlightens his readers on the lack of interest from hygienists for the endangered bodies of workers at that time, as the machines were seen as an element of improvement in the general work conditions, compared to former crafts. Paradoxically, Le Roux shows how mechanisation in industry lead to an optimistic and ambiguous discourse of hygienists about the industrialisation of society, quite indifferent toward the worker's suffering body and hiding to a large extent the harmful effects of work.

Finally, two articles address what can be called 'Atlantic crossings' and include a focus on transnational debates about occupational health and safety. The comparative approach implemented by Judith Rainhorn between the French and US experiences about white-lead use in paint makes possible the reassessment of the historical process of regulating the use of toxic products for workers in an industrial context. The slow disclosure of the toxicity of lead in industrial paint (for workers both manufacturing and using the paint) gives way to different pathways for facing this great professional risk in France and the United States in the early twentieth century. Between legal prohibition and financial dissuasion, the author enlightens two ways of getting rid of the harmful white lead, emphasising the role of reform circles in raising public awareness of this process, along with the slow penetration of the state into the private space of the factory.

The links between pollution inside and outside the factory are also addressed by Florence Hachez-Leroy in her article on the French aluminium industry. She argues that the issue of risk associated both with metal production and consumption has evolved during the twentieth century from a joint approach, supported by different levels of actors, from international scientific circles to local actors. Being controversial, the making and use of aluminium in food spread during the twentieth century, triggering many scientific debates and public worries. Considered from a transnational point of view, the issues of occupational health and public health were addressed differently on both sides of the Atlantic, as the international organisations became increasingly more involved in the debate.

Finally, we hope this special issue of the *European Review of History*, through the manifold issues addressed by the authors, will contribute to further enlightening the prevailing issues and modestly participate in the on-going debates on the renewal of the history of the industrial workplace.

Notes

1. Burgmann, "The Strange Death of Labour History"; Süß, *Kumpel und Genossen*, 9–17. See also the special issue of *Australian Historical Studies* 25, no. 100 (1993): "Is Labour History Dead?"
2. This is what Christopher Sellers and Joseph Melling call the history of industrial hazards in their recent introduction to *Dangerous Trade*, 4.
3. See for example Rainhorn, "Workers Against Lead Paint," 137–61.
4. Sellers, "Cross-nationalizing History of Industrial Hazard."
5. See for example the articles in *Journal of Modern European History* 7, no. 2 (2009), a special issue entitled "Health and Safety at Work. A Transnational History." See also Lengwiler, *Risikopolitik im Sozialstaat*.
6. See Rosental, "Health and Safety at Work"; Conrad, "Social Policy History after the Transnational Turn," 218–40. Van Daele et al., "ILO Histories."
7. For a short overview of these historiographic approaches, especially in the United States and the UK see McIvor and Johnston, *Miner's Lung*, 14–26.
8. Uhl and Bluma, "Arbeit – Körper – Rationalisierung," 12–17. See also the other articles in Bluma and Uhl, *Kontrollierte Arbeit*.
9. http://www.sslh.org.uk/
10. Omnès and Pitti, *Cultures du risque au travail*; Bruno et al. *La santé au travail;* Omnès and Rosental, "Les maladies professionelles"; Rosental 2009.
11. Kocka, *Work in a Modern Society*.
12. Kocka, "Work as a Problem," 1.

Bibliography

Bluma, Lars, and Karsten Uhl, eds. *Kontrollierte Arbeit – Disziplinierte Körper? Zur Sozial- und Kulturgeschichte der Industriearbeit im 19. und 20. Jahrhundert*. Bielefeld: transcript, 2012.

Bruno, Anne-Sophie, Eric Geerkens, Nicolas Hatzfeld, and Catherine Omnès, eds. *La santé au travail, entre savoirs et pouvoirs, 19e et 20e siècles*. Rennes: Presses universitaires de Rennes, 2011.

Burgmann, Verity. "The Strange Death of Labour History." In *Bede Nairn and Labor History, Labor History Essays*, Vol. 3 edited by Bob Carr, et al., 69–81. Sydney: Pluto Press, 1991.

Conrad, Christoph. "Social Policy after the Transnational Turn." In *Beyond Welfare State Models. Transnational Historical Perspectives on Social Policy*, edited by Pauli Kettunen and Klaus Petersen, 218–40. Cheltenham: Edward Elgar, 2011.

Kocka, Jürgen, ed. *Work in a Modern Society. The German Historical Experience in Comparative Perspective*. New York: Berghahn Books, 2010.

Kocka, Jürgen. "Work as a Problem in European History." In *Work in a Modern Society. The German Historical Experience in Comparative Perspective*, edited by Jürgen Kocka, 1–15. New York: Berghahn Books, 2010.

Lengwiler, Martin. *Risikopolitik im Sozialstaat. Die schweizerische Unfallversicherung 1870–1970*. Köln: Böhlau, 2006.

McIvor, Arthur, and Ronald Johnston. *Miners' Lung. A History of Dust Disease in British Coal Mining*. Aldershot: Ashgate, 2007.

Omnès, Catherine, and Laure Pitti, eds. *Cultures du risque au travail et pratiques de prévention – La France au regard des pays voisins*. Rennes: Presses universitaires de Rennes, 2009.

Omnès, Catherine, and Paul-André Rosental. "Les maladies professionnelles: genèse d'une question sociale (XIXe-XXe s.)." *Revue d'histoire moderne et contemporaine* 56, no. 1 (2009).

Rainhorn. "Workers Against Lead Paint: How Local Practices Go Against Prevailing Union Strategy – France at the Beginning of the 20th c." In *Kontrollierte Arbeit*, edited by Bluma and Uhl, 137–61.

Rosental, Paul-André. "Health and Safety at Work: An Issue in Transational History – An Introduction." *Journal of Modern European History* 7, no. 2 (2009): 169–73.

Sellers, Christopher. "Cross-Nationalizing History of Industrial Hazard." *Medical History* 45 (2010): 315–40.

Sellers, Christopher, and Joseph Melling, eds. *Dangerous Trade: Histories of Industrial Hazard Across a Globalizing World*. Temple University Press, 2012.

Süß, Dietmar. *Kumpel und Genossen. Arbeiterschaft, Betrieb und Sozialdemokratie in der bayerischen Montanindustrie 1945 bis 1976*. Munich: Oldenbourg, 2003.

Uhl, Karsten, and Lars Bluma. "Arbeit – Körper – Rationalisierung. Neue Perspektiven auf den historischen Wandel industrieller Arbeitsplätze." In *Kontrollierte*, edited by Bluma and Uhl, 19–31.

Van Daele, Jasmien, Magaly Rodriguez Garcia, Geert Van Goethem, and Marcel Van Der Linden, eds. *ILO Histories. Essays on the International Labour Organization and Its Impact on the World During the Twentieth Century*. Bern: Peter Lang, 2010.

The hygienic movement and German mining 1890–1914

Lars Bluma

German Mining Museum, Bochum, Germany

This article examines the scientific and medical objectification of workers' bodies in mining on the Ruhr as an integral part of the formation of a modern care and control regime. This specific control regime had been established with the modernisation of health insurance for miners at the end of the nineteenth century. The central thesis of this article is that in the German Empire new knowledge about the miner's body arose within the scope of the categories and paradigms of the hygiene movement. Above all this means that the miner's body, in particular his productivity and health, was analysed and categorised in relation to his working and everyday life environment. This specific form of hygienic objectification of the miner aimed at the production of a healthy environment as well as at the production of a hygienic subject. Indeed, this environmental-hygienic approach was to be complemented by a new scientific discipline at the turn of the century, namely bacteriology or more precisely, bacteriology-oriented hygiene. The fight against hookworm disease around 1900 and the extension of the medical infrastructure of the health insurance for miners will be taken as examples of this important turning point for biopolitics in industrialised Germany.

The working practices established by industrialisation in factories and large-scale enterprises – with their machine-supported, concentrated regime of production – led to new health risks in the working process.[1] In addition, in the beginning, protecting the health of industrial workers was not an important objective of state authorities, parliaments or other public institutions. In the nineteenth century, industrial working conditions caught civil social reformers' attention only when women and children were concerned, because both groups were seen as in need of special protection.[2] In direct contrast to a lack of concern for adult male workers, who were for the most part blamed for accidents at work because of their putative carelessness,[3] bourgeois morality called for special, state-organised protection of women and children at the workplace. Governmental activities for the protection of children and women, particularly the ban on child employment which became effective in England in 1833 and in Prussia in 1839, were not essentially an appreciation of health as a quality in its own right to be protected by the state, but rather an expression of the paternalistic state, as well as a response to the state's interest in enforcing general compulsory education and in the determination of fitness for military service of young recruits.[4] Now the field was prepared for the increasing regulation of industrial workplaces within the framework of state-run control. This supervision of the workplace became, in conjunction with the public debates around the protection needs of women and children, an important point of intervention for engineers and doctors who dealt with the health risks of industrial work and their prevention.[5]

Since the middle of the nineteenth century, hygiene as a new scientific discipline had entered the stage and soon dominated the debates about the unhealthy conditions of industrial labour. Furthermore, hygiene was not limited to occupational health but rather targeted the problem of public health in a comprehensive manner, including problems of sanitation in the growing industrial cities, control of epidemics, the fight against alcoholism, individual hygiene, and so on. Within this hygiene movement industrial hygiene, which dealt especially with the hygiene of industrial workplaces, was established as a subdiscipline. Industrial hygiene examined the evident social intertwining of industrial production with the health of the workers.[6] Important hygienists like Rudolf Virchow in Germany pushed for a state-regulated health-care policy which was seen as an efficient way to get the hygiene problems of an industrialised society under control.[7] However, the Prussians took a liberal standpoint within the process of growing trade legislation in the 1860s; that meant, with regard to occupational health, very weak regulation, which demonstrated the firm conviction that health is a private affair and not a public issue.[8]

Indeed, the problematisation of the industrial workplace as a state-run intervention for protecting workers did not become a major concern in Germany until the founding of the German Empire and Bismarck's social-insurance legislation setting up health insurance (1883), accident insurance (1884) and disability and old-age insurance (1889) as compulsory and obligatory institutions. With it came an interventionist welfare state which organised the regulation of risks specific to occupation within the scope of social insurances.[9] It is noteworthy that before the introduction of this social-security system in Germany, public health care became one of the first spheres of activity of the German Empire through the foundation of the Reichsgesundheitsamt (Imperial Health Authority) in 1876.[10] Hygiene as a modern medical concept was settled institutionally at the highest level and played a major role in establishing a distinct national identity for the emerging German Empire. Furthermore, hygiene as a set of sanitary knowledge and practice was now the dominant approach of public health care. Its attractiveness was not coincidently based on a close linkage between scientific knowledge and bourgeois morality, favouring a clean and moral life.

Although the medical care of miners has a long tradition tracing back to the foundation of Knappschaften as mutual insurances in the Middle Ages, the hazardous and harmful working conditions itself were not the focus of medical experts. This did not change fundamentally until the turn of the twentieth century, when hygiene ideas entered the debate on the working conditions in coal mining in the Ruhr. This article examines the problematisation of hygiene and the beginnings of the transformation of the coalminers' workplace underground in the Ruhr area around 1900. The first part will examine why the infiltration of modern hygiene into coal mining in the Ruhr was delayed until the end of the nineteenth century and why discussions on the miners' workplaces were neglected until then. The main thesis of this article is that the problematisation of the hygiene of working conditions in German coal mining was neither an effect of the beginnings of the mechanisation of subterranean industry nor as a reaction to the growing cases of illness, but, rather, a consequence of a new health threat: the hookworm which invaded the European coal mining districts at the end of the nineteenth century. Thus, the hookworm epidemic and its effect on the now hygiene-oriented health care in mining will be discussed in the second part of this article, especially the problem of controlling the miner's body as a biopolitical strategy. The Knappschaft on the Ruhr founded modern sanatoria and hospitals exclusively for miners at the turn of the twentieth century. This issue will be discussed in the third part, not only as a simple expansion of medical infrastructure, but as a realisation of a hygienic utopia shared by both employers and employees and, therefore, was a crucial element of hygiene biopolitics in industrialised mining.

Health care and the neglected problematisation of the miner's workplace

In German mining we can find a tradition of health care reaching far back into the Middle Ages. The miners founded mutual social-insurance funds, later called Knappschaften, to support ill workers as well as widows and orphans of miners killed in accidents.[11] But these more Christian-oriented brotherhoods were far from being modern insurance companies. With the General-Privilegium für die Bergleute (General Privilege of the Miners) in 1767, coal mining in the Ruhr area was put under royal protection, which permitted above all the setting up of compulsory Knappschaften, which were so far totally unknown in the Ruhr region. The Knappschaften offered several insurances, which compensated the special illnesses and accident risks of the miners. In addition, payments of benefits for illness and disability pensions, just as for health-resort expenses and the free delivery of drugs, were made. On top of that, the new mining insurances established a medical infrastructure initially including specialised physicians for first aid, pre-employment medical examinations and the general medical supply of ill miners. At the turn of the nineteenth century this was complemented by hospitals and pharmacies exclusively for the demand of the miners. In comparison with other industrial sectors, the miners had the best insurance protection until the passing of Bismarck's social-insurance legislation for all workers. Nevertheless, the modernisation of the Knappschaften as a challenge for the growing coal-mining sector took place in the middle of the nineteenth century with the deregulation of state-organised mining in Prussia, even though the responsibility for and inspection of miners' health was still in the hands of the state-run mining authority.

As a consequence of the above, the Allgemeine Knappschaftsverein zu Bochum (AKV) became one of the major stakeholders in this process. Paying insurance benefits in cases of sickness, disability and retirement, the AKV had a legitimate interest in meeting the new challenges. Caring for the health of miners in this context was not only seen as a project to transform the workplace of the miners, but also a means to build up an adequate medical infrastructure beyond the gates of the coal mine. The AKV, established in 1890 in a merger of three smaller Knappschaften on the Ruhr, could draw upon many years of experience with a well-established system of specially trained physicians, who had served the miners on the Ruhr since 1767.[12] In 1840, this medical infrastructure of the Knappschaft was organised into a system of district-based care.[13] That means that a sick miner could only consult his district doctor, as freedom of choice with regard to one's medical practitioner was not possible in German mining until 1970.

Because health care means not only a normative frame of rules and laws or a set of scientific knowledge, but mainly the implementation of a distinct practice to regulate bodies in terms of health, care and productivity, these special trained medical experts were important actors within the health-care system of the AKV. The role of the physicians working for the Knappschaft changed dramatically at the end of the nineteenth century because of the general professionalisation of workers' insurance in the course of Bismarck's social legislation. Now, beside the classical role of the doctor as a curative authority, the medical consultants, including the doctors and their expert knowledge, possessed decisive power over the payment of benefits for the insured miners.[14] Therefore, an important part of the Knappschaft's doctors' work was not only the treatment of the sick miner and the prescription of medication, but also the writing of medical reports, especially in case of disability and on-the-job accidents, as well as the certification of the inability to work. Following the jurisdiction of the Reichsversicherungsamt (Imperial Office of Insurance), a miner was incapable of work if he was unable to do the job he did immediately before the onset of his illness, or if further work was likely to worsen his state of health. This definition allowed various interpretations concerning the physical and mental ability of the disabled miner to carry out his work. Within the social-insurance system and in particular within the AKV, medical estimates on disability, in which the degree of occupational disability was the focus of the reports, played a major role, because here more long-term and therefore more costly benefits than sick pay were concerned. In fact, the doctor's report was responsible for the financial security of sick and disabled miners. Under these social, economic and organisational circumstances it is no surprise that the harmful impact of the working conditions in mining on the Ruhr attracted the AKV's officials' attention. But nevertheless the workplace of miners was not a crucial factor in the disputes and conflicts between employers and employees. Although a new phase of social politics centred on the so-called 'Arbeiterschutz' (protection of workers) was pushed by the Prussian government after the mining strike in 1889,[15] the problematisation of the workplace conditions continued in an orderly and conservative fashion. Central topics of the Berlin international conference on the protection of labour championed by the German Emperor Wilhelm II in 1890, for example, discussed the well-known problems of child, youth and female labour in mining, but the overall problem of occupational diseases was elided.[16]

Although playing a crucial part in German industrialisation as a key branch with corresponding public attention and strategic importance for the German Empire, mining was not a typical industrial sector.[17] The industrialisation of coal mining, or more specifically, the mechanisation of the mining industry, and with it new challenges in health care, started in Germany in the 1870s; it was still a very slow process which gained momentum in the 1920s.[18] The first tests with semi-mechanical, pneumatic coal-cutting machines were made in 1875, but these machines initially achieved only a limited significance for the advancement of the industry and not for the intrinsic extraction of coal.[19] The most important development for the mining workplaces had been the establishment of conveyors at the beginning of the twentieth century, which demanded a complete reorganisation of work processes underground and replaced the stoop and room work by filled flat-back stoping.[20] With this mechanisation and reorganisation of the workplace by conveyors, new health risks for the miners arose, especially by moving conveyors, which was necessary every day. In the initial phase of this new technology, faults were the rule rather than exceptions and the working conditions of coal mines using conveyors changed generally for the worse. Additionally, miners complained about the higher degree of control and pressure to increase their working performance; at the very least the use of conveyors led to a heightened discord between miners and foremen. The mining companies simply inhibited all serious discussion about the advantages and disadvantages of the conveyors and their complex effects on the working process. And with it, scientific reflection about working conditions in terms of Taylorism or occupational medicine could not result from the process of the mechanisation of mining; it was just as well, as mechanisation was not a catalyst for considerations about a more corporate-oriented arrangement of industrial relations in German mining.

Moreover, the pneumatic pick was only slowly adapted before the First World War. Thus traditionally successful methods like shooting and hard manual work with the mattock dominated the work of miners.[21] Standing in the long tradition of hard work in mining, occupational diseases, regardless of being caused by new technologies or by well-known harmful effects of the work, were widely seen as inevitable. Only the spectacular mass accidents caused by coal-dust explosions and the explosion of fire damp received sustainable attention before the turn of the century,[22] although the extent of occupational diseases in mining was well known and is documented in detail in the statistics of the AKV. Occupational health risks were not so much ignored, but the whole system of mining medical care was centred around financial compensation and medical care after a miner got seriously ill; preventive strategies were, however, widely neglected with the exception of the obligatory medical examination of workers before setting-on.[23] Mining has a long history of dealing with health issues, but there was no powerful idea of prophylaxis that included the workplace layout.

Now the question arises of why the neglect of hazards caused in the special environmental conditions underground gave way to an extensive problematisation of the miners' workplace in terms of hygiene around 1900. When it was neither a response to the process of mechanisation nor the result of a logical process of scientific/medical professionalisation within the miners' insurance nor a moral discussion about child and female mining labour in the Ruhr, what was the driving force that stimulated the growing discussions about, for example, toilets underground, the usefulness of showers for cleaning after work and about the working conditions in mining in general? Why was the workplace of miners transformed into a laboratory for physicians and hygienists after 1900? There is a simple answer: the fear of the hookworm, a new parasite that entered onto the mining stage at the end of the nineteenth century.

The hookworm and the hygienic body of miners

Around 1900 the hookworm (*ancylostoma duodenale*), invaded German coal-mining areas along the Ruhr and with it the bodies of the miners in such an alarming manner that only the combined efforts of different groups such as physicians, health-insurance companies, scientists, government agencies and mining corporations could mitigate the hazard.[24] The hookworm is a parasite which is to be found everywhere in humid tropical regions. The first large-scale appearance of the hookworm in Europe was documented in the 1870s during the construction of the Gotthard tunnel in the Alps. A high number of tunnel workers, who showed symptoms of anaemia as a result of the hookworm infestation, died of this epidemic, which had so far been unknown in Europe.[25] From the Alps the parasite spread out across the coal-mining areas of Eastern Europe, France and Germany. The epidemic specialists at that time supposed that the tunnel miners especially, who became active in the coal-mining industry after working at the Gotthard tunnel, were responsible for the spread of the hookworm; but likewise, Belgian brick makers were suspected. The brickyards, as well as the working conditions during the construction of the Gotthard tunnel and the coal-mining areas of the Ruhr all had similar conditions in common which promoted the spread of the hookworm: darkness, high temperatures coupled with high air humidity, and muddy ground contaminated by excrement. The parasite reached the human small intestine by getting through the skin and penetrating the blood vessels of the infected, causing symptoms of anaemia.

Scientists in the late nineteenth century were quickly convinced that not only physical circumstances such as temperature, humidity and soil conditions were responsible for the spread of hookworm, but also the social conditions of the workplace. In the special case of hookworm this specifically meant the lack of adequate levels of sanitation and personal hygiene. The German biologist Adolph Lutz, exploring the hookworm in Brazil around

1880, declared that the highly objectionable hygiene situation, caused by a common and indifferent attitude of Brazilian natives to sanitary problems, favoured the spreading of the parasite.[26] Thus, the ancylostomia epidemic was not only seen as a biological or physical problem but also as a social and moral one. Infected with hookworm, these social and moral reproaches were applied to the workers of the European mining industry.[27] In matters of hygiene, miners were equated with Brazilian natives.

In 1892 two cases of hookworm infection were diagnosed at a pit in the Ruhr area (Zeche Graf Schwerin). The responsible Knappschaft, the Allgemeine Knappschaftsverein zu Bochum (AKV), immediately started an examination of the concerned pit staff, especially of miners with anaemic symptoms.[28] Together with the physicians of the Knappschafts-Berufsgenossenschaft, the German occupational insurance association of mining, the excrement of the miners was analysed with microscopes and hookworms were found in 18 samples.[29]

The AKV was so worried about these few cases that it reacted quickly and sent immediate warnings to the mining management. As a result the royal mining authority in Dortmund commissioned the medical head of the Knappschafts-Berufsgenossenschaft, Ferdinand Löbker, to give his expert opinion on the extent of the worm illness in the Ruhr area and the necessary action to combat the epidemic. Löbker suggested several measures that were immediately implemented at the infected coal mine:[30]

(1) Miners, pit management and doctors of the Knappschaft should be educated about the hookworm illness.

(2) Medical examination of potential carriers (that is, miners with anaemic symptoms). The confirmation of the existence of worm eggs in the excrement was to be followed up with microscopic investigations. Every case was to be re-examined after the first anthelmintic therapy some weeks later, until there was a complete certainty of recovery.

(3) Reports of all suspected and ill miners were to be sent to a central office of the AKV, including reports of workplace changes of the infected workers. (The frequently practised work-place change was a big problem for epidemic containment).

(4) Special medical check-ups for all foreign miners and brick makers before employment.

(5) Improvement of the sanitary conditions underground, especially with regard to the toilets and a ban on the deposit of excrement in the coal clearances, as well as the cleaning of the damp ground.

(6) Common bathtubs for the miners should be substituted with shower facilities. (It was feared that the contaminated sludge gathered in the bathtub could be a source of infection if swallowed by the miners).

Because the infection was strictly limited to miners working underground, the medical experts focused their actions on the epidemic in the mining workplaces; unhygienic circumstances were especially examined. For the next few years this was the *status quo* for combating hookworm. But all these medical and hygiene instructions controlled by the mining authority could not prevent the outbreak of an epidemic, which grew into a serious threat to mining in the Ruhr. The statistics from the AKV for 1903 show a dramatic increase in the number of ill miners due to infection with hookworm; the outbreak of an epidemic was now obvious.[31] The hookworm caused at least 16% of all sickness-related absenteeism in the Ruhr mining area.

Löbker's suggestions were obviously inadequate. This was partly due to the fact that he and the physicians of the AKV, but also the whole international community of medical and hygiene experts, knew only little about the spread and means of distribution of the hookworm in the miner's body and its environment. The knowledge that the infestation occurred through the skin only slowly became accepted truth in the medical community.[32] Instead, experts discussed the role of bad air and horse manure,[33] the possibility of adding citric acid to the drinking water[34] and the effect of drinking alcoholic beverages or eating herring.[35] However, it is more important that Löbker, and with him the head of the medical department of the AKV, August Tenholt, thought that it was sufficient to examine only miners with anaemic symptoms.[36] By doing so, the physicians ignored the large number of worm carriers who still showed no visible signs of illness.[37] Consequently, only the anaemic workers received a de-worming treatment. The miners who showed no symptoms, but were already infected with hookworm, were not removed from work and could still spread the parasite underground. This paralleled the insurance logic of the Knappschaft as a health insurance that at that time had to pay sickness benefits as compensation for the miner's wage in the case of illness. A look at the expenditure for claims made to the AKV shows that the payment of sickness benefits was the biggest expenditure for the AKV's health insurance. In 1894, for example, statutory sick pay alone amounted to nearly 7 million Mark with an overall benefit level of approximately 9.8 million Mark.[38] With a percentage between approximately 60% and 70% of the total expenditures from 1901 to 1903, these sickness benefits were the centre of attention of the AKV administration as an area where potential savings could be made within the health-insurance system. Sickness benefit was paid when incapacity for work was attested, but for an infected miner without visible illness symptoms who was still able to work, this did not apply. Furthermore, the financial charges of the AKV would have risen enormously with the acceptance of all worm-infected miners as diseased and not able to work. This seems to be contrary to the efforts of the AKV for preventive measures against hookworm. But Tenholt was convinced that the fight against hookworm should basically only be fought with hygienic and technical means, by installing toilets underground, by draining the wet areas of the mine and improving ventilation to regulate the temperature.[39] However, these preventive measures required not only technical realisation, but also a change in the habits of the miners. They had to use the toilets underground, but this was not self-evident and the necessary behavioural changes were not easy to achieve.[40] Different objectives of the miners became conflicted when it came to pit security. Indeed, the miners did pay attention to their health; after all their bodies were their only capital. However, they were also ready to accept the risk of illness or an accident to raise the commission wage of the mining team, the so-called *Gedinge*. Going to a far-away toilet meant an interruption of the working process and with it a loss of income. In the case of the toilets, the enforcement of the hygiene regulations also failed completely: with their use, the bad smell increased, while burying the excrement had previously prevented this.[41] The health experts discussed this problem in great detail and tried to solve it by improving the toilets. Nevertheless, a simple metal bucket with a lid was the favoured solution for this problem on the Ruhr.

Tenholt then developed a new medical-hygiene action programme which was aimed less at the body of the miner and more at the environmental conditions in the pit, which he defined as a principal place for intervention in the fight against the parasites: 'The contagion does not occur by transmission from a sick worker to his close neighbour, as we can see by infectious diseases, but through the pit.'[42] Tenholt's target was a readjustment of the workplace as a techno-natural environment. Three measures especially were in the centre of his next plan: the lowering of the temperature underground to 22 degrees; the draining of the coal clearances; and their disinfection.

Until then the different groups, like AKV, the miners, the mining authority and the mining companies worked together with only little friction. But with the outbreak of an actual epidemic, scathing criticism of Tenholt's plan was heard, and the mining companies expressed their dissatisfaction emphatically. In 1902, the pit owners demanded the addition of a new agent, the Institut für Hygiene und Bakteriologie in Gelsenkirchen (Institute of Hygiene and Bacteriology in Gelsenkirchen), to fight the disease.[43] The institute had been founded following the advice of the famous scientist and microbiologist Robert Koch, who had investigated a typhoid epidemic in the Ruhr district in 1901.[44] The Institut für Hygiene und Bakteriologie was responsible for supervising the canalisation and water supply of the local-authority districts in the Ruhr area and to set up an epidemic guard.

The head of the institute, Hayo Bruns, then proposed a catalogue of measures contrary to Tenholt's plan. In committees and at scientific conferences, partially initiated by the German Reichstag, and, therefore, on top of the political agenda, Bruns promoted a bacteriology-oriented control of the hookworm epidemic analogous to the fight against typhoid, cholera, dysentery, and so on.[45] What did this bacteriological approach mean in practice? What Bruns wanted was a systematic microscopic examination of excrement from all miners in the Ruhr who were endangered by hookworm disease.[46] For him it did not matter if a miner had anaemic symptoms or not. What was important, and this is the basic message of the bacteriological approach, was the infection with the worm. Bruns applied his bacteriological knowledge to the problem of the hookworm epidemic. Consequently, he demanded that all worm-infected miners, regardless of visible signs and symptoms or ability to work, should be removed from their workplaces and immediately de-wormed. This was a fundamental biopolitical intervention that concerned not only miners as single subjects, but as a whole group. The former individual diagnosis, which had been based on external, visible symptoms, was to be substituted for a complete microscopic serial examination. Bruns wanted to attack the hookworm in the body of the miners, a clearly defined position. In contrast, Tenholt and the AKV intended to fight the hookworm at the miners' workplace underground by a slow transformation of hygiene standards. This was anything but a clearly defined battlefield. In fact Tenholt dissipated his energies, and his efforts were without quick success.

Now the opponents of this conflict tried to support their theories with intensive research.[47] The miner's workplace was converted to a medical experimental ground. The physicians and microbiologists examined the pits with regard to temperature, air humidity, soil conditions and ventilation to specify the ideal breeding conditions for the hookworm. The mines were searched thoroughly for hookworm eggs and larvae to track down possible paths of infection; at the same time the hookworm was investigated experimentally in the laboratories of the AKV and the Institut für Hygiene und Bakteriologie.[48] These competitive experiments of the two institutions at the miners' workplace were complemented by research in medical laboratories and scientific tests which included self-experiments conducted by the staff.[49] This intensive research produced new knowledge about the hookworm and with it also a new understanding of the body of the miner and its interrelation with the workplace environment.[50]

The production of scientific facts was important, indeed, but it was not crucial for the final success of Bruns' bacteriological approach because the etiological knowledge among the two opponents was nearly identical and the two different strategies derived from this knowledge were both rational and logical. What really helped Bruns' concept was the formation of a new network and the social compatibility of his approach with the main players, especially the mining authority and the coal-mining companies. For example in 1903, the pit owners, when an official conference decided to pursue Bruns' plan,[51] were not really interested in a slow project to establish hygiene and medical standards underground at that time. Although they were convinced that the hygienic transformation of the workplace was an important measure to prevent further epidemic hazards in the long run, they wanted a quick and definite solution for the hookworm problem there and then. And Bruns could offer such a solution. By contrast, Tenholt could only offer an uncertain plan whose targets could only be met in the remote future. Thus the crucial point for the success of Bruns' intervention was not an advance of etiological knowledge but an advance in effectiveness.

Furthermore the mining authority opposed the hygiene project. One important request of Tenholt's concept was the avoidance of sludge production by sprinkling underground. But it was absolutely clear that the mining authority would never agree with this suggestion due to safety reasons. The sprinkling of pits was necessary to avoid dust explosions, which were a problem for many pits on the Ruhr. Another problem was that the behaviour of the miners, despite all official orders, changed only slowly. Although the mining authority formulated detailed rules and applied sanctions against miners who didn't use the toilets underground, for a long time infringements were the rule, not the exception. That had to do with the very limited influence the authorities had on the working teams underground. The mining authorities and pit owners, therefore, not only had to establish external social control measures based on severe sanctions but also attempt to impart an internalisation of hygienic norms in the miners. In Tenholt's concept it was necessary that, without exception, all miners used the toilets at the workplace. But as his opponent Bruns emphasised, it would have only needed one irresponsible sloven, leaving his excrement on the ground, to pose a genuine risk to his colleagues' health.[52] Therefore, fitting the pits with an adequate number of toilets was a long-term project as well, without offering a quick solution for the hookworm problem.

Indeed, with permanent medical-hygienic control by the screening of large groups and obligatory medical examinations before enlisting a miner, moral-hygienic behaviour of the miners was preferable but not mandatory. The hygienic subject of bacteriology is above all a dangerous subject who can infect other people, and was seen solely as a physical and biological entity, as a kind of transit station in the life cycle of the hookworm. Instead of educating the miners to change their behaviour, the contagion programme of the bacteriologists meant above all an incapacitation of the miners by mass investigations. The fact that this remained not without resistance does not surprise. The collection of the miner's faeces, as ordered by Bruns, for the microscopic analysis which was organised by toilets specially built up for this purpose, could be carried out successfully only by extensive control of the intimate act by pit foremen and medical staff.[53]

The accompanying educational measures, which were meant to improve the morality of the workers, counted as a central element of the hygiene-oriented biopolitics of the German Empire. In 1897, senior medical officer Emanuel Roth outlined the general opinion that the worker was a hygienically deficient creature thus: 'The protection of workers is a postulate not only of humanity and morality, but above all also of national health; the more the worker learns to protect himself by complying with an efficient as well as a morally and physically wholesome lifestyle, the bigger will be the success rates of public and private attempts to improve working-class well-being.'[54] Consequently, the excessive consumption of alcoholic beverages, especially on Sunday, which was seen as a day for physical and moral regeneration, was also criticised as moral misconduct as serious as the poor nutrition and unsanitary housing conditions of German workers. The industrial hygiene of the Empire attached special importance to two origins of occupational diseases: the workers' lifestyle as an effect of the specific labour relations and the hazardous working conditions.[55]

The miners and their unions were only very hesitantly and dismissively responsive to the debate. Even though the workers' demands for the improvement of working conditions was not new, it was nonetheless unusual that health issues got such an outstanding role within industrial relations, which were overshadowed by discussions on working time, wages and unfair treatment by foremen. A police report on a public miners' meeting discussing the measures to fight hookworm documented the worries of the miners very well.[56] It was mainly the loss of wages in the case of a hookworm infection and the subsequent therapy which was criticised. Otto Hue, the famous Social Democratic labour leader, noted that the mining companies were exclusively responsible for the hygienic nuisance and consequently had to pay compensation. In any case, the Gewerkverein Christlicher Bergarbeiter (Union of Christian Miners) published periodical grievances on the unacceptable working conditions underground, but linked these appraisals with the demand for more wages and a reduction of working hours as the most effective measurements to keep up the health of the miners.[57]

In the end, the bacteriological approach of Bruns supported by the mining companies was successful. The comprehensive microscopic examination of underground miners on the Ruhr and the systematic de-worming of all infected miners caused a rapid reduction of the hookworm illness after 1903.[58] The occupational physician Ludwig Teleky appraised this success in his 'History of Factory and Mine Hygiene' some decades later as 'a phenomenal triumph of well-planned epidemiological control'.[59] But that this 'well-planned' fight against the hookworm epidemic was the result of a hard and intense discussion was unspoken in his book. Nevertheless, after this quick success, the long-term project of a hygienic transformation of miners' workplaces, suggested by Tenholt and the AKV, became a major paradigm in the German mining industry to prevent further risk of infection of any kind. This was also supported by Hayo Bruns, who never neglected the general significance of underground hygiene and preventive actions for the health of the miners. In the words of Peter Baldwin, who analysed the different preventive strategies of contagionists and sanitationists in Europe: 'Between these two outlying positions, however, stretched a broad middle range where etiological conceptions and preventive tactics coexisted in polymorphous perversity.'[60]

To sum up, there are some fundamental changes the hookworm epidemic caused for mining in the Ruhr. First of all, we can see the rise of a new modern dispositive that linked industrial coal mining with the gathering of new medical knowledge about the miner's body, its productivity and vulnerability at the workplace. In a long-term perspective the process of the mechanisation of German coal mining after the First World War was not only an effect of a rational organisation of industrial production, but also powered by discussions on industrial health risks dealing with concepts like hygiene, bacteriology and occupational disease at that time. Therefore, the hookworm was responsible for a long-lasting process of a hygienic and bacteriological transformation of the miners' workplace. The examination of miners' excrement to avoid further hookworm epidemics, especially that of foreign workers from Eastern and Southern Europe who were seen as precarious hygienic subjects, remained a common practice in German mining until the 1970s. Furthermore, hygiene in mining was a comprehensive concept integrating quite different fields of action: the fight against typical occupational diseases like hookworm, nystagmus and silicosis; the prevention of explosion hazards; the provision of a medical and first-aid infrastructure; the installation and organisation of toilets in the pits; as well as hygiene outside the workplace, embedding housing conditions and all parts of urban infrastructure especially sewerage and water supply, sanitary facilities, and so on.

This medical dispositive, established around the problem of the hookworm epidemic, produced deep insights into the relationship between the miner's body and its ambient conditions at work. Consequently, it was necessary to attain greater knowledge about the working body and its environment to gain control over the working process. This medical knowledge was not only linked to new technologies of industrial production but also to new social technologies to control the behaviour of miners, which was a necessary precondition for the success of this biopolitical dispositive. The Knappschaft produced not only health but also a governmental rationality resting on discipline and the internalisation of behavioural rules and norms to avoid and combat health risks in mining. In fact, the hygienic and bacteriological view of the miner's body in conjunction with bourgeois moral presumptions supported at first the paternalistic regime of the mining companies; later the construction of the miner's body as an object of medical and scientific scrutiny was the starting point for new biopolitics based on the rationality of risk prevention and modern insurance. It was the prime mover for a new network incorporating workers, companies, medical experts, the government and institutions like the AKV, the Knappschafts-Berufsgenossenschaft and others, such as the Institut für Hygiene und Bakteriologie.[61] As Michel Foucault stressed in his biopolitical works, it is the body that was socialised by capitalism as a factor of productive force.[62] Furthermore, at the end of the nineteenth century, medicine and hygiene were important biopolitical strategies to gain control over individual workers.

Hygienic utopia: the hospitals of the AKV

Although the doctors of the AKV were important for the general health of the miners, the district-based system reached a functional limit at the end of the nineteenth century where clinical treatment was necessary for the cure of the patient. The Ruhr area, with its insufficient level of urbanisation in general, had been characterised by a distinct lack of hospitals for a long time. Indeed, the confessional hospitals established by the Catholic and Protestant churches since the middle of the nineteenth century, together with a few private and municipal hospitals, offered a medical infrastructure which had been operating reasonably effectively since the beginning of industrialisation of the Ruhr area in the mid-nineteenth century.[63] But the population explosion at that time caused by growing migration to the Ruhr area created a situation in which the management of the AKV reasoned that the existing hospital infrastructure was no longer able to fulfil the medical needs of the population working as miners.[64] Everywhere along the Ruhr, the AKV heard growing complaints about an unmet demand for medical care for its own, insured, miners. Besides, it was criticised that the hospitals with which the AKV had signed contracts knew only a little about the illnesses specific to mining and without it an adequate medical care of the miners could not be guaranteed.[65] The established hospitals' owners necessarily reacted to the legitimate complaint of the AKV's management with a documented increase in the number of hospital beds between 1890 and 1914, the technical modernisation of the existing hospitals and the obvious specialisation in emergency medicine, so that they were able to perform surgery on miners hurt in accidents.[66]

Nevertheless, from 1901, the AKV started the planning process to build its own hospitals, which were to offer medical services exclusively for miners. Indeed financial considerations played a decisive role in this decision as well, because the daily rates for nursing charged by the Christian hospitals were a constant source of irritation to the AKV. The AKV-run hospitals were based on two important models, namely the Knappschaften in Upper Silesia and in the Saarland, which had begun to open hospitals for their insured miners in the middle of the nineteenth century, and, secondly, the other very important biopolitical force in the Ruhr area, the miners' accident insurance, the Knappschafts-Berufsgenossenschaft, which had been running an emergency hospital named Bochumer Bergmannsheil at an extraordinarily high technical and scientific level since 1898.[67] However, the demands of the AKV exceeded the facilities of specified emergency hospitals, such as the Bochumer Bergmannsheil. As a health-insurance provider, the AKV management wanted to offer the whole spectrum of inpatient health care to their insured miners, thus the AKV planned the founding of general hospitals with a wide range of medical facilities.

In 1905, the first hospital of the AKV was opened in Gelsenkirchen-Ückendorf, followed a year later by the Knappschaftskrankenhaus Recklinghausen. Both hospitals contained state-of-the-art technical and hygiene equipment and offered X-ray machines, therapy rooms with artificial light, machines for physiotherapy and orthopaedic treatments, baths and massage equipment as well as medical laboratories and modern aseptic operating theatres: in other words, the whole spectrum of medical technology and therapy forms at that time.[68]

In 1905/6, the X-ray room in the Knappschaft's hospitals in Gelsenkirchen and Recklinghausen was not, however, a special feature of those two hospitals, although X-ray apparatuses were by no means standard in all the hospitals along the Ruhr. It is obvious that the hospitals of the AKV complied with the technical standard at the time, but they were by no means the forerunner of a mechanised hospital medicine. Cutting-edge technology was also used in other hospitals, even though the abundant technical equipment in Knappschaft-run hospitals impressed the public.[69] The equipment found in the X-ray rooms of both hospitals of the AKV was not used exclusively for diagnostic and therapeutic purposes, but also fulfilled functions specific for insurance needs. In this context one has to stress again that the hospitals were locations of further investigation in case of suspected misdiagnosis by the district doctors and unknown causes of disease. Also, they were responsible for medical reports regarding pension and disability benefits as well as for the observation of possible malingerers. The hospitals' X-ray departments and all the other diagnostic equipment played an important role in the decision-making process of the doctors. Therefore, the technical equipment was an essential part of the AKV's control system, including not only the control of the miners but also of the district doctors who were not able to acquire such expensive technology for their own use. Furthermore, running their own hospitals was another key factor in stabilising the system of the AKV's health insurance as a closed system. The miner could ideally be medicated and examined as a patient within the frame of the medical system of the Knappschaft alone. Together with the system of district doctors without free choice, the AKV's hospitals concurred with the aim of the insurance administration to keep the miners under comprehensive control.

The hospitals of the AKV can be interpreted as spatial hygiene utopias, because the mechanisation of the hospitals was top of the hygienists' agenda. The AKV met the demands of the hygienists and planted a large garden, created corridors flooded with light and sun verandas, and offered healthy food as well as rooms for religious contemplation. Therefore, the AKV's hospitals created a hygienic utopia which stood in deliberate contrast to the injurious miners' workplace.

This applied to an even greater degree to the convalescent homes of the AKV, which were naturally not established in the Ruhr area, but in a nearby rural region, the Sauerland, which is characterised by its abundant forests. A convalescent home for sick miners suffering from various respiratory problems had opened in Beringhausen, a small village of the Sauerland in 1904, even before any of the hospitals in Gelsenkirchen and Recklinghausen started providing medical care. A publication commemorating the opening of the Auguste Viktoria Knappschafts-Heilstätte in Beringhausen points out the strong contrast between miners' lives and their work environment in the industrialised Ruhr area and this sanatorium for consumptives: 'As the best area for the sanatorium, the region of the Sauerland was chosen because of the favourable environment. Notably the fresh, dust-free mountain air, the woodland far away from noisy industry and the absence of smoky emissions produced by the chimney stacks ensure the healing of the sick miners at the sanatorium.'[70] Also, the medical treatment of the miners suffering from lung diseases there followed certain hygiene concepts, namely the hygienic-dietary approach which recommended in particular extensive solar baths on the verandas and the breathing of fresh air. As an aside, it is no surprise that August Tenholt after his hookworm disaster became the director of this hygienic utopia. His environmental approach as a sanitationist fitted well with his new field of activity. At least for the short time of their health-resort stay, the miners with respiratory diseases were able to exchange the dirty and dark environment of their workplace with the clean, bright environment of AKV's remedial site and take a therapeutic solar bath on the veranda. But after physical recovery the miner had to return to work: Paradise lost!

Even though the special importance of the environment and the location of the sanatorium in the Sauerland for the ill miners had been stressed repeatedly, these convalescent homes were no mere nature utopias. Like the Knappschaft's hospitals, the Auguste Victoria Knappschaft Sanatorium contained state-of-the-art medical facilities: 'On the ground floor are the offices, the surgery rooms including the laboratories, the pharmacy and a dental laboratory. In the basement one may find the sputum disinfection chamber, the X-ray room, two inhalation rooms based on Wassmuth and Senninger, the tailor shop, the shoemaker and the upholsterer's workshop.'[71] Besides all that, chief physician Tenholt lists the utility buildings, especially the machine hall with its three steam generators and two dynamos, the sanatorium's own metalworking shop, the laundry room, central electric facilities, pump station, drainage and water-supply systems. Right down to the industrial potato peelers, these facilities paint a very clear picture of the scale of mechanisation of the sanatorium, which resembled completely autonomous, highly industrialised machinery located in beautiful, natural surroundings. The duality of the sanatorium, its doubling as a technological utopia and at the same time its setting inside a natural paradise, showed an interesting structural resemblance to the miners' normal working environment, but only as an inversion of each other because in mining, the environment was hostile and extremely dangerous.

Despite their image as rest homes in stark contrast to the conditions underground, those sanatoria remained part of the work-minded and performance-oriented culture of mining, resulting in only a temporary heterotopia for the miner, not a permanent one. Moreover, the sanatoria not only reflected the existing social structures, as shown in the room allocations and the weekly menu, which were both organised according to the miner's hierarchy, but also a concept of order which aimed to keep the miner under constant control. All patients were made to wear a standard-issue uniform which was meant to stop the spread of lice and spotted fever.[72] Long before any miner arrived at the sanatorium, during the selection process of those who might qualify for tuberculosis treatment, the doctors had to take great care to select only those who 'could be expected to act according to the doctor's orders and who are likely to see the treatment through to the end'. So, not only did the doctors have to diagnose tuberculosis, they also had to examine the social competencies of the miners in question, which, of course, should be more than what can reasonably be expected of any objective medical examination.[73]

The supervision of the ill miner included both the coexistence of doctors, patients, nurses and other staff, which was organised by a list of house rules, and the medical practices of diagnosis, therapy and patient supervision. Put together, these measures were intended to guarantee complete medical transparency of the miner's body. The spatial organisation of the sanatoria therefore produced a localised medical authority which could then carry out its functions efficiently. At work, and especially underground, this supervision was only possible to a very limited extent, if at all. There, the miners were able to retain some level of autonomy. This, however, was to become highly restricted in the medical facilities of the Knappschaft with the introduction of norms, codes of conduct and controls. That was the price the miners had to pay for these localised health utopias.

In fact, the hospitals and sanatoria of the AKV played a crucial role in the biopolitics of the mining industry in the Ruhr. Beside their functions to cure ill miners and reintegrate them into the working regime as productive workers, the medical infrastructure as described above additionally offered a social, hygiene-driven utopia for the employee as well as for the employers. Whereas the ill miners became acquainted with considerate medical care, a clean environment and the hope that it is possible to overcome occupational diseases, the pit owners thought that the hospitals realised their vision of a strong social order by exercising control over the miners' behaviour and bodies. Again, hygiene was the scientific discipline which could satisfy the claims of employees and employers to a social as well as a medical utopia.

Summary

With the enforcement of hygiene as a specific form of the bourgeois objectification of worker–environment relations at the end of nineteenth century, the whole system of medical care in mining also changed. This was not an effect of new health risks resulting from the mechanisation and reorganisation of the miners' workplace, and it was not a response to rising number of sick certificates. It was the hookworm epidemic which transformed the medical-care system of the Knappschaft in the Ruhr and which led to new strategic alliances of heterogeneous actors. The production of knowledge about the sanitary conditions of coal-mining workplaces within the frame of hygiene was initially overwhelmed by the general conflict between sanitationists and contagionists, which also affected the fight against the hookworm epidemic and with it the problematisation of the working conditions underground. With establishing mass examinations of the miners' faeces, bacteriological-oriented hygiene could push its biopolitical strategy, but the hygienic transformation of the miners' workplace environment, favoured by the Knappschaft, was still on the agenda as a long-term project. This mangle of biopolitical practice led to a comprehensive knowledge about the interaction between the worker's body and its workplace. The miner's body, its health and productiveness, was now an object of systematic research and biopolitical action.

Medical care was one side of the coin: increasing control, regulation and monitoring the other. Miners had to internalise the new hygienic norms and they were under constant suspicion of breaking the rules. Furthermore their bodies were now a scientific object of investigation and the physicians of the AKV tried to get total knowledge about the working body of the miners. A similar 'mixed blessing' could be found in the establishment of sanatoria and hospitals for miners of the Ruhr area around 1900, which fulfilled the hygienic standards at that time. This medical infrastructure was intended to fight the occupational diseases of the workers, both for care and economic reasons, but they were also seen as realisations of a perfect social order to control the behaviour and the bodies of the miners. The crucial point is that the hygiene movement, however, could act as a joint reference for all involved social groups and, therefore, the dominant and long lasting problematisation of workplaces in German mining was a hygienic one.

Notes

1. On the history of occupational safety see Weber, *Arbeitssicherheit*.
2. Schmitz, "Die Begründung eines spezifischen Frauenarbeitsschutzes durch die Gewerbehygiene."
3. Kaudelka, "Hygiene im Arbeitsleben," 123. See also Le Roux's article in this issue, 255–70.
4. Weber, *Arbeitssicherheit*, 88–96.
5. Wulf, *Der Sozialmediziner Ludwig Teleky (1872–1957)*, 33–5.
6. On the history of industrial hygiene in Germany see Klein and Miles, "Gewerbehygiene und soziale Sicherheit"; Labisch, "Neuere Beiträge zur Sozialgeschichte der Arbeitsmedizin in Deutschland"; Müller and Martin, "Institutionalisierung und Professionalisierung der Arbeitsmedizin in Deutschland."
7. Balkhausen, *Der Staat als Patient*.
8. Labisch, *Homo Hygienicus*, 105.
9. This was not only a phenomenon in Germany but also in France: Ewald, *Der Vorsorgestaat*.
10. Hüntelmann, *Hygiene im Namen des Staates*.
11. The different Knappschaften as regional, mutual-benefit institutions for miners were transformed in the eighteenth century into obligatory, state-controlled organisations. In the Ruhr area Knappschaften were founded after enacting orders for mining in 1766 and 1767. The Knappschaftsvereine at the Ruhr merged into a single Knappschaft so called Allgemeiner Knappschaftsverein zu Bochum (AKV) in 1890 which stands in the foreground of this article. After uniting the multitude of Knappschaftsvereine in Germany on a national level by founding the Reichsknappschaft in 1924, the regional organisations were nevertheless still working and had in many cases freedom of decision, for example by choosing different arrangements for health care. In the Ruhr the AKV was renamed the Ruhrknappschaft. The Knappschaft still exists today for health and pension insurance but is now open to all insured. On the history of the Allgemeine Knappschaftsverein zu Bochum (AKV) see: Lauf, *Der Allgemeine Knappschaftsverein zu Bochum (1890–1923)*. The history of the Reichsknappschaft is described in a broad social political frame by Geyer, *Die Reichsknappschaft*. On the early history of the Knappschaften in the Ruhr see: Brinkmann, "Die Geschichte der Knappschaft im Ruhrgebiet", see also Fessner, Bartels, and Slotta, *Auf breiten Schultern*.
12. On the medical system before 1851 see Balster, *Medizinische Wissenschaft und ärztliche Praxis im Leben des Bochumer Arztes Karl Arnold Kortum (1745–1824)*. Boventer, "Zur Geschichte der Knappschaftsärzte im Steinkohlenbergbau"; Müller, "Kortum als Arzt, Alchemist und Volksaufklärer."
13. Wrede, *Geschichte des Knappschaftsarztes an der Ruhr*, 10.
14. Britze, *Der Arzt in der Knappschaftsversicherung*, 19.
15. Weber, *Gescheiterte Sozialpartnerschaft – Gefährdete Republik?*, 40–4.
16. Internationale Arbeiterschutzkonferenz, *Die Protokolle der internationalen Arbeiterschutzkonferenz*.
17. Weisbrod, "Arbeitgeberpolitik und Arbeitsbeziehungen im Ruhrbergbau," 107–10. On the transformation of coal mining in the Ruhr by the process of industrialisation see Tenfelde, *Sozialgeschichte der Bergarbeiterschaft an der Ruhr im 19. Jahrhundert*.
18. Wächter, "Bergbau und industrielle Revolution in Deutschland," 256.
19. Burghardt, *Die Mechanisierung des Ruhrbergbaus 1890–1930*, 137–8.
20. Burghardt, *Die Mechanisierung des Ruhrbergbaus 1890–1930*, 115–31; Trischler, *Steiger im deutschen Bergbau*, 120–4; Tenfelde, "Der bergmännische Arbeitsplatz während der Hochindustrialisierung," 313–18.
21. Tenfelde, "Der bergmännische Arbeitsplatz während der Hochindustrialisierung," 311–12, 320.

22. Farrenkopf, *Schlagwetter und Kohlenstaub*.
23. Köhne, *Die deutschen Knappschaftsvereine, ihre Einrichtung und ihre Bedeutung*, 40.
24. For details see Bluma, "Der Hakenwurm an der Ruhr"; Langenfeld, *Die Ankylostomiasis im Ruhrgebiet*.
25. Löbker, *Die Ankylostomiasis und ihre Verbreitung unter den Bergleuten im Oberbergamtsbezirk Dortmund*, 4.
26. Lutz, "Ueber Ankylostoma duodenale und Ankylostomiasis," 2311–17.
27. See for example the book of the French physician and bacteriologist Albert Calmette: Calmette and Breton, *L'ancolostymiase*.
28. Martin, *Arbeiterschutz und Arbeitsmedizin im Ruhrbergbau 1865–1914*, 430.
29. Löbker, *Die Ankylostomiasis und ihre Verbreitung unter den Bergleuten im Oberbergamtsbezirk Dortmund*, 19.
30. Ibid., 29–30.
31. Tenholt, *Die Ankylostomiasis-Frage*, 36.
32. This path of infection was discovered by Artur Looss in 1901. But Tenholt, for example, revised his opinion that the hookworm penetrated the human body by mouth not until 1906. Looss, "Ueber das Eindringen der Ankylostomalarven in die menschliche Haut"; Looss, "Weiteres über die Einwanderung der Ankylostomen von der Haut"; Tenholt, "Ueber die Wurmkrankheit der Bergleute (Anchylostomiasis)."
33. Mills, *Regulating Health and Safety in the British Mining Industries, 1800–1914*, 173; Anonymous, "Mittel zur Bekämpfung der Wurmkrankheit," 714.
34. Goldmann, *Die Ankylostomiasis*, 42–4; Barbier, *La Lutte controle l'Ankylostomasie*.
35. Dieminger, *Beiträge zur Bekämpfung der Ankylostomiasis*, 3 4.
36. Langenfeld, *Die Ankylostomiasis im Ruhrgebiet*, 68–70.
37. Tenholt, *Die Ankylostomiasis-Frage*, 5–6.
38. Allgemeiner Knappschafts-Verein zu Bochum, *Verwaltungs-Bericht für das Jahr 1903*, 33.
39. Ibid., 7–13.
40. Langenfeld, *Die Ankylostomiasis im Ruhrgebiet*, 56.
41. Tenholt, *Die Ankylostomiasis-Frage*, 13–14.
42. Ibid., 17.
43. Bruns, *Die Bekämpfung der Wurmkrankheit* (Ankylostomiasis) *im rheinisch-westfälischen Ruhrkohlenbezirk*, 3.
44. Wüstenberg, "50 Jahre Hygienisches Institut im Ruhrgebiet"; Wüstenberg, *75 Jahre Hygiene-Institut des Ruhrgebiets Gelsenkirchen*.
45. Bruns, *Versuche über die Einwirkung einiger physikalischer und chemischer Agentien auf die Eier und Larven des Ankylostoma duodenal*, 2–3; Bruns, *Die Bekämpfung der Wurmkrankheit* (Ankylostomiasis) *im rheinisch-westfälischen Ruhrkohlenbezirk*, 21–22.
46. Bruns, *Die Bekämpfung der Wurmkrankheit* (Ankylostomiasis) *im rheinisch-westfälischen Ruhrkohlenbezirk*, 4.
47. It is an interesting notice that this conflict between sanationism and contagionism/quaratinism followed a similar dispute some years ago, when the Pettenkofer School as a proponent of the sanationism approach, and the Koch School represented by Bruns acrimoniously discussed the causes of a typhoid fever in Gelsenkirchen 1901. One effect of this dispute was the founding of the Gelsenkirchener Hygiene-Institut. Bluma, "Die Hygienisierung des Ruhrgebiets": Weyer-von Schoultz, *Die Gelsenkirchener Typhusepidemie und ihr gerichtliches Nachspiel*. On the dichotomy between Max Pettenkofer and Robert Koch see Baldwin, *Contagion and the State in Europe*, 143–9.
48. Tenholt, *Die Ankylostomiasis-Frage;* Bruns, *Versuche über die Einwirkung einiger physikalischer und chemischer Agentien auf die Eier und Larven des Ankylostoma duodenal*.
49. Tenholt, "Ueber die Wurmkrankheit der Bergleute (Anchylostomiasis)," 14.
50. Bluma, "Der Hakenwurm an der Ruhr," 319–20.
51. Anonymous, *Verhandlungen, betreffend Maßregeln zur Bekämpfung der im Oberbergamtsbezirke Dortmund herrschenden Wurmkrankheit*.
52. Bruns and Gärtner, *Gutachten über den derzeitigen Stand und die weitere Bekämpfung der Ankylostomiasis im Oberbergamtsbezirk Dortmund*, 29.
53. Bruns, *Die Bekämpfung der Wurmkrankheit* (Ankylostomiasis) *im rheinisch-westfälischen Ruhrkohlenbezirk*, 4.
54. Roth, "Gewerbehygiene und Fabrikgesetzgebung," 3.

55. Rubner, *Lehrbuch der Gewerbehygiene*, 722.
56. Timmerbeul, *Polizeibericht (Fuß-Gendarm Timmerbeul) über eine öffentliche Bergarbeiterversammlung zur Wurmkrankheit.*
57. Imbusch, *Arbeitsverhältnis und Arbeiterorganisationen im deutschen Bergbau*, 628–9.
58. Bruns, *Die mikroskopische Untersuchung des Fäzes in ihrer Bedeutung für die Bekämpfung der Ankylostomiasis*, 398.
59. Teleky, *History of Factory and Mine Hygiene*, 254–5.
60. Baldwin, *Contagion and the State in Europe*, 525.
61. On the formation of this network see: Trischler, "Arbeitsunfälle und Berufskrankheiten im Bergbau 1851 bis 1945."
62. Foucault, *The History of Sexuality*, 139–45 and with close reference to medicine Foucault, "The Birth of Social Medicine."
63. Thomsen, "Katholische Krankenhäuser im Ruhrrevier 1830–1914."
64. Lauf, "Knappschaftskrankenhäuser und -kureinrichtungen im Ruhrkohlenbergbau bis zum Ende der 1920er Jahre," 302; Thüer, *Das Prosper-Hospital Recklinghausen im wirtschaftlichen und sozialen Wandel 1848–1998*, 52.
65. Tenholt, *Das Gesundheitswesen im Bereiche des Allgemeinen Knappschaftsvereins zu Bochum*, 125–6.
66. Bluma, "Heterotope Orte," 71; Scheele, "Einhundert Jahre Chirurgie in der Huyssen-Stiftung."
67. Martin, "Medizintechnik im Ruhrgebiet."
68. Bluma, "Heterotope Orte," 76–9.
69. On the technical equipment of AKV's hospitals see in detail: Bluma, "Heterotope Orte," 69–80.
70. Allgemeiner Knappschaftsverein zu Bochum, *Die Auguste Viktoria Knappschafts-Heilstätte in Beringhausen bei Meschede i.W.*, 7.
71. Die Auguste Viktoria Knappschafts-Heilstätte in Beringhausen bei Meschede in Westfalen. Chefarzt Dr. Tenholt, Geh. Med. -Rat., Stadtarchiv Meschede, B 2525.
72. Thüer, "Die Recklinghäuser Krankenhäuser im Industriezeitalter," 255.
73. Allgemeiner Knappschaftsverein zu Bochum, *Geschäftsanweisung für die Knappschaftsärzte des Allgemeinen Knappschafts-Vereins zu Bochum*, 36.

Bibliography

Allgemeiner Knappschafts-Verein zu Bochum. *Verwaltungs-Bericht für das Jahr 1903. 1. Teil.* Bochum: Eigenverlag des AKV, 1903.

Allgemeiner Knappschaftsverein zu Bochum, ed. *Die Auguste Viktoria Knappschafts-Heilstätte in Beringhausen bei Meschede i.W, Denkschrift zur Feier der Eröffnung der Anstalt.* Berlin: W. Greve, 1904.

Allgemeiner Knappschafts-Verein zu Bochum, ed. *Geschäftsanweisung für die Knappschaftsärzte des Allgemeinen Knappschafts-Vereins zu Bochum.* Bochum: Eigenverlag des AKV, 1911.

Anonymous, "Mittel zur Bekämpfung der Wurmkrankheit." *Glückauf* 25, no. 30 (Juli 1903): 714.

Anonymous. *Verhandlungen, betreffend Maßregeln zur Bekämpfung der im Oberbergamtsbezirke Dortmund herrschenden Wurmkrankheit. Konferenz am 4. April 1903.* Berlin: Norddt. Buchdruck, 1903.

Baldwin, Peter. *Contagion and the State in Europe, 1830–1930.* Cambridge: Cambridge University Press, 1999.

Balkhausen, Irmtraud. *Der Staat als Patient. Rudolf Virchow und die Erfindung der Sozialmedizin von 1848*. Marburg: Tectum, 2007.

Balster, Wolfgang. *Medizinische Wissenschaft und ärztliche Praxis im Leben des Bochumer Arztes Karl Arnold Kortum (1745–1824). Medizinhistorische Analyse seines Patiententagebuches*. Bochum: Univ. Diss., 1990.

Barbier, A. *La Lutte contre l'Ankylostomasie*. Brussels: Adamant Media Corperation, 1903.

Bluma, Lars. "Der Hakenwurm an der Ruhr. Umwelt, Körper und soziale Netzwerke im Bergbaus des Kaiserreichs." *Der Anschnitt: Zeitschrift für Kunst und Kultur im Bergbau* 61, no. 5/6 (2009): 314–29.

Bluma, Lars. "Heterotope Orte: Raumhistorische Dimensionen des knappschaftlichen Krankenhauswesens im Ruhrgebiet." In *Berufliches Risiko und soziale Sicherheit*, edited by Christoph Bartels, 67–98. Bochum: Selbstverlag des Deutschen Bergbau-Museums, 2010.

Bluma, Lars. "Die Hygienisierung des Ruhrgebiets: Das Gelsenkirchener Hygiene-Institut im Kaiserreich." In *Seuche und Mensch. Herausforderung in den Jahrhunderten*, edited by Carl Christian Wahrmann, Martin Buchsteiner, and Antje Strahl, 347–67. Berlin: Duncker & Humblot, 2012.

Boventer, Karl. "Zur Geschichte der Knappschaftsärzte im Steinkohlenbergbau." In *Sudhoffs Archiv für Geschichte der Medizin und der Naturwissenschaften* 48 (1964): 54–62.

Brinkmann, Heinrich. "Die Geschichte der Knappschaft im Ruhrgebiet." *Der Kompass. Zeitschrift für Sozialversicherung im Bergbau* 6 (1967): 175–99.

Britze, Hans. *Der Arzt in der Knappschaftsversicherung*. Engelsdorf-Leipzig: Vogel, 1929.

Bruns, Hayo. *Die Bekämpfung der Wurmkrankheit (Ankylostomiasis) im rheinisch-westfälischen Ruhrkohlenbezirk. Separatabdruck aus der Münchener medizinischen Wochenschrift 15 & 16 (1904)*. Munich: J.F. Lehmann, 1904.

Bruns, Hayo. *Versuche über die Einwirkung einiger physikalischer und chemischer Agentien auf die Eier und Larven des Ankylostoma duodenal, nebst Bemerkungen über die Bekämpfung der Krankheit im Ruhrkohlengebiet*. Jena: Fischer, 1904.

Bruns, Hayo. *Die mikroskopische Untersuchung der Fäzes in ihrer Bedeutung für die Bekämpfung der Ankylostomiasis. Ein Bericht über den Stand der Wurmkrankheit im Ruhrkohlengebiet nach 10jähriger Bekämpfung. Seperat-Abdruck aus der Zeitschrift für Hygiene und Infektionskrankheiten 78 (1914)*. Leipzig: Springer Berlin, 1914.

Bruns, Hayo, and August Gärtner. *Gutachten über den derzeitigen Stand und die weitere Bekämpfung der Ankylostomiasis im Oberbergamtsbezirk Dortmund*. Jena: Thaden & Schmemann, 1914.

Burghardt, Uwe. *Die Mechanisierung des Ruhrbergbaus 1890–1930*. Munich: C.H. Beck, 1995.

Calmette, Albert, and M. Breton. *L'ankylostomiase: maladie sociale (anémie des mineurs): biologie, clinique, traitement, prophylaxie*. Paris: Masson, 1905.

Dieminger. *Beiträge zur Bekämpfung der Ankylostomiasis. Nachtragsbericht an die Kgl. Regierung zu Arnsberg*. Jena: G. Fischer, 1905.

Ewald, Francois. *Der Vorsorgestaat*. Frankfurt a.M. Suhrkamp, 1993.

Farrenkopf, Michael. *Schlagwetter und Kohlenstaub: das Explosionsrisiko im industriellen Ruhrbergbau (1850–1914)*. Bochum: Selbstverlag des Deutschen Bergbau-Museums, 2003.

Fessner, Michael, Christoph Bartels, and Rainer Slotta, eds. *Auf breiten Schultern. 750 Jahre Knappschaft. Katalog der Ausstellung des Deutschen Bergbau-Museums Bochum 1. Juli 2010-20. März 2011*. Bochum: Selbstverlag des Deutschen Bergbau-Museums, 2010.

Foucault, Michel. *The History of Sexuality. Volume 1: An Introduction*. New York: Vintage Books, 1990.

Foucault, Michel. "The Birth of Social Medicine." In *Essential Works of Foucault 1954–1984, Volume 3: Power*, edited by James D. Faubion, 134–56. London: Penguin Books, 2002.

Geyer, Martin H. *Die Reichsknappschaft. Versicherungsreformen und Sozialpolitik im Bergbau 1900–1945*. Munich: C.H. Beck, 1987.

Goldmann, Hugo. *Die Ankylostomiasis. Eine Berufskrankheit des Berg-, Ziegel- und Tunnelarbeiters*. Vienna/Leipzig: W. Braunmüller, 1900.

Hüntelmann, Axel C. *Hygiene im Namen des Staates, das Reichsgesundheitsamt 1876–1933*. Göttingen: Wallstein, 2008.

Imbusch, Heinrich. *Arbeitsverhältnis und Arbeiterorganisationen im deutschen Bergbau. Eine geschichtliche Darstellung*. Essen: Verlag des Gewerkvereins christlicher Bergarbeiter, 1908.

Internationale Arbeiterschutzkonferenz. *Die Protokolle der internationalen Arbeiterschutzkonferenz. In amtlichem Auftrag.* Leipzig: Duncker & Humblot, 1890.

Kaudelka, Karin. "Hygiene im Arbeitsleben. Zwischen persönlicher Verantwortung und staatlicher Regulierung." In *"Sei sauber...!" Eine Geschichte der Hygiene und öffentlichen Gesundheitsvorsorge in Europa,* edited by Marie-Paule Jungblut, 120–31. Cologne: Wienand, 2004.

Klein, Paul, and Dietrich Miles. "Gewerbehygiene und soziale Sicherheit. Konzepte und Perspektiven in Deutschland vor 1933." In *Beiträge zur Geschichte der Arbeiterkrankheiten und der Arbeitsmedizin in Deutschland,* edited by Bundesanstalt für Arbeitsschutz, 501–13. Dortmund: Wirtschaftsverlag NW, 1984.

Köhne, August. *Die deutschen Knappschaftsvereine, ihre Einrichtung und ihre Bedeutung.* Hannover: Helwing, 1915.

Labisch, Alfons. "Neuere Beiträge zur Sozialgeschichte der Arbeitsmedizin in Deutschland." In *Beiträge zur Geschichte der Arbeiterkrankheiten und der Arbeitsmedizin in Deutschland,* edited by Bundesanstalt für Arbeitsschutz, 26–45. Dortmund: Wirtschaftsverlag NW, 1984.

Labisch, Alfons. *Homo Hygienicus. Gesundheit und Medizin in der Neuzeit.* Frankfurt am Main: Campus, 1992.

Langenfeld, Heiner. *Die Ankylostomiasis im Ruhrgebiet: ein Beitrag zur Geschichte der medizinischen Parasitologie.* Frankfurt a. M./Bern: Lang, 1981.

Lauf, Ulrich. "Knappschaftskrankenhäuser und –kureinrichtungen im Ruhrkohlenbergbau bis zum Ende der 1920er Jahre." *Der Anschnitt: Zeitschrift für Kunst und Kultur im Bergbau* 61, no. 5/6 (2009): 302–13.

Lauf, Ulrich. *Der Allgemeine Knappschaftsverein zu Bochum (1890–1923). Mythos und Wirklichkeit.* Bochum: Selbstverlag des Deutschen Bergbau-Museums, 2009.

Le Roux, T. "Hygienists, workers' bodies and machines in nineteenth-century France." *European Review of History* 20, no. 2 (2013): 255–70.

Löbker, Ferdinand. *Die Ankylostomiasis und ihre Verbreitung unter den Bergleuten im Oberbergamtsbezirk Dortmund.* Wiesbaden: Bergmann, 1896.

Looss, Arthur. "Ueber das Eindringen der Ankylostomalarven in die menschliche Haut." *Zentralblatt für Bakteriologie* 29 (1901): 733–9.

Looss, Arthur. "Weiteres über die Einwanderung der Ankylostomen von der Haut aus." *Zentralblatt für Bakteriologie* 33 (1903): 330–43.

Lutz, Adolph. "Ueber Ankylostoma duodenale und Ankylostomiasis." *Sammlung Klinischer Vorträge in Verbindung mit deutschen Klinikern* (1885): 255–256, 265, 2295–2350; (1886), 2467–2507.

Martin, Michael. *Arbeiterschutz und Arbeitsmedizin im Ruhrbergbau 1865–1914,* PhD diss., Ruhr University Bochum (microfiche) 2000.

Martin, Michael. "Medizintechnik im Ruhrgebiet. Vom Bergmannsheil zur Life Science Industry." In *Technikgeschichte im Ruhrgebiet – Technikgeschichte für das Ruhrgebiet,* edited by Manfred Rasch and Dietmar Bleidick, 875–91. Essen: Klartext, 2004.

Mills, Catherine. *Regulating Health and Safety in the British Mining Industries, 1800–1914.* Farnham: Ashgate, 2010.

Müller, Irmgard. "Kortum als Arzt, Alchemist und Volksaufklärer." In *Carl Arnold Kortum. 1745–1824, Arzt, Forscher, Literat,* edited by Kortum-Gesellschaft, 92–103. Bochum e.V. Essen: Pomp, 1995.

Müller, Irmgard, and Michael Martin. "Institutionalisierung und Professionalisierung der Arbeitsmedizin in Deutschland." *Archiwum Historii I Filozofii Medycyny* 61, no. 2–3 (1998): 129–44.

Roth, Emanuel. "Gewerbehygiene und Fabrikgesetzgebung." In *Handbuch der Hygiene. Achter Band: Gewerbehygiene, mit besonderer Rücksicht auf Fabrikgesetzgebung, Unfallschutz und Wohlfahrtseinrichtungen,* edited by Theodor Weyl, 1–78. Jena: Verlag von Gustav Fischer, 1897.

Rubner, Max. *Lehrbuch der Hygiene. Systematische Darstellung der Hygiene und ihrer Untersuchungs-Methoden.* 5th edition Leipzig: Franz Deuticke, 1895.

Scheele, Karl. "Einhundert Jahre Chirurgie in der Huyssen-Stiftung." *100 Jahre Huyssens-Stiftung. Evangelisches Krankenhaus Essen 1854–1954,* 56–73. Essen: Girardet, 1954.

Schmitz, Birgit. "Die Begründung eines spezifischen Frauenarbeitsschutzes durch die Gewerbehygiene." In *Beiträge zur Geschichte der Arbeiterkrankheiten und der Arbeitsmedizin in Deutschland,* edited by Bundesanstalt für Arbeitsschutz, 425–37. Dortmund: Wirtschaftsverlag NW, 1984.

Teleky, Ludwig. *History of Factory and Mine Hygiene*. New York: Columbia University Press, 1948.

Tenfelde, Klaus. "Der bergmännische Arbeitsplatz während der Hochindustrialisierung (1890 – 1914)." In *Arbeiter im Industrialisierungsprozeß. Herkunft, Lage und Verhalten*, edited by Werner Conze and Ulrich Engelhardt, 283–335. Stuttgart: Klett-Cotta, 1979.

Tenfelde, Klaus. *Sozialgeschichte der Bergarbeiterschaft an der Ruhr im 19. Jahrhundert*. 2nd edition Bonn: Neue Gesellschaft GmbH, 1981.

Tenholt, August. *Das Gesundheitswesen im Bereiche des Allgemeinen Knappschafts-Vereins zu Bochum. General-Bericht des Knappschafts-Oberarztes Regierungs- und Medizinalrath a.D. Dr. Tenholt*. Bochum: Stumpf, 1897.

Tenholt, August. *Die Ankylostomiasis-Frage. Zusammenfassende Uebersicht*. Jena: G. Fischer, 1903.

Tenholt, August. "Ueber die Wurmkrankheit der Bergleute (Anchylostomiasis)." *Berliner Klinik* 213 (1906): 1–22.

Thomsen, Arne. "Katholische Krankenhäuser im Ruhrrevier 1830–1914." In *Berufliches Risiko und soziale Sicherheit*, edited by Christoph Bartels, 99–108. Bochum: Klartext, 2010.

Thüer, Christoph. *Das Prosper-Hospital Recklinghausen im wirtschaftlichen und sozialen Wandel 1848–1998*. Recklinghausen: Bitter, 1998.

Thüer, Christoph. "Die Recklinghäuser Krankenhäuser im Industriezeitalter." In *Recklinghausen im Industriezeitalter*, edited by Klaus Bresser and Christoph Thüer, 247–70. Recklinghausen: Bitter, 2000.

Timmerbeul. "Polizeibericht (Fuß-Gendarm Timmerbeul) über eine öffentliche Bergarbeiterversammlung zur Wurmkrankheit und die Erlangung des vollen Krankengeldes in Altenbochum vom 2.8.1903." Transcription, Landearchiv NRW Abt. Westfalen, RA 14377. In *Das Ruhrgebiet – Ein historisches Lesebuch in zwei Bänden, Bd. 1*, edited by Klaus Tenfelde and Thomas Urban, 258–9. Essen: Klartext, 2010.

Trischler, Helmuth. *Steiger im deutschen Bergbau. Zur Sozialgeschichte der technischen Angestellten 1815–1945*. Munich: C.H. Beck, 1988.

Trischler, Helmuth. "Arbeitsunfälle und Berufskrankheiten im Bergbau 1851 bis 1945. Bergbehördliche Sozialpolitik im Spannungsfeld von Sicherheit und Produktionsinteressen." *Archiv für Sozialgeschichte* 28 (1988): 111–51.

Wächter, Eberhard. "Bergbau und industrielle Revolution in Deutschland – Gedanken zum Thema." In *Montan- und Industriegeschichte. Dokumentation und Forschung, Industriearchäologie und Museum*, edited by Stefan Brüggerhoff, Michael Farrenkopf, and Wilhelm Geerlings, Paderborn: Ferdinand Schöningh, 2006.

Weber, Petra. *Gescheiterte Sozialpartnerschaft – Gefährdete Republik? Industrielle Beziehungen, Arbeitskämpfe und der Sozialstaat. Deutschland und Frankreich im Vergleich (1918–1933/39)*, 247–259. Munich: R. Oldenbourg Verlag, 2010.

Weber, Wolfhard. *Arbeitssicherheit. Historische Beispiele – aktuelle Analysen*. Reinbek: Rowohlt Taschenbuch Verlag, 1988.

Weisbrod, Bernd. "Arbeitgeberpolitik und Arbeitsbeziehungen im Ruhrbergbau. Vom "Herr-im-Haus" zur Mitbestimmung." In *Arbeiter, Unternehmer und Staat im Bergbau. Industrielle Beziehungen im internationalen Vergleich*, edited by Gerald D. Feldman and Klaus Tenfelde, 107–62. Munich: C.H. Beck, 1989.

Weyer-von Schoultz, Martin. "Die Gelsenkirchener Typhusepidemie und ihr gerichtliches Nachspiel." In *Stadt, Krankheit und Tod. Geschichte der städtischen Gesundheitsverhältnisse während der Epidemologischen Transition (vom 18. bis ins frühe 20. Jahrhundert)*, edited by Jörg Vögele and Wolfgang Woelk, 317–35. Berlin: Duncker & Humblot, 2000.

Wrede, Hubert. *Geschichte des Knappschaftsarztes an der Ruhr*. Bochum: Hoose, 1978.

Wüstenberg, Joachim. "50 Jahre Hygienisches Institut im Ruhrgebiet." In *Festschrift zum 50jährigen Bestehen des Vereins zur Bekämpfung der Volkskrankheiten im Ruhrkohlengebiet und seines hygienischen Instituts*, edited by Joachim Wüstenberg, 11–52. Gelsenkirchen: Bertenburg, 1952.

Wüstenberg, Joachim. *75 Jahre Hygiene-Institut des Ruhrgebiets Gelsenkirchen*. Gelsenkirchen: Verein zur Bekämpfung der Volkskrankheiten im Ruhrkohlengebiet, 1977.

Wulf, Andreas. *Der Sozialmediziner Ludwig Teleky (1872–1957) und die Entwicklung der Gewerbehygiene zur Arbeitsmedizin*. Frankfurt am Main: Mabuse Verlag, 2001.

The banning of white lead: French and American experiences in a comparative perspective (early twentieth century)

Judith Rainhorn

Université Lille-Nord de France (Valenciennes, Calhiste) - Institut universitaire de France - Esopp, EHESS

Since the early nineteenth century, white lead has been identified as a harmful agent responsible for creating toxicity affecting workers in plants and painting sites. Its use nevertheless increased dramatically in major industrialised countries, making lead poisoning one of the most widespread occupational diseases. This article aims to examine and compare the stakeholders, the processes and chronological trends through two historical experiences (France and the United States) on the issue of occupational lead poisoning in the paint industry in the early twentieth century. It emphasises two different national approaches to achieving the same goal: reducing – and eventually eliminating – the use of lead paint during the inter-war period. Investigating decision makers at different levels, the article seeks to explain the limited public awareness and public participation in the debate on occupational diseases, in order to assess the disclosure and process of giving up white-lead paint in both countries.

> *Raise your voice in song from North to South and East to West*
> *Sing the praises of the lead you know to be the best;*
> *Don't take any substitute when you go to invest,*
> *After you've gone from Alabama [...].*
> *Tell them in the North and South of its opacity,*
> *Tell them East and West it is the lead of quality,*
> *Tell them how it covers – of its great capacity,*
> *After you've gone from Alabama.*

Song by the Carter Quartet, advertising the Carter White Lead paint (Chicago, 1906).[1]

Introduction

This article examines the reality and, more to the point, the perceptions of the occupational-health risks at the beginning of the twentieth century by comparing the situations in France and the United States. The goal of this comparison is to place the national struggles and stakes in a transnational and comparative perspective, just as the (mostly US) scholars publishing in previous decades – as well as the most recent developments in historical research on occupational health and safety, especially in Europe[2] – have invited us to do. As Sellers states, 'in the history of industrial hazards, further investigation is needed of the different ways in which toxins and their effects have been viewed across times and places other than our own', inviting scholars to a 'cross-nationalizing study' of lead.[3]

Through the emblematic case of lead paint, I do not so much draw up a detailed inventory of the proliferation of lead poisoning in industrial workers in France and the United States, as I try to clarify the decision-making processes, chronological patterns and principal players in the prohibition of white lead (PbCO3) in paint in the first half of the twentieth century. The question of lead poisoning seems to be a particularly good example of the slow progressive development of the social rhetoric about occupational health and safety and occupational diseases at the turn of the twentieth century. Thus, examining the case of lead poisoning allows us to consider these issues both in a comparative perspective, which will be done here, and a transnational perspective due to the great importance of the circulation of ideas and international scientific debates which have partly been assessed elsewhere.[4]

At the beginning of the twentieth century, France was engaged in an extremely animated discussion about lead poisoning involving health-care professionals and industrial hygiene and health specialists in both the political and professional spheres. A few years earlier, intense debates led to the law of 9 April 1898, which recognised employers' liability in occupational hazards. The US context was quite different in that the United States was relatively silent about the issues of occupational health and safety: until around the 1920s, publications were rare and essentially limited to a few very restricted professional spheres. Thus, comparing the working conditions in France and the United States in terms of health and the risks of industrial poisoning on the one hand, and the public awareness and discourse about this issue on the other, will allow us to frame the issues in many ways:

(1) We can step back from national history, to place the discussion in a larger historical context of transnational exchanges and the circulation of ideas. This perspective allows the often simplistic opposition between national patterns to be called into question: in this case, the French prohibition approach and the US dissuasion approach to occupational health.

(2) We can take occupational health and safety out of the traditional binary conflict between capital and labour that has long been part of discussions about labour history, which seems to me to be relatively unproductive.

(3) We can explore the complex problem of decision-making levels with respect to legislation, social transformation and reform. In France, the national government and the legislators appeared early as the authority that regulated conflicts related to working conditions, whereas in the United States, workers and their representatives only had recourse to laws later on, working with decision-making levels that ranged from state to federal government, and that varied over time.

Anchored in these methodological concerns, my contribution successively tackles three issues in a comparative perspective. First, it evokes the massive industrialisation at the end of the nineteenth/beginning of the twentieth century, which had a high social cost in terms of occupational health in the two geographic areas. Both areas had different time frames, with the industrial shockwave moving more rapidly and more powerfully in the United States than in Europe. In the paint sector, the extensive use of white lead and other lead pigments made the work unhealthful, both for manufacturing and using the paint, thus generating serious workplace risks. Secondly, there is a relatively large time gap between the two countries in terms of when the debate about this problem erupted in the public domain, and when it started attracting serious attention. In France, as early as the 1880s, the problem of workers' lead poisoning began generating protests on the part of health-care professionals and industrial-hygiene specialists, followed by workers and trade unions, together with policy makers. However, in the United States, public opinion was almost indifferent; at least most observers and the press remained silent about the problem of industrial poisons before the 1920s, except for a few notable individuals and isolated pressure groups. Lastly, I will assess how the divergent processes and the time gap that characterise the treatment of this problem nonetheless produced similar results, albeit by different paths: the almost total abandonment of lead paint in France and the United States in the 1940s. But the reasons given for this change, the implementation mechanisms, the methods used to raise public awareness, and the mobilisation of the political authorities are quite different in the two countries.

I. Victims of lead poisoning in the paint industry: similar realities on both sides of the Atlantic

At the beginning of the twentieth century, the poisoning of house painters by the lead oxides contained in certain colour pigments, particularly white lead, was not a new issue in the industrial countries of Europe. Many observers had already identified this problem in artisans and industrial workers alike. For two centuries, these observers had directly accused lead as being the cause of 'lead colic', also called 'painter's colic'.[5] Since the middle of the nineteenth century, its intense whiteness, strong covering capacity and weather resistance had made the use of white lead increase, at the same time as rapid urbanisation greatly heightened the need for paint in construction projects.

The early French reaction

After being imported from Holland and England for half a century, white lead was then manufactured in France from the early nineteenth century, mainly in the Lille region, where approximately 500 workers worked in a dozen plants around 1900. Among the most important establishments were Faure, soon bought by Expert-Bezançon, Théodore-Lefebvre and Veuve Pérus. The last few decades of the nineteenth century occasioned a fierce combat between the white-lead manufacturers in Lille and Paris and the hospital, local and prefectural authorities, who were trying to put an end to the lead-poisoning epidemic in the workers in this sector. White-lead workers, often falling sick after only a few days or weeks on the job, were filling the wards in all the Lille hospitals due to the unhealthy working conditions, made worse by the lack of protective clothing.[6]

Surrendering to the power of the authorities, the white-lead manufacturers were forced to greatly modify their industrial installations. If the hospital sources at the beginning of the twentieth century can be believed, these modifications very likely helped to make the working conditions in the white-lead factories healthier and caused a dramatic reduction in the risk of lead poisoning in these factories.[7] Still, the prevalence of lead poisoning remained significant among workers using white lead (still close to 100% according to some authors[8]), but now it was the house painters that attracted the attention of the doctors and the public authorities. In fact, although the risk of developing visible signs of lead poisoning was clearly lower for the painters than for white-lead factory workers, the number of painters in the population of blue-collar workers was much greater. As a result they always appeared at the top of the list of workers affected by this disease on a national scale; alone, they made up approximately 50% of the victims of lead poisoning.[9] Despite the obscurity of the available statistics, which are always partial and rarely reliable due to the non-existence of sources for evaluating the epidemic, it is clear that the painters, sanders and finishers, who were in daily contact with white lead, constituted the bulk of the lead-poisoning patients.

For this reason, these workers were the first to be subjected to protective measures, implemented at the local and national levels at the very beginning of the twentieth century:

(1) The prohibition of the use of white lead by some ministries (national decrees) and some municipalities (local laws) in the public-works projects under their control between 1900 and 1902;

(2) The decree of 18 July 1902, stipulating the use of white-lead paste rather than powder on work sites (article 1), which reduced the risk of inhaling lead dust; the same decree prohibited the bare-handed manipulation of white lead (article 2) and the dry scraping of paint (article 3);

(3) The 1903 vote by the French Parliament on a proposed law that totally prohibited the use of white lead in all painting projects, which launched a legislative process that ended in – after a long series of parliamentary and ministerial manoeuvres – the first law prohibiting the use of white lead: this law was finally passed in 1909 and envisioned the suppression of white lead in 1915, leaving the manufacturers the time to switch over rapidly to another product. Even if the law was not properly implemented before the 1926 ratification of the ILO convention, as we will argue, France can be acknowledged as an early actor in the recognition process of white-lead hazards among industrialised countries.[10]

The late US concern

Global statistics about the extent of worker lead poisoning for the United States are even less available than for France.[11] This can be partially explained by the size of the country, the geographic distribution of its industry and especially the lack of public discussion about the issues of occupational diseases and occupational health and safety. In truth, the US paint industry had not been frequently called into question in the nineteenth century; on the contrary, it had been developing massively. The first white-lead factory was set up in 1804 in Philadelphia by Samuel Wetherhill. The War of 1812 between the United States and Great Britain, by provoking a blockade around the east coast, encouraged the emergence of local industry to the detriment of British imports. Between 1815 and 1830, white-lead factories sprouted up all over the country and soon merged into the National Lead Company.[12] The country then experienced an unprecedented urban and industrial revolution in the two decades following the Civil War. At the beginning of the twentieth century, the paint industry became one of the most prosperous in the United States, manufacturing over 100 million gallons of paint per year and using almost half the lead the country produced to do so.[13] Indeed, 150,000 tons of lead pigments, to which must be added 70,000 tons of zinc pigments, were produced each year by the principal factories in Chicago (Carter White Lead Company: 14,000 tons), New York City (Atlantic White Lead and Linseed Oil Works: 12,000 tons), and Cincinnati (Eagle White Lead Company: 12,000 tons).[14] These pigments entered the composition of the paint produced in United States at the beginning of the twentieth century.

Most of the US white-lead factories used a manufacturing process called the 'Dutch process', which was similar to the process used in France, except that the latter had been improved with respect to health conditions, under the impetus of the French medical and political authorities. Such improvements hadn't necessarily reached the US companies.

According to the available eyewitness reports, the manufacturing conditions in the United States were rudimentary; the workers lacked protective equipment and transported shovels, wheelbarrows and tipcarts full of white-lead powder through air permeated with white-lead dust, without the benefit of masks, gloves or protective clothing. In the *Illinois Report on Occupational Diseases* (1911), Dr Alice Hamilton, appointed as general investigator for the industrial survey by the Governor of Illinois[15], noted the impracticality of keeping white-lead factories safe, because of the dust produced by the process:

> Even in the two factories where the managers are doing all that they believe possible to render the work safer there still remain processes which are very dangerous, such as the emptying of the stacks and of the drying pans and the heading up of the barrels. So far no method has been devised for rendering these processes safe. Only one of the three factories [visited in Illinois] has done away with hand trucking altogether, in the other two trucks are still emptied by hand. [. . .] Dry sweeping [is] the rule.[16]

The improvements in the US white-lead industry at the turn of the twentieth century seemed to be more along the line of enhancing the chemical-manufacturing process itself. For example, in the final years of the 1890s, Carter of Chicago invented a process that reduced the transformation of lead into white lead from 20 days to around 12 days thanks to acetic acid, thus considerably accelerating production. In just a few years, Carter sold his patented process to some of his competitors and became the leader in the white-lead market in the United States, spreading the most dangerous process of manufacturing white lead.[17]

Here as in France, house painters rapidly became the most endangered profession among industrial lead users. Although the onset of lead poisoning was slower among painters than among white-lead workers (making symptoms developing during apprenticeship quite rare) it frequently appeared after several years, leading to fatal paralysis. In Illinois, in the 1910s, a quarter of the lead-poisoned workers in industry were painters, sandpapering being the most dangerous task, because of the significant amount of lead dust filling the atmosphere of the workplace:

> This sandpapering produces clouds of very fine white lead dust, which the workmen breathe in. It is done usually inside a building, in interior work in houses, in the painting of railway cars, street cars, carriages, coaches, automobiles and even wagons. The room in which the work is done is tightly closed to keep out drafts of air, which might scatter dust on freshly painted surfaces. There is never any exhaust system to carry off the dust [. . .]. The paint which is sanded often contains as much as 80 per cent white lead, the putty, which is also sanded, may be 95 per cent white lead.[18]

Responsible for very rapid and severe forms of lead poisoning, sandpapering was also frequently done by unskilled workers; often these were new immigrants mostly from Europe with no idea of the danger connected with their work. The danger was explained to the workers in English, when it was explained at all. Moreover, the nexus seems very important between the unprecedented scale of immigrant manpower in the US industrial system on the one hand, and the deafening silence on sanitary working conditions in the early twentieth century on the other.

II. The situation of lead poisoning in the public debate

During the nineteenth century, a subject of (very) limited concern

The problem of lead poisoning in the workers who manufactured white lead and the painters who used it was, for a long time, only a subject of concern for the medical profession and the industrial-health movement. In France, as in other European industrialised countries such as Great Britain and Germany, the nineteenth century was an era when considerable scientific knowledge about occupational diseases was amassed, knowledge that reflected the evolving concerns about occupational health and safety under the conditions of industrialisation.[19] Specialised journals, such as the *Annales d'hygiène publique et de médecine légale* (Annals of Public Hygiene and Forensic Medicine), the *Revue d'hygiène et de police sanitaire* (Review of Hygiene and Sanitation Police) or the *Gazette médicale de Paris* (Paris Medical Gazette), published in this era an abundance of articles on occupational diseases (about 100 between 1829 and 1880), and gave limited attention relatively early, echoing the increasing interest in industrial poisoning and professional wear-and-tear. These periodicals published many articles about the health of workers in all the trades using lead (for example, painters, printers, porcelain workers, enamellers, and so on) as early as the 1830s and even more from 1880.[20] Although one of the main concerns about occupational health and safety in the industry, the white-lead issue nevertheless remained restricted to a circle of doctors, hygienists and public-health-related professionals, before the early years of twentieth century.

The attention paid to lead poisoning seems to have arrived significantly later in the United States. In fact, there was no significant publication denouncing this professional affliction before the beginning of the twentieth century, when a limited number of articles began appearing and continued throughout the following decade. In 1909, the American Clifford Holley wrote a 340-page book about the use of lead oxides in paint without any mention, even in the footnotes, of the eminently toxic nature of these substances or the precautions that needed to be taken when using them.[21] With no pressure from public communications and no compulsory reform legislation, the journal *The Carter Times*, published by the Carter white-lead company in Chicago, could obviously not be expected to denounce white lead. However, it certainly could have given information on precautions when using the product it promoted. Without opposing views, *The Carter Times* was able to present the manipulation of white-lead pigment and lead paint as totally inoffensive as late as the 1930s: painters mixing white lead, oil and paint with their bare hands, children manipulating the product, even babies proudly playing with their *'papa's lead'*

Figure 1. In The Carter Times (Carter White Lead Company, Chicago), no. 1, March 1906. Source: Courtesy of New York Public Library.

Figure 2. In The Carter Times (Carter White Lead Company, Chicago), Autumn 1909. Source: Courtesy of New York Public Library.

(Figure 1 and Figure 2). This is admittedly a trade publication; however, advertisements for the general public frequently vaunted the merit, the quality and the resistance of lead paint as late as the 1940s. Wherever it appeared, propaganda in favour of white lead seemed to promote no contradiction by diminishing or even concealing the serious risk of irreparable harm from the product. This definitely reveals a wide discrepancy between our two national cases.

1900 to the Great War: the French press and the public debate on lead poisoning

The time gap between France and the United States with respect to the appearance of the debates on industrial poisoning deserves special attention. In France, the huge scientific knowledge mentioned above was slow to be provided with legal status and force; in truth, legal measures and regulations regarding occupational health and safety were adopted at a very slow pace at the turn of the twentieth century.

After half a century of scientific discussions, the problem of white lead being poisonous had achieved national recognition, thanks to the vigorous campaign in the press that started in 1901 and increased in the following years. The issue of industrial poisons never competed with national political issues as did the School quarrel or the separation of Church and State, but it gained attention in the general press. In August 1904, the many damaging editorials by Clémenceau denouncing the owners of white-lead factories in L'Aurore were bolts from the blue[22], as was the special issue of L'Assiette au Beurre, a satirical popular paper, in 1905, entirely dedicated to this economic and social scandal (Figure 3). The intense debate within the government for the first decrees mentioned above gave the people supporting the prohibition of white lead a favourable national context. The first years of the twentieth century saw phenomenal growth in articles in the press, satires, expert reports, conferences and books in which ardent opponents of white lead, and its equally ardent defenders, tried to convince diverse segments of the public of the reality or illusory nature of the lead-poisoning epidemic among house painters.

Figure 3. Front cover of the *Assiette au Beurre* satirical paper, special issue on the white-lead industry, no. 210, 1905. All rights reserved.

The French parliamentary context obviously gave the problem a national platform when the members of Parliament passed a law prohibiting the use of white lead in paint in June 1903. This initiative set in motion the back-and-forth process between the two chambers of Parliament that resulted, after six years, in the final text of a law and launched a public debate. The decision of the Senate, conservator of the interests of employers and industry, was suspended pending the results of a parliamentary inquiry that was considered by many to be dilatory, even more so because the inquiry was confided to Senator Alcide Treille[23], famous for his hostility to public intervention in health and sanitation matters. In just a few months, this senator became the person that the adversaries of white lead loved to hate.

It was thus a veritable concert of mutual denunciations that appeared in France with the new century. In the decade preceding the First World War, the public debate about the prohibition of white lead was relatively high profile and led to the long collective consideration of social legislation, especially the assimilation of occupational diseases into the legal definition of industrial accidents. This public debate explains the important role that France, working through the International Labour Organization, played in the internationalisation process of the issue of lead poisoning shortly after the First World War, as we argue below. Long acknowledged as a pioneer in the fight against white lead[24], France situated the issue of lead poisoning in a professional context, which is a curious contrast to the deafening silence that reigned over this issue on the other side of the Atlantic.

The lack of public debate on occupational health and safety issues in the United States

The great industrial boom and the explosion of urban manufacturing centres that the United States had generated by the turn of the twentieth century had dramatic consequences, making 'the American workplace among the most dangerous in the world' as Rosner and Markowitz argue.[25] Beyond the sympathetic interests and the murmurs of protest one can find here and there, the whole nation seemed to be quite unconcerned about the occupational health and safety issue. As one observer reported in 1907: 'How many [people are killed], none can say exactly, for we [are] too busy making our record breaking production to count the dead.'[26]

An exhaustive examination of two large New York newspapers, the *New York Times* and the *Brooklyn Eagle*, on the subject of lead poisoning between 1880 and 1914 confirmed this statement on the lack of public awareness and interest in the issue of industrial poisoning in the United States.[27] However, the situation is, in fact, more complex. A few rare articles, most often only paragraphs, report that cases of lead poisoning occurred in the companies of this great industrial metropolis during the last two decades of the nineteenth century. When these articles rapidly relate the legal proceedings brought by workers against their employers, the story is always the same: the worker's complaint is always rejected, while the employer is completely exonerated of the charges brought by the court. The verdict is clear. As the *Brooklyn Eagle* declared: 'An employee takes his chances and must know the risks.'[28] Generally treated as human-interest stories, these articles are put at the back of the paper with the anecdotes. Much more rarely, these stories lead to reflections, with very few references, on blue-collar working conditions in an era of massive industrialisation and the consequences for worker health.[29] Far from condemnation, even less a call for social and legislative reform, these articles mostly content themselves with callously noting the dreadful health and safety conditions in certain trades.

The tone of the New York press changed radically after the turn of the twentieth century. From treating the lead poisoning of workers in the lead and paint industries as a marginal problem, the press moved on to what had become the central problem: the risk of poisoning in the general public. Articles about lead poisoning due to dish use, food and drink packaging, the use of cosmetics and the deterioration of interior paint abound. While workers, victims of lead poisoning in the workplace, attracted only a vague compassion coloured by a reproach for their imprudence or their guilty negligence, an odour of scandal floated over the 'innocent' victims of lead poisoning in daily life, a scandal that the press seized with great vigour.

Thus, in the 1890s and even in 1900, a sizable number of articles in the press denounced the mortal danger that menaced Americans, with all the exaggeration that the media are famous for. Each one in turn – porcelain plates, tin cans, soda fountains or cosmetic creams – was accused of insidiously poisoning the people and of being the cause of numerous deaths. The tone was now the denunciation of a public scandal that threatened the whole population. The American citizens mobilised, pushed by those that President Theodore Roosevelt called 'muckrakers' – a not very flattering word used to refer to journalists that scraped the bottom of the barrel – and the result was the Pure Food and Drug Act of June 1906.[30]

As a result, the relative acceptability of occupational diseases, acknowledged as the deplorable but predictable consequence of a risk that responsible workers knowingly took, opened the way for public recognition of the totally unacceptable risk of disease and death that 'innocent' citizens unknowingly encountered. However, by provoking the adoption of normative legislation about the conditions of manufacturing, packaging and labelling of food and medicine with the intent to protect consumers, this consumer movement gradually generated interest in occupational health and safety conditions.[31] Thus, the collective recognition of occupational diseases by urban US society seems to have passed through a stage of denouncing the health threats affecting the general public, who were apparently the only ones capable of massively raising public awareness.

Revealing the scourge of industrial poisons, the lead-poisoning 'scandal' in the general population carried in its wake an increased awareness, nonetheless still limited to the world of progressives, of the need to improve working conditions in the industries that used lead and heavy metals. Around 1910, occupational diseases were considered, for the first time in general articles in the press, as an appallingly scandalous result of a modern civilisation that was out of control. Here and there, the suffering endured and the brutality of industrial poisons was compared to the tortures of the Inquisition and the subtle venoms of the Borgia family.[32] All at once, the flax ropemakers' dermatitis, the matchmakers' phosphorus necrosis of the jaw (familiarly called 'phossy jaw'), the miners' pathologic nystagmus and the house painters' lead poisoning were denounced as modern afflictions that enlightened US citizens must help to combat. Nonetheless, US society's mobilisation is thin on the ground, and the combatants are less diverse than in France.

Who is protesting against lead poisoning?

As mentioned above, until the beginning of the twentieth century, in France, the problems of lead poisoning specifically and occupational diseases generally remained the concern of the medical profession and the hygienist movement. It was necessary to wait until these problems were exposed in the press and through legislative action for the interest to gain sufficient momentum to trigger concrete action. Surprisingly, neither the work world nor the trade unions were leading the mobilisation efforts. Although the problem of white-lead poisoning was appearing regularly in the French professional broadsheet *L'Ouvrier peintre* (published by the Confédération générale du travail [CGT][33] starting in 1900 and intended for union house painters), working hours and salary were much more important issues for the French trade unions than healthy working conditions. As it has been argued elsewhere, the victory against lead paint in France was less a result of a trade-union combat than the mobilisation of diverse social and political spheres, involving doctors, legislators, workers and members of what the sociologist Topalov called '*nébuleuse réformatrice*', that is, the reform circles/community.[34]

According to the archival sources, the US trade unions seem hardly more combative than their French counterparts on the problem of lead poisoning. The first painter trade unions, which were founded in the 1830s in Philadelphia, Boston and New York City, generally focused their primary demands on wages. The health danger posed by white lead seems to have been vastly underestimated and was seen more fatalistically (that is, the notional 'risks of the trade'). The danger was nonetheless well known: in June 1910, the *Painters' Journal* highlighted the possibility of substituting lead in the paint with zinc, considered to be less toxic.[35] At the beginning of the twentieth century, falling from ladders and scaffolding was considered at the top of the list of the dangers for house painters, but lead poisoning was a close second. An investigation into house painting conducted by a Chicago trade union in the 1910s indicated that one out of six painters had more or less severe cases of lead poisoning, more than double those who declared work accidents.[36]

However, beyond the knowledge of the reality of lead poisoning, denial remained widespread, including among workers themselves. Discussions about this issue within the house-painters' unions remained rare.[37] In 1913, the trade-union journal, *Painter and Decorator*, denounced the toxicity of white lead, while admitting that the painters themselves constituted 'the chief obstacle to abandoning the use of white lead'.[38] On this specific issue of the workers' denial, the US situation was ultimately no different than the situation in France or Belgium, for example. Thus, one cannot look to the workers' movement for evidence of early or effective social mobilisation to improve the health and safety of house painters' working conditions. The occupational health and safety issue seems to have been linked to wider public-health issues, for example, tuberculosis or diphtheria among the workers and their family, even in the labour-union discourse. Finally, the role of some of the individual actors in the collective mobilisation seems to be more essential in the gradual emergence of the debate, but even then, not occurring at the same times on the different sides of the Atlantic.

On the French side of the Atlantic, the personality of Abel Craissac – a former house painter himself and treasurer of the CGT house-painter trade union in Paris before he was excluded for ideological reasons – was fundamental in establishing the anti-white-lead discourse within the sphere of the French trade unions, for which he apparently played a role of *trompe-l'œil*.[39] At the beginning of the twentieth century, the convergence of opinion-leadership forces as powerful as the press, parts of the philanthropic and medical world, freemasonry and the 'reform circles' around Craissac succeeded in getting the public to discuss the problem of industrial poisons (of which lead was at the top of the list). To a large extent, this was due to Craissac's untiring action for the prohibition of white lead. His crusade against lead paint made the issue of white lead the core issue for mobilising public opinion against industrial poisons and health conditions at work. In his case, the painter's scaffolding leads to ministerial offices: the personal itinerary of Abel Craissac reflects the progressive evolution of exposing the problem of white lead during the *Belle Epoque* of France, from the recognition of the problem to the banning legislation for which he worked so tirelessly. Reconstituting this mobilisation also allows the importance of the local scale and the individual actor in the historical process to be understood.

In the United States, there was also an exceptional person who fought early and hard against white lead: Dr Alice Hamilton, the first female physician to join the faculty at Harvard University (1919) and, as of 1911, the delegate to the US Bureau of Labor in Washington. After reading the early survey conducted by Dr Thomas Legge in the paint and pigments factories in England, she was made aware of the harmful effects of white lead on workers' health.[40] Visiting factories and work sites, she diagnosed precisely the shocking state of the US white-lead and paint industry (both paint manufacturing and paint use), with regard to industrial poisoning. For example, in the 25 white-lead companies in the United States, she discovered in 16 months 388 lead-poisoning cases, from which 16 people died (1911). At Wetherill & Brothers, the oldest factory in Philadelphia, Alice Hamilton described interior and exterior walls encrusted with white lead, which floated in clouds in the buildings on the wind. She found that workers ate lunch daily in a workshop covered with lead dust. The Philadelphia hospitals always treated multiple cases of lead poisoning from this company.

Published in 1911 by the US Bureau of Labor, Alice Hamilton's study long remained pioneering research.[41] When, as a US delegate, she went to the Second International Congress on industrial accidents and occupational diseases (Brussels, 1910) to speak about the white-lead industry in the United States, she was quite embarrassed by the statements of a Belgian doctor, who declared to those in attendance: 'It is well known that there is no occupational hygiene in the United States.' Relating this anecdote in her memoirs, she acknowledged that the Brussels congress was not, 'for an American, [. . .] an occasion for national pride'.[42] For around two decades, the intense debate that held sway in most European countries on the subject of industrial poisons and occupational health had, in fact, largely bypassed the US public.

Clearly an undeniable time gap existed between the French and the US experience on this issue. Additionally, the process of raising public awareness and converting this awareness to action on industrial poisoning risks was quite different in light of the widely dissimilar social, economic and political contexts; this was in spite of the flow of ideas circulating between France and the United States.

III. Two paths towards abandoning white lead

Different processes were at work on either side of the Atlantic. More precisely, to reach a generally similar result – the almost universal abandonment of lead paint in the 1930s/40s – France and the United States took quite different paths. It is interesting to compare them in order to highlight the variety of available processes for mobilisation, political decision-making and economic implementation that reach comparable results.

Starting from environmental concerns

In France, as in other European industrialised countries, awareness began with environmental concerns. As scholars have recently shown, it was first the fears of those that lived near the factories that generated an interest in the pollution *outside* the factory, already a concern since the end of the eighteenth century.[43] In turn, that led to mobilisation against the harmful effects and industrial pollution *inside* the factory, finally leading to broad concerns for overall occupational health and safety. Fearing that the toxicity in the industrial environment would 'overflow' and lead to pollution of the human and urban environment, the factories' neighbours ended up, much, much later, concerned with the pollution that industrial activities generated within their own territory.

This slow evolution from interest in the *outside* of industrial establishments to interest in the *inside* signalled the very slow penetration of the State into the private relationships that govern labour and the hitherto closed, sovereign space of the company at the turn of the nineteenth and the twentieth century. Earlier in this article it was shown through the New York City newspapers that, with a 50-year gap, these environmental concerns had relatively great significance for US public opinion, as Christian Warren has also argued.[44] In France, it was also through the general population's perception of the harmful effects on the environment that the people involved would later shift public opinion toward industrial accidents and occupational health and safety. As in the white-lead sector in the North of France, which was the core of the national output around 1900, complaints mostly emerged about the harmful effects of the plant on the neighbourhood, rarely about the health of workers themselves.[45] The results are similar on both sides of the Atlantic, but the pace of change is quite different.

Towards legal prohibition in France

At the beginning of the twentieth century, the militancy of a few actors and the gradual evolution of public opinion due to the factors mentioned above rapidly succeeded in

France in forcing a political intervention, albeit timid at first. Beginning in 1900, numerous local laws forbade the use of white lead in municipal public-works projects. At the national level, the decrees of 1902 and 1908 governed the use of lead paint and the conditions under which it could continue to be used. After several alerts and detours (that is, legislation proposed by the French Parliament that led to the senatorial inquiry directed by A. Treille), legislation was passed in 1909 prohibiting the use of white lead. Thus, in France, a prohibition process had begun, even though only the use of white lead was outlawed, not its production – a strange state of affairs requiring further examination. However, in order to permit the industrialists involved in white-lead production to convert their factories gradually, the law of 1909 stated that white-lead prohibition would take effect in 1 January 1915. Ultimately, this date was set back again by the First World War and the consequent industrial intensification, causing this early prohibition to fail.

After the war, the debate about white lead reappeared. The massive mobilisation before the war had the likely effect of facilitating the passage of the law of 25 October 1919, which created a compensation system for victims of occupational diseases and put lead poisoning among the diseases at the top of the list (the early list included only two diseases: lead and mercurial poisonings). Europe was mobilised around these health and safety issues in the first years of the twentieth century. The internationalisation of the debates and the harmonisation of the national laws, still very relative, took a new dimension due to the creation of the International Labour Organisation (ILO) by the League of Nations in Geneva in 1919. As Heitmann states: 'Whether or not to ban, restrict or regulate white lead became a central question for the newly-created ILO.'[46] In fact, the ILO rapidly gravitated towards the issue of white lead, in which it seems relatively clear that France was a driving force in favour of prohibiting white lead, especially within the Third International Labour Conference taking place in Geneva in 1921. The ILO archives on this issue provide evidence that Director-General Albert Thomas had taken the white-lead cause as personal, following the International Congress of Painters' Trade Unions in 1920 calling for the total prohibition of white lead in any kind of work. Thomas' deep and close links with Abel Craissac definitely helped to implement the 1921 convention in France.[47]

With respect to the ratification of the 1921 international convention against white lead (13th convention of the ILO), the French Parliament prohibited the use of lead paint by some categories of house painters in February 1926, not including artisans or self-employed persons, who made up a large number of the total at risk. It was thus a legal half-measure on the way to the definitive acknowledgement of the harmful nature of white lead. It was not until 1948 that white lead was totally banned for interior paint jobs, for both employees and artisans, thus leading to the almost total disappearance of white lead used to paint walls inside buildings. In any case, the intervention of the legislature and of politics in general – first at the local level with the municipalities in the first years of the twentieth century, then at the national level with the decrees of 1902, 1908, 1913 and the 1909 law, and finally at the international level with the 1921 convention followed by the 1926 French ratification – led gradually to the total prohibition of white lead, always using as the primary argument that the state must protect the health and safety of its workers.

Reducing the use of white lead by economic deterrence

In the United States, the rapid turnover of industrial workers – with a sizeable proportion of recent European immigrants increasing the invisibility of the critical epidemiological situation in the workplace – made a smokescreen and disguised the importance of occupational diseases for a long time in a period of expanding industrial activity. With more cynicism, one could go as far as to say that the precariousness of the workers in some of the most dangerous sectors were the most obvious instruments in industrial-disease 'prevention', making disease more elusive. For this reason, in the 1910s and 1920s, by showing that US factories had higher morbidity and mortality rates due to lead poisoning than European factories, Alice Hamilton gradually weakened the myth of the superiority of US industry, a myth that was the doctrine of the 'Progressive Era' and the decades prior to the Great Depression. Still, she barely changed the opinions of the general public, for whom these stakes remained far off and – like almost all US doctors according to Hamilton – the subject was 'tainted by socialism or feminine sentimentalism in favor of the poor'.[48]

Despite the reports by Alice Hamilton about the varnishers and the enamellers, about the workers that painted car bodies and those who worked on the batteries in the car factories in Detroit, mobilisation on the issue of industrial poisons was still then restricted to the world of the reformers. Quite diverse but gaining a powerful role, the often politically radical reform circles got involved in the occupational health and safety issue, as part of a wider struggle for social change. In June 1910, the first National Conference on Industrial Diseases was held in Chicago, promoted by the American Association for Labor Legislation. The harsh reality of the extent of the work to be done to ensure acceptable working conditions, in terms of health and safety, for US industrial workers was reported, and the critical lack of statistics on this issue in the United States was severely criticised. In addition, an international congress on occupational hygiene only mobilised a few Americans, and when the issue was internationalised after the First World War, the United States, which did not belong to the League of Nations, partly isolated itself from the European debates. As in Great Britain, the powerful US paint industry insisted on the ineffective substitutes for white lead, as there was no consensus on this technical issue, especially for exterior works. Moreover, Rosner and Markowitz make the interesting point that the emergence of the 'Safety First' movement, together with the decline of the reform movement after the War, contributed to restrict the occupational-health issue to a narrow expert circle, away from the public arena.[49] In fact, the US reform movement acted less to prohibit dangerous products – it admittedly had little opportunity to act in a country that preaches almost total economic liberalism – than it did to regulate the economic system itself.

Thus, Alice Hamilton's work had an impact mostly on the reform movement and the social workers in Chicago, who pushed the Governor of Illinois, the Democrat Charles S. Deneen, and the state legislators to act. It was thus at the state level, more than the federal level, that the mobilisation occurred. As had occurred similarly in its industrial neighbour Wisconsin two years before, and due to the powerful Chicago reform movement and the presence of a Governor willing to engage reforms, in 1913 Illinois voted in a law indemnifying occupational diseases, the Workmen's Compensation Act, associating occupational diseases and work accidents. So did 25 US states in the 1910s: they did not employ prohibitionist logic, which would have forbidden toxic products, but rather financial dissuasion towards the employers. By drawing the economic and financial stakes into the equation in the form of insurance premiums, this law had a major impact on occupational health and safety conditions in the United States, as had the laws voted in numerous industrial states in the following years. The powerful insurance companies, which until then had no data on disease rates in US factories, exhibited a feverish desire for statistics in order to adjust the premiums that they required from businessmen to the rates of accidents and disease in their companies. Many entrepreneurs, themselves worried about reducing their premiums, worked to improve the health and safety conditions in the factories, as Alice Hamilton observed, almost 25 years after her original inquiry, when she conducted her second inquiry into the health and safety of people working in paint factories.[50]

Henceforth, lead paint was almost totally abandoned for interior jobs, furniture, cars, boats, trains, trucks and tractors; in fact, it was progressively abandoned in all the sectors that were seriously affected by the epidemic of lead poisoning at the beginning of the twentieth century. Although the Carter factories in Chicago continued to present the manipulation of white lead as totally harmless – showing the painter using the raw product with neither gloves nor respirator in 'Directions for use' – the national market contracted significantly. Sales of lead paint fell by half between 1928 and 1934.[51] However, according to the figures available, this reduction in use did not necessarily mean a rapid reduction in illness for two major reasons: (1) the length of exposure before displaying the initial symptoms; and (2) technical innovations in the trade, especially the rapid development of spray-painting techniques, which produced projections that were even more dangerous than brush techniques and consequently increased the harmful effects of the product.

From 1911 to 1920, most of the US industrial states adopted workmen's compensation laws, following the model of the early Wisconsin and Illinois legislation. Step by step, through economic and financial dissuasion instead of a prohibition process, the risk of industrial poisoning was reduced for the workers in most paint factories and workshops. These legislative advances were combined with technical transformations that modified professional behaviour and the required qualifications and work procedures. The question of industrial risk would reappear later, but in other forms, for example, other harmful substances and other poisoning vectors.

Comparing two national experiences bears witness to the fact that, while the medical and epidemiological/health diagnosis is approximately the same in the two industrial countries, the issue of occupational health and safety is regarded differently. This discrepancy is mostly due to the fact that the economic and political stakes are not the same in France and the United States. In particular, the rules governing the work world don't pass through the same channels nor the same decision-making levels. The contrast seems vivid between France, on the one hand, where the long process towards prohibition occurs in a context in which the State begins to be perceived as the protector and the promoter of public health, as well as the regulator of the work world (albeit later than in some other countries, such as Germany). The State is thus called upon to put an end to the scandal of industrial poisoning for 'humanitarian' reasons. The path chosen ranges from inspecting the industrial workplace to informing the professional associations and the general public and finally to prohibiting white lead by law. In the United States, on the other hand, a system that is based on rapid turnover of industrial workers is breached by the states through legislative measures using economic dissuasion, more than feared prohibition.[52] These legislative measures encouraged entrepreneurs to take occupational health and safety conditions into account. The path taken by Wisconsin and Illinois was quickly adopted by many other industrial US states, which mostly passed legislation that associated occupational diseases and work accidents in order to compensate the workers. Thus, the federal government, working through such institutions as the Bureau of Labor or the Office of Industrial Hygiene (part of the US Public Health Service created in 1912), intervened primarily with information (for example, industrial surveys like the ones by Dr Hamilton). The insurance system was part of the equation; it encouraged industrialists to abandon the most dangerous industrial products or processes for reasons of economic viability, since the compensation for damage was first and foremost a private affair. The state government only intervened when the private compensation scheme failed. Also, the leading part France took in the adoption of the 13th international convention outlawing lead paint in interiors (1921) and the late participation of the United States to the ILO (1934) have to be emphasised to understand the discrepancy between the process in both countries.[53]

This contrast probably must be investigated more in order to better understand what mechanisms played a role, how information circulated and what reciprocal and transnational influences were at work in this parallel evolution. However, this contrast at least positions the comparative strategy and proposes an analysis framework for the evolving situations and laws about professional risks in the twentieth century.

Notes

1. The song was written for the 22nd Annual Convention of the International Association of Master House Painters and Decorators of the United States and Canada, which took place in Birmingham, Alabama, in February 1906. Quoted in *The Carter Times* [Carter White Lead Company, Chicago], 1906, no. 1.
2. See in particular Rosental and Omnès, "Les maladies professionnelles: genèse d'une question sociale." Research in US historiography is far ahead of European research: see the numerous publications by David Rosner and Gerald Markowitz or, more recently, *Brush with Death. A Social History of Lead Poisoning* by Warren and the works by Sellers.
3. Sellers, "Cross-nationalizing the History of Industrial Hazard," 322.
4. For more information about the transnational nature of the history of occupational health and safety, the interested reader can consult Topalov, *Laboratoires du nouveau siècle*; Rosental, "Special Issue: Health and Safety at Work. A Transnational History."; Moret-Lespinet, and Vincent Viet (eds) *L'Organisation internationale du Travail*; Van Daele, et al. (eds), Essays on the International Labour Organization; or Rasmussen, "L'hygiène en congrès (1852–1912)." On the British experience, see Heitmann, "The ILO and the Regulation of White Lead in Britain."
5. The first was by a Paduan doctor, Bernardo Ramazzini, in *De morbis artificum diatriba*.
6. On this particular issue, see Lestel, "Comment concilier développement industriel et protection de l'ouvrier"; J.–P. Barrière, "Le patron, le médecin et l'ouvrier."
7. Departmental archives of the *Nord* (now ADN), 96 J/Q 938 (Saturnins, 1884–1914), 96 J/M 1238[4] (Saint-Sauveur, patient information sheets, 1900–1905), 96 J/M1241[2] (Hôpital de la Charité, Saturnins, 1901–1904). The reduction in the number of patients in the hospitals in Lille is greater than the one mentioned in the very approximate statistics established by the Seine Health and Sanitation Council (approx. 50%). See "Comptes-rendus des travaux du Conseil d'hygiène et de salubrité de la Seine, 1894 et 1902", cited in Orliac and Calmettes, *La lutte contre le saturnisme*, 221–6.
8. Orliac and Calmettes, *La lutte contre le saturnisme*, 65.
9. Ibid., 65, or Roch, "Le saturnisme, maladie evitable," 2.
10. On the British case and the early 1915 *Report of the Departmental Committee Appointed to Investigate the Danger Attendant on the Use of Paints containing Lead in the Painting of Buildings*, London, HMSO, see Heitmann, "The ILO and the Regulation of White Lead in Britain."
11. The only serious study, produced by the US Department of Labor in 1915, is the one by Alice Hamilton, which examined four US hospitals and determined that 25% of the cases of lead poisoning concern painters, two thirds of them in New York City. See below.
12. First National Lead Trust, founded in 1887, was transformed into National Lead Company in 1891.
13. According to Holley, *The Lead and Zinc Pigments*, v.
14. All these figures were cited by Holley, *The Lead and Zinc Pigments*, 32–3.
15. No recent monograph exists on Dr Alice Hamilton. I am preparing a book on her role in the emergence of industrial medicine in the US and in international health organisations after the

First World War. See Sicherman, *Alice Hamilton. A Life in Letters* and Rainhorn, "L'épidémiologie de la bottine".

16. Hamilton, *Report of Commission on Occupational Diseases*, 32–3.

17. All manufacturing processes for lead oxides were presented in detail in Holley, *The Lead and Zinc Pigments*, as well as in Georges Petit, *Céruse et Blanc de zinc*.

18. Hamilton, *Report of Commission on Occupational Diseases*, 37.

19. On the constitution of this scientific knowledge about "occupational health and safety" see Moriceau, *Les douleurs de l'industrie*, and Thomas Le Roux, "Hygienists, workers' bodies and machines in nineteenth-century France." *European Review of History* 20, no. 2 (2013): 255–70.

20. See Moriceau, *Les douleurs de l'industrie*.

21. Holley, *The Lead and Zinc Pigments*.

22. Georges Clémenceau (1841–1929), a famous radical politician, had been one of the first to stand up for captain Dreyfus during the Dreyfus affair, and published Emile Zola's « J'Accuse » in his paper *L'Aurore*. As a physician, he was also involved in the fight to improve the health conditions of workers. At that time (1904), he was a Senator, well known for his anti-clerical and anti-colonialist opinions.

23. Doctor and Senator from Constantine (French Algeria) from 1897 to 1906. Very conservative, he was already well known for his virulent opposition – in the name of communal liberty – to the law proposed by Jules Sigfried, establishing the generalisation and obligation of the smallpox vaccination, the declaration to the health authorities of all contagious diseases, and the adoption of communal rules to facilitate the fight against insalubrious housing.

24. In fact, this agitation started in France. Belgium, Switzerland, Germany and Italy acknowledged the pioneering nature of the role that France played in the movement against white lead. I am currently conducting research aimed at illuminating the role of French delegates in the process of the international convention, voted within the ILO, that banned white lead in interior paint in 1921.

25. Rosner and Markowitz, *Dying for Work*, xi.

26. B. Reeve, "The Death Roll of Industry," *Charities and the Commons* 17 (1907): 791, quoted in Rosner and Markowitz, *Dying for Work*, xii.

27. These sources were examined thanks to the collaboration of Elizabeth Monahan, a Master's student in History at Manhattan College in New York. I want to thank here Elizabeth and her professor, Prof. Jeff Horn, for their work and help.

28. *The Brooklyn Eagle*, 20 June 1882.

29. See, for example, "Dangerous Occupations," *New York Times*, 18 January 1880 or "Unhealthy Trades: Outdoor Labor Compared with Indoor Work," *Brooklyn Eagle*, 28 February 1886.

30. Among them, Upton Sinclair, who acquired a considerable reputation with his novel *The Jungle* (1905), denounced conditions in the animal slaughtering and meatpacking industries. The public-opinion campaign that followed the publication of this book led to passing the *Meat Inspection Act* in the same year.

31. For more information about the influence of consumer organisations in the adoption of manufacturing standards (and thus working-condition standards) in the consumer-goods industries in Anglo-Saxon countries, the interested reader would do well to consult Chessel, *Consommateurs engagés à la Belle Epoque*, especially 33–58 and "Women and the Ethic of Consumption"; also see Vincent, "La réforme sociale à l'heure du thé."

32. See "Civilization has Created a Long List of New Diseases," *New York Times*, 9 October 1910.

33. Confédération générale du Travail (CGT) was the biggest labour-union federation in France, born in 1895, gathering hundreds of local unions from different trades. See Michel Dreyfus, *Histoire de la CGT*.

34. I have argued this in Judith Rainhorn, "Workers against Lead Paint." (in French as "Les ouvriers contre la peinture au plomb"). The question of the implication of trade unions in the fight against work-related diseases at the beginning of the twentieth century is open to debate. For the debate in France, also see Devinck, "Pour une histoire par en bas de la santé au travail." The reference for Topalov is '*Laboratoires du nouveau siècle*'.

35. This substitution was at that time partly done in most European countries.

36. Runnberg, *Statistical Report to Painters District Council*, 13–18.

37. See *One Union: A History of the International Union of Painters & Allied Trades*, 29.

38. *Painter and Decorator*, February 1913, cited in *One Union* ....

39. The role of Abel Craissac is explained in Rainhorn, "Workers against Lead Paint."
40. Sir Thomas Legge, *Report on the Manufactures of Paints and Colours Containing Lead.*
41. Study by Alice Hamilton on lead poisoning, in *A Half Century of Public Health. Jubilee Historical Volume of the American Public Health Association.*
42. Hamilton, *Exploring the Dangerous Trades.*
43. See Le Roux, *Le laboratoire des pollutions industrielles*, Geneviève Massard-Guilbaud, *Histoire de la pollution industrielle, France (1789–1914)*, and Le Roux, Letté (eds), *Débordements industriels.*
44. In *Brush with Death*, especially p. 116 and the pages that follow.
45. See the white lead files in the Archives départementales du Nord (Lille), M 417 serie in particular.
46. Heitmann, "The ILO and the Regulation of White Lead in Britain," 269.
47. ILO Archives, Hy 500/1/0/22, correspondence between Albert Thomas and Abel Craissac, 1925–7. I am at the moment conducting research on Thomas-Craissac's correspondence and the implementation of the ILO 13th international convention on white lead in France.
48. *Bulletin of the American Academy of Medicine* 15, Oct. 1914, 304.
49. Rosner and Markowitz, *Dying for Work*, xv.
50. Hamilton, *Recent Changes in the Painters' Trade.*
51. Ibid.
52. Lead paint wasn't legally prohibited in the United States until 1977.
53. See Heitmann, "The ILO and the Regulation of White Lead", and my personal research (in progress) on the whole process of the adoption of the 13th international convention about white-lead use in interior paint,

Bibliography

Barrière, Jean-Paul. "Le patron, le médecin et l'ouvrier: le procès des Hospices de Lille contre un cérusier lillois dans le dernier tiers du XIXe siècle." In *La gloire de l'industrie, XVIIe-XIXe siècles. Faire de l'histoire avec Gérard Gayot*, edited by Corine Maitte, Philippe Minard, and Matthieu De Oliveira, 317–334. Rennes: Presses universitaires de Rennes, 2012.

"Le blanc de céruse." special issue of *L'Assiette au Beurre* 210 (April 1905).

Chessel, Marie-Emmanuelle. "Women and the Ethic of Consumption in France at the turn of the Century." In *The Making of the Consumer: Knowledge, Power and Identity in the Modern World*, edited by Frank Trentmann, 81–98. London: Berg, 2005.

Chessel, Marie-Emmanuelle. *Consommateurs engagés à la Belle Epoque. La Ligue sociale d'acheteurs*. Paris: Presses de Sciences Po, 2012.

Devinck, Jean-Claude. "Pour une histoire par en bas de la santé au travail." *Mouvements* 58 (2009): 68–78.

Dreyfus, Michel. *Histoire de la CGT: cent ans de syndicalisme en France*. Bruxelles: Complexe, 1995.

A Half Century of Public Health. Jubilee Historical Volume of the American Public Health Association, in Commemoration of the Fiftieth Anniversary Celebration of its Foundation. New York: American Public Health Association, 1921.

Hamilton, Alice. *Report of Commission on Occupational Diseases, to his Excellency Governor Charles S. Deneen.* Chicago: Warner Printing Company, 1911.

Hamilton, Alice. "The Economic Importance of Lead Poisoning." *Bulletin of the American Academy of Medecine* 15 (1914).

Hamilton, Alice. *Recent Changes in the Painters' Trade.* Washington: U.S. Dpt of Labor, U.S. Govt. Print. Office, 1936.

Hamilton, Alice. *Exploring the Dangerous Trades. The Autobiography of Alice Hamilton, M.D.* Boston: Little, Brown and Cy, 1943.

Heitmann, John. "The ILO and the Regulation of White Lead in Britain during the Interwar Years: an Examination of International and National Campaigns in Occupational Health." *Labour History Review* 69, no. 3 (2004): 267–84.

Holley, Clifford D. *The Lead and Zinc Pigments.* New York: Wiley, 1909.

Le Roux, Thomas. *Le laboratoire des pollutions industrielles. Paris, 1770–1830.* Paris: Albin Michel, 2011.

Le Roux, Thomas. "Hygienists, workers' bodies and machines in nineteenth-century France." *European Review of History* 20, no. 2 (2013): 255–70.

Le Roux, Thomas and Michel, Letté. *Débordements industriels. Environnement, territoire et conflit, XVIIIe-XXIe siécles.* Rennes: Presses universitaires de Rennes, 2013.

Legge, Thomas. *Report on the manufactures of paints and colours containing lead, as effecting the health of the operatives employed.* London, 1905.

Lestel, Laurence. "Comment concilier développement industriel et protection de l'ouvrier: le cas de la céruse en France au xixe siècle." *Archiv für Sozialgeschichte* 43 (2003): 79–99.

Massard-Guilbaud, Geneviève. *Histoire de la pollution industrielle, France (1789–1914).* Paris: Éditions de l'EHESS, 2010.

Moret-Lespinet, Isabelle, and Vincent Viet, eds. *L'Organisation internationale du Travail. Origine, développement, avenir.* Rennes: Presses universitaires de Rennes, 2010.

Moriceau, Caroline. *Les douleurs de l'industrie. L'hygiénisme industriel en France.* Paris: Editions de l'EHESS, 2010.

One Union: A History of the International Union of Painters & Allied Trades, 1887–2003. s.l. Aspatore, 2004.

Orliac, A., and Emile Calmettes. *La lutte contre le saturnisme.* Paris: Berger-Levrault, 1912.

Petit, Georges. *Céruse et Blanc de zinc.* Paris: Gauthier-Villars, s.d., [1907 ?].

Rainhorn, Judith. "Le mouvement ouvrier contre la peinture au plomb: stratégie syndicale, expérience locale et transgression du discours dominant au début du XXe siècle." *Politix* 91 (2010): 9–26.

Rainhorn, Judith. "Workers Against Lead Paint. How Local Practices Go Against the Prevailing Union Strategy. France at the Beginning of the 20th Century." In *Kontrollierte Arbeit – Disziplinierte Körper ? Zur Social- und Kulturgeschichte der Industriearbeit in 19. und 20. Jahrhundert,* edited by Lars Bluma and Kasten Uhl, 137–161. Bielfeld: Transcript Verlag, 2012.

Rainhorn, Judith. "L'épidémiologie de la bottine ou l'enquête médicale réinventée. Alice Hamilton et la médecine industrielle dans l'Amérique du premier XXe siècle." *Gesnerus. Swiss Journal of the History of Medicine and Sciences* 70/1 June 2013(forthcoming).

Ramazzini, Bernardino. *Des maladies du travail.* 1700, reprinted Valergues: Alexitère, 1990.

Rasmussen, Anne. "L'hygiène en congrès (1852–1912): circulations et configurations internationales." In *Les hygiénistes. Enjeux, modèles et pratiques,* edited by Patrice Bourdelais, 213–239. Paris: Belin, 2001.

Roch, René Dr. "Le saturnisme, maladie évitable. À propos des saturnins traités à l'hôpital cantonal de Genève en 1907, 1908 et 1909." *Revue suisse des accidents du travail,* Year IV, 3.

Rosental, Paul-André ed. "Special Issue: Health and Safety at Work. A Transnational History." *Journal of Modern European History* 2 (2009).

Rosental, Paul-André, and Catherine Omnès, eds. "Les maladies professionnelles: genèse d'une question sociale." *Revue d'histoire moderne et contemporaine* 56, no. 1 (2009).

Rosner, David, and Gerald Markowitz, eds. *Dying for Work. Workers's Safety and Health in Twentieth-Century America.* Bloomington: Indiana University Press, 1987.

Runnberg, John A. *Statistical Report to Painters District Council no.14.* Chicago: s.d. [between 1910 and 1915].

Salls, Carroll M. "How to Eliminate the Hazard of Lead Poisoning in Paint Factories." New York State Department of Labor. *Industrial Hygiene Bulletin,* 12 (1) (1925): 1.

Sellers, Christopher. *Hazards of the Job. From industrial disease to environmental health science*. Chapell Hill: University of North Carolina Press, 1999.

Sellers, Christopher. "The Dearth of the Clinic. Lead, Air and Agency in Twentieth-Century America." *Journal of the History of Medicine and Allied Sciences* 58 (2003): 255–291.

Sellers, Christopher. "Cross-Nationalizing the History of Industrial Hazard." *Medical History* 54 (2010): 315–340.

Sicherman, Barbara. *Alice Hamilton. A Life in Letters*. Urbana: University of Illinois Press, 1984.

Topalov, Christian, ed. *Laboratoires du nouveau siècle. La nébuleuse réformatrice et ses réseaux en France (1880–1914)*. Paris: Editions de l'EHESS, 1999.

Van Daele, Jasmien, Magaly Rodriguez Garcia, Geert Van Goethem, and Marcel van der Linden, eds. *Essays on the International Labour Organization and Its Impact on the Work During the Twentieth Century*. Bern, Berlin, Bruxelles, New York, Oxford: Peter Lang, 2010.

Vincent, Julien. "La réforme sociale à l'heure du thé: La porcelaine anglaise, l'empire britannique et la santé des ouvrières dans le Staffordshire (1864–1914)." *Revue d'histoire moderne et contemporaine* 56-1 (2009): 29–60.

Warren, Christian. *Brush with Death: A Social History of Lead Poisoning*. Baltimore: John Hopkins University Press, 2000.

Aluminium in health and food: a gradual global approach

Florence Hachez-Leroy

Centre de Recherches Historiques, EHESS / CNRS, Institut Universitaire de France, Université Lille Nord de France, Artois, France

The history of occupational diseases and environment gives little consideration to pathologies related to the use of artefacts. Furthermore, materials are seldom the centre of studies. In this article, aluminium is used as an example for understanding the processes of user acceptance and rejection. The issue of user confidence over long periods of time is raised from the actors' perspective and with respect to the relationships between companies, scientists, public actors, citizens and users. Since the time that aluminium was first produced, it was subjected to physicochemical tests. Scientists concluded that it was harmless. With mass production, starting in 1886, the debate was reopened, in particular because of its use for military purposes. Simultaneously, the arrival of new smelters caused local public reaction against pollution and occupational diseases. From the 1960s, the development of mass pollution generated a geographical widening of the debates. Companies had to confront national associations of ecologists and public organisations. From the 1970s, broad suspicion hit aluminium with the dialysed of Denver, and, about 10 years later, with Alzheimer's disease. In the 1990s, the 'Aluminium and Health' issue within the general metal-production and consumption domain became a global and international issue.

Introduction

For the last 10 years, occupational diseases and environmental history have been the subject of ground-breaking studies. Some of them focus on the complexity, standardisation and inter-relationships of these fields.[1] In these studies men and women at work or at home are mostly presented as victims of small-scale and industrial activities. In both cases, the historians' perspective is most often established at the industrial-production level. At the other end of the economic chain, historical research focused on consumption and consumers in an attempt to understand their nature, practices and organisation.[2] In contrast to these studies, we decided to concentrate on the materials, and not only on certain plants or firms, that is to say from production to implementation and consumption in different periods of time.

This study starts with a consideration of the nature of critical opinions concerning aluminium, a material that has become symbolic of the second industrial revolution.[3] We chose to focus on two points: environmental issues, including pollution and occupational diseases; and food utensils. This choice is justified by the analysis of sources at both ends of the time period: the first scientific book on aluminium in 1859 and the 1997 international report on health in the aluminium industry. By analysing events and actors, we seek to explore the public-health risks, true or not, and their representations; we want to understand the nature of suspicions and responses, from the vantage point of constantly changing scientific and technological knowledge.[4] We will exclude bauxite production and alumina processing, the upstream sector of aluminium production, which belong to the mining and chemical sectors.[5]

The emergence of aluminium as a new material in the nineteenth century opened a new field of science and technology. This period was important for the construction of knowledge. But the public, as a viewer and user, also perceives and receives these new materials with a feeling of reluctance and/or acceptance and/or rejection, according to an overlapping chronology. The issue of risk and consumer confidence is perceptible in key documents affecting the history of aluminium and systematically come up whenever and wherever aluminium is produced. The question is: can we trust aluminium? What are the dangers caused by its industrial production and its use in kitchen utensils?

In the case of aluminium, I argue that a comprehensive approach was initially used to study production and consumption and that the question of risk, until the early twentieth century, was supported by two levels of actors: the international scientific community and the local actors in production zones. This period is characterised by the predominance of scientific questioning to prove the innocuousness of aluminium. In the second period, from the inter-war period until the 1960s, this issue was decoupled; new fields of expertise, impermeable to each other, were developed with a clear distinction being made between problems of production and consumption. Business companies were the dominant actors. This period is characterised by efforts to build up consumer confidence. Last, starting in the 1970s, the problem took on a more global dimension: aluminium related to public and professional health entered the public debate, and scientific research was co-ordinated on a worldwide scale. The question of the harmlessness of aluminium, in both metallic and non-metallic form, was seen in terms of the whole commodity chain, from production to consumption. The approach became unconditionally global. Consumers' associations and popular-science journals played a crucial role in the emergence of distrust of everything that was aluminium.

Several types of sources have been used in an attempt to draw up a history of scientific questioning, confidence and suspicion: the scientific reports and journals, newspapers and popular-science books, the general press and consumer magazines are the first corpus. Public records and business archives constitute the second corpus. Company records are good sources for information on the development of attention to aluminium in relation to occupational diseases, and environmental and public-health problems since they provide details on controversies, legal disputes and claims and progress in scientific research.

Can aluminium be trusted?

The first steps in aluminium research: the toxicity risk

Research on alumina and aluminium resulted from work started in the eighteenth century, in a more general movement of natural sciences on plants, soil and the human body.[6] Research on the composition of clays and plants led to the discovery of alumina (before aluminium), and to an evaluation of quantities in their natural state in soil, water and plants. This was the beginning of interest in understanding material and in non-metallic forms of aluminium, a fundamental step in understanding the path followed by the scientists. It is characterised by careful thought to determine the safety or danger of substances ingested directly or indirectly by man, on the basis of quantities and chemical forms. Although aluminium did not yet exist in a metallic form, it was present in the scientific debate for scientific and intellectual reasons, through its metal oxide, alumina. Theodore de Saussure, in 1801 and in 1804[7], devoted many pages of fundamental importance in terms of methods and results, emphasising the strong presence of alumina in plants. Work in this direction ceased almost for 40 years, until 1844: research picked up again and gained considerable momentum as of 1855. Alumina was then considered as an abundant element in the earth and plants, and its presence in the human body as natural.

The first process for producing aluminium was developed in France in 1854 by the chemist Henri Sainte-Claire Deville[8] who finally revealed its metallic nature by a new process. Aluminium ingots were presented in Paris at the World Exhibition of 1855, and samples were sent to academies of science around the world.[9] The work by Sainte-Claire Deville was of fundamental importance. The texts he published on aluminium between 1854 and 1859 show amazing scientific breadth, which included knowledge of the metal in different fields: the production process and its difficulties; its harmful effects such as pollution; the chemical and physical analysis of the metal; as well as its possible uses. The question of the safety of the metal was at the heart of these last two aspects. Sainte-Claire Deville then considered the new material from very different angles that were especially relevant to the questions of his time.

Technical difficulties and environmental problems were outlined in 1856 and reprinted in his reference book *De l'aluminium* in 1859.[10] In 1860, production was transferred to a chemical-production site in Salindres, a rural area in the south of France where it was difficult to specifically identify nuisances associated with this new production line. Records apparently do not mention specific health problems for the workers. This factory was owned by the Pechiney Company.

As for the uses of metal, scientists paid special attention to metal from the time it first appeared, even before it was put to any use. Sainte-Claire Deville not only invented the first process for aluminium production but also devoted much of his work to the related industrial development and scientific knowledge. In 1854, in his brief submitted to the Academy of Sciences, his conclusion was very clear: 'Midway between the base metals and precious metals, because of some of its properties, it is better than the former for use in households because of its absolute safety when combined with weak acids.'[11] Two years later, in another article explaining the implementation of the industrial process, Sainte-Claire Deville confirmed his earlier analysis: 'Its inalterability and perfect safety have been tested and in the tests, aluminium has been even better than I could have predicted.'[12] Finally in 1859, in his main book, *De l'aluminium*, Sainte-Claire Deville described the various stages for implementing his invention, and the results of his work on the metal. He published the first reliable synthesis of physico-chemical knowledge on aluminium.[13]

The question of the use of aluminium in kitchen utensils was controversial from that time. Some negative results were justified by referring to the impure metal that was used many years before when the process was not yet well controlled. The presence of copper affected the analysis and some scientists recommended that aluminium not be used for cooking or storing beverages.[14] But during that period, aluminium alloys, the main one at the time being aluminium bronze, were, nevertheless, already applied in uses requiring complete safety. Tests such as cooking roast beef on an aluminium plate were carried out, and aluminium cooking utensils, cutlery and so forth were manufactured.[15] In church silver, the symbolism of materials is prominent; this includes the idea of purity. The use of aluminium was accepted in 1866 by a rescript of Pius IX. An article written in 1869 referred to the Pope who expressed striking support through his approval on 'aluminium, either pure or mixed with other metals'.[16] Similarly, in 1864 in the medical world, we find advertisements for aluminium dentures.[17] Literature of this period reflects growing trust, as shown in this passage from a scientific lecture in 1868: aluminium and aluminium bronze 'compete with other precious metals, first, to provide households with more hygienic utensils for the very reason that the substance of which they are formed does not lead to the production of poisonous bodies'.[18]

The period from 1854 to 1888/9 is fundamental in the social construction of aluminium, which was hoped for, expected, then described and supported as 'the' most hygienic metal. In the scientific context of the middle of the nineteenth century, the question of the harmlessness of materials in contact with food is far from unimportant: in the vast problem of food adulteration, the role of materials for containers or kitchen utensils is the object of debate among scientists. The scientific journals of this time report the difficult fight to have pots galvanised with fine tin, and copper removed from kitchen utensils. The questions about metals and research are also applied to aluminium. The technical frame, used by Wiebe J. Bijker,[19] is extremely wide, and brings together many actors: scientists from different disciplines, users of kitchen utensils and beverage containers, doctors faced with poisoning and legislators who attempt to legislate. Sainte-Claire Deville undoubtedly knew the importance of this issue and sent some aluminium samples to chemists around the world, for example, to Liebig, the expert on food adulteration in Germany. In the United States, Dr A. A. Hayes recognised the scientific progress through the following words in 1856: 'So as soon as the genius of Deville enabled him to throw the clear light of experimental results on this subject, chemists saw that he had not only rendered more sure what was known, but he had created as it were a new assemblage of characters to be included under the term aluminium.'[20] That is to say, Sainte-Claire Deville established the chemical characteristics of aluminium and its innocuousness; he had made a major step. The popular-science journals played a very important role in the social construction. One of the best known in France, L'Année scientifique et industrielle by Louis Figuier, reported scientific information and conveyed it to a vast public. Its overall purpose is also to convey positivism, as defended by Auguste Comte: science is a source of technological, economic and social progress. Political power also plays a role in this technical framework. Sainte-Claire Deville benefited indeed from the personal financial support of Emperor Napoleon III to continue his research on aluminium. Unlike Parkesine or Bakelite, aluminium was a new material that Sainte-Claire Deville immediately identified as a metal that could be used for food. He enthusiastically studied its lack of odour (another difference from iron and Bakelite), and its chemical and physical properties.

Issues of public health and industrial pollution linked to aluminium have been raised ever since the metal was produced. However, the small quantities produced and the limited variety of uses has limited the number and extent of the conflict. A new industrial process changed this situation, but the resulting conflict was rapidly and sustainably controlled by businesses.

A new industrial process and the emergence of big polluters

In 1886, a new electrolysis process, developed by P. Héroult in France and C.-M. Hall, in the United States, opened the way for mass production and made aluminium very inexpensive. In France and Switzerland, the first plants were established in the alpine mountains because large amounts of energy were available for hydroelectric power since electricity was not yet carried over long distances. It was the same in North America around Niagara Falls. The chronology of industrial and commercial development on both sides of the Atlantic is quite similar.

The installation of this new production plant provoked some early negative reactions, characterised by a double approach that included environmental pollution and occupational diseases. In the French case, doubt convinced a scientist to enter the public debate. But his action only concerned the production plant and its close territory. The role of the expert became essential in answering accusations. During that same period of time, civil society organised itself and brought in its own experts. The debate lasted for 10 years, starting in 1902, with a turning point in 1907.

Because of technical difficulties, the first plant was slow in starting production and only exceeded 1000 tons per year in 1901.[21] By 1902, resident populations were alarmed about the pollution to surrounding vegetation. At that time, negotiations were underway for the installation of other plants along the Arc River. The public concern was legitimate. The issue was submitted to the Board of Health of Savoy[22] and to three types of experts: a medical doctor, a Water and Forests Warden, and a mining engineer. All of them concluded that aluminium production was safe for the environment and workers. The debate was temporarily closed.

The construction of a new plant in 1905 revived people's attention and pushed the protesters to organise themselves to make their voice heard. The 1905 *commodo & incommodo* survey was joined by the farmers who demanded, in particular, that 'dust and smoke from the factory be collected'. They were alluding to a system developed in Switzerland after residents complained in 1893.[23] Under pressure from the farmers' union, the plant was equipped with two towers to recover gaseous emanations.[24]

Around 1907, the conflict reached a turning point. A pharmaceutical doctor took the initiative to study and identify hazards.[25] He became the *de facto* expert of the plaintiffs' camp. His work was of a new scale and scope, since he dealt not only with pollution and environmental damage, but also with the distress of the workers, against the interests of the powerful industry.[26]

The pharmaceutical doctor combined damage to the environment and to the people, including the factory workers. This attitude was not common at the time, but some others examples existed. Massard-Guilbaud, for example, mentions a similar situation in Figueroa, around 1851, where a doctor was the leader of the complaint's movement against environmental pollution. His father lived next to a lead factory, and observed some special diseases that he felt were related to lead. Massard-Guilbaud insists that very often the experts were clearly more familiar with and favourable to businesspeople than the local citizens.[27] Rainhorn also emphasises that nobody worried about the factory workers when producing white lead in Lille.[28]

The next *commodo & incommodo* survey sought the expertise of the County Labour Inspector. He only partly agreed with the doctor's opinion. His report indicated that no special diseases could be attributed to the aluminium industry, despite the fact that the workers' health was bad. Dr Hollande gave a more precise and terrible description of the workers' health: 'Little by little, under the effects of the mixture of carbonic acid gas, carbon monoxide, hydrogen fluoride... they lose weight, feel unquenchable thirst, nausea, and dizziness, and some of them have trismus, contracture, nosebleeds, or pneumonia. Some of them vomit blood, and several of them have diabetes... My conclusions are thus far from being in conformity and in perfect harmony with the statement which the company director made at your subcommittee on hygiene.'[29]

This very local debate, without relay at the national level, can be explained by the characteristics of this industry in the early twentieth century. There were very few aluminium factories in France: only five were operating in 1906. They employed a small workforce, including many seasonal workers from Italy who left in the summer, when the flow rate of the streams was not sufficient to produce electricity. By 1908, there were eight factories, located between the Alpine and Pyrenean massifs.

Working conditions were extremely harsh: the heat was around 140–158°F, with very strong emissions of toxic gas and dust. In addition to fluoride, there were also tar fumes used in manufacturing cathodes. The human body was subjected to harsh conditions in the various operations that had not yet been mechanised. There were many accidents, especially burns, and pulmonary problems that were usually fatal because of the large differences in indoor and outside temperatures, especially in winter.[30]

This document was devastating for the industry, and the author's position and scientific expertise could not be questioned. The Saint-Jean-de-Maurienne court recognised the expert opinion of Dr Paul Hollande, but it was limited to a traditional professional field of a pharmacist: the study of vegetation. The court ordered him, in 1910, to make a study he entitled 'Plant Pathology of the Hydrofluoric Acid'. To carry out his investigation, Dr Hollande tried to estimate the quantities of fluorinated gases released, but he was refused access to the smelters. His survey made it possible to measure the effects of fluorine on vegetation in the Maurienne Valley. It subsequently served as a reference for determining the compensation to be paid to farmers and ranchers. Issues of occupational health were excluded from the debates, which were focused exclusively on environmental issues. Until the 1960s, environmental problems were settled through mutually agreed financial compensation between the factories and unions of agricultural producers.[31]

Building trust and examining the issue

Safe food utensils: a transnational approach from the 1890s to the 1940s

With the new Hall-Héroult process, the aluminium industry began large-scale development activities downstream of the metal production. The light metal got out of the Parisian world's manufacturers of confidential semi-luxury items to become an ordinary metal, processed and used by a growing number of consumers.[32] The use of aluminium for cookware (and for soldiers' packs) was developed especially between the 1890s and the Second World War.

One of the tools used has been the creation of scientific and technological laboratories devoted partly or totally to aluminium, both in the military and in the civilian fields. A scientific community dedicated to this metal gradually emerged. The army first had a positive role in pushing innovation. The scientific community started analysing this metal and studying the possibilities of reducing the weight of the soldiers' equipment. Germans were the first to test the potential of aluminium in this field. In the 1890s, international efforts to define the physical and chemical characteristics were intensified. The development of the new aluminium-production process led to a new wave of activity and new scientific debate, against a backdrop of Franco-German political rivalry. The debate was launched with an article by the German chemists Lubbert and Roscher in 1891, which warned against aluminium water bottles, especially for soldiers. The reactions to this assertion were international.[33] In France, Joseph Balland analysed the aluminium material used by French soldiers during the expedition to Madagascar in 1890 and concluded that the metal stood up well.[34] Four years later, the *Service de l'Intendance* decided to create a laboratory, under the auspices of the War Administration, and made Balland the manager. In 1896, in Germany, L. Lewin, professor at Berlin University, published a treatise on toxicology in which aluminium appeared among other metallic substances. The book, published in French in 1903, guaranteed the safety of the light metal and became a reference book in France.[35] France and Germany were the leaders in this scientific field.

The industrial world was directly affected by the controversy, just at a time when the market was weak and slowly progressed. It had to find a strategy to quash the rumour.

Finally, an independent expert was chosen. In France, the largest aluminium producer, Société électrométallurgique française (SEMF), became a leading manufacturer. This downstream development strategy has been adopted in order to develop the market on the basis of new uses. SEMF produced aluminium pans. Faced with persistent rumours on the safety of the metal, in 1897 SEMF recruited Auguste Trillat, a chemist who was working for a pharmaceutical company and in 1905 became department manager at the Pasteur Institute in Paris. Trillat published the results of his work in 1915 in a long article in which he spoke of – and discredited – the motives of the opponents of aluminium. He especially cited the work of Alfred Ditte, which, he said, was carried out on impure aluminium components, containing large quantities of copper.[36] After concluding unequivocally that the metal was safe, Trillat continued working with the industry for many years, especially on developing aluminium for use in the brewery sector.[37] The proximity of the Pasteur Institute to a business firm was not unusual; at that time there were other similar examples in, for example, the canning industry.

During this same period, national public institutions, namely the Council of Hygiene and Safety and the Standing Committee for the Prevention of Fraud at the Department of Agriculture, also vouched for the safety of aluminium for use in food utensils. These decisions, as well as Trillat's works, were largely disseminated by the firm SEMF, especially in its journal, the *Revue de l'Aluminium*, created in 1923.[38]

The movement was similar in the US market.[39] According to Georges D. Smith, cooking utensils were the fastest growing application until the 1910s, and the application best known by the general public. Alcoa, the US aluminium producer, tried, from the mid-1890s, to enter this market by selling metal to manufacturers. Because the quality of the manufactured pots and pans was poor, and the consumers were discouraged, Alcoa decided in 1901 to buy an aluminium-utensil production plant. In 1912, it had 75% of the US market. As with the SEMF, Alcoa relied on an external expert, Joseph W. Richards. In 1886, Richards had published the first version of his famous book, *Aluminium: its History, Occurrence, Properties, Metallurgy & Applications, Including Its Alloys*. It was the first book in English dedicated to aluminium. Electrochemist and metallurgical engineer, he was an academic expert on aluminium, at Lehigh University in Pennsylvania. He became the Alcoa official expert, funded by the company, and was a fervent supporter of aluminium.[40]

The 1896 edition gives a good summary of scientific knowledge at that time. Richards, as a strong supporter of aluminium for domestic use, also mentions the interest expressed by the US military. He is a promoter of metal and defends it by referring to the increasing popularity of aluminium: six firms made cooking utensils in the United States, with success, because of the 'non-poisonous' quality of aluminium.[41] All of Richards' arguments were not scientific. Without imagining any collusion between the interests of the metallurgist and those of the aluminium manufacturers, one can underline the very strong empathy for this new material. This attitude is comparable to the French case.

The two companies, Alcoa and SEMF, had relationships. Héroult and Hall knew each other; Héroult visited the US factories and the Alcoa president, E. Hunt, came to France to see the La Praz factory in 1895. Both companies collaborated inside an international cartel founded in 1901 called the Aluminium Association. Although the electrolytic process issues were confidential, real collaboration existed for the development of the market. US, French, British and Swiss companies took part in this cartel from the beginning. After the First World War, Alcoa left, but the Canadians participated, and so did the German companies. In 1927, the International Office for Aluminium was created to provide information and promote new applications. Alcoa participated in it. In France, the laboratory of L'Aluminium Français, which had been in charge of French market development since 1918, took special care to look for new applications throughout in the world.[42] This organisation, with many different and durable cartels and agreements, is typical of the aluminium industry. That was important in the social construction of aluminium, because extensive agreement gave the companies an exceptional capacity to conduct research, extend patent rights, publish books and journals on aluminium, and so forth. The scope was extremely wide and effective, adapted to each product or each sector of application.

It seems that safety and trust in scientific progress made it possible to calm people's anxiety and eliminate criticism in France. In the 1930s, the famous Parisian Home Exhibition (Salon des Arts ménagers) reflected the growing success of aluminium in cooking utensils and appliances. The metal had indeed found its market and seemed to have gained the trust of consumers.[43] In the 1950s, its innocuousness had been confirmed by the official authorities: the Superior Council of Public Hygiene (Conseil supérieur de l'hygiène publique) issued a report on the maximum aluminium content acceptable in food and concluded that aluminium was not a toxic metal and that it was in a natural state in food.[44] In 1952 and 1956, the French Association for Standardisation accredited the choice of alloys to be used in the equipment of a delicatessen or a kitchen. Both the public authorities and the consumers seemed very confident.

Invisible polluters?

As we said, until the Second World War, factories and unions of agricultural producers in France settled the environmental problem through financial compensation. Occupational diseases did not arouse other claims or disputes. A hypothesis is that Pechiney, in the inter-war years, established a health service in each factory; the workers benefited from exemplary medical care. Suitable clothing had been gradually provided, as in the Saint-Jean plant, where gloves and leather aprons were used during the First World War. This situation, combined with significant turnover in the plants at that time, also probably contributed to the absence of any claims. There are very few historical studies on occupational diseases in the aluminium industry. The monographs by plant or company underestimate this aspect. In Canada, according to Duncan C. Campbell,[45] Alcan began to become interested in this topic during the Second World War. In the United States, the situation was much the same, and the social policy of the Alcoa Company was similar to that of France.[46] It was also stressed that the workers' attitude should have reinforced the company's position. In Italy, Guido de Luigi suggests that workers in the Mori aluminium factory, between 1928 and 1938, always argued that their health was not in danger, despite the major environmental disaster. They defended their jobs while at the same time many children and adults were hospitalised.[47] Nevertheless, work and scientific publications on the pollution caused by aluminium factories to nature and animals continued on an international scale. Fluoride poisoning was in the headlines again during the First World War with the survey by Cristiani and his team, who conducted studies around the Alusuisse smelters in the Swiss Valais and gave fluorosis its name.[48] In 1934, a new series of studies was made, particularly as a result of Slagsvold's observations on the Norwegian aluminium smelters. It led to the identification of skeletal fluorosis in man. Two years later, Kaj Roholm from Denmark published a major work on the history of this disease: *Fluorine Intoxication.* In France, the toxicologist René Truhaut wrote a reference book on fluorosis and its impact on industrial hygiene and food in 1948. The book includes a remarkable bibliography of 290 titles. Following this increase in research, in 1952 the

International Conference on Safety at the Workplace recommended that all participating countries enter industrial fluorosis in the list of compensable diseases. Fluorosis was recognised as an occupational disease in Switzerland in 1953. The International Labour Office in 1955 issued an information note on this subject.[49]

Trust, doubt and debate: from the 1960s to the 1990s

Mass pollution and enlargement of the debate

The issue of occupational health in the aluminium industry seemed to be absent from public debate in France until the 1970s.[50] But the considerable increase in production in the Alpine smelters, particularly in the 1970s, gave rise to more pollution problems in both France and Switzerland. This period was also characterised by a strong awareness of environmental issues by the population as a whole, which resulted in demonstrations and trials against the polluting industries, with, for France and Switzerland, the active presence of very dynamic environmental organisations.[51] The contribution of veterinary science to the debate on fluorosis was essential in France.[52] The French aluminium industry, at that time, seemed to be taking these problems into account, especially since industrial projects abroad were subject to more stringent environmental law, for example, in the Netherlands. The pioneering work of Daniel Boullet on this issue did not address the problem of occupational diseases, which the company did not talk about until the 1970s.[53]

The thesis by André Mazel from the Veterinary School of Toulouse was a key element in the debate and sensitisation about industrial fluorosis.[54] He addressed the issue of human fluorosis in both plants and animals and advanced his arguments carefully, but nevertheless suggested the existence of fluorosis in France 'in man and not only among the smelter workers working in the atmosphere of the smelters, but also in children who grow up in the polluted adjacent areas'. In addition to fluorosis, Mazel went on to say, with very alarming words: '[It is] especially among the workers in the aluminium smelters that we observe the highest rate of tuberculosis mortality and cancer.'[55] Fluorosis, cancer and tuberculosis could thus become three diseases caused by the aluminium industry. His thesis made a great stir in public spheres, and his international bibliography evidenced the timeliness and relevance of his research.

At the international level, some countries already had taken steps to provide compensation for fluorosis, including Belgium, Switzerland and Italy. In 1962, the European Economic Community published a European list of the occupational diseases in which fluorine was included in the category of toxic chemical agents. In France, diseases related to fluoride and its compounds were put on the list of occupational diseases in 1963.[56] The French National Institute of Safety published a review of the literature on this subject in 1965. The paper focused exclusively on occupational fluorosis; industrial fluorosis was excluded (that is, outside the factory, and due to contamination of water and plants by fumes and polluted water from smelters) and endemic fluorosis (that is, of hydro-telluric origin). Although the international context imposed it – that was obvious – France (like Great Britain), did not systematically include occupational fluorosis among the occupational diseases, thus avoiding any compensation for the patient.

In 1975, Pechiney, the leading European producer, spoke of this subject for the first time in its internal newsletter *Bulletin Aluminium Pechiney*. In an interview, Dr Coulon, the Medical Officer of Aluminium Pechiney, took stock of health issues in smelters. The article was written to reassure the Pechiney staff and is interesting because it demonstrates the need to discuss the subject. But it was not only a question of informing the employees sporadically: a second article explained that the company, henceforth, would systematically check workers' health.

The company's argument to repeal criticism is based on five elements. First, the effects of pollution on plants and animals are judged to be significantly decreasing, thanks to progress in the fume-collection system, and there will be no effects on people if they refrain from consuming the plants or animals. Second, the existence of 'natural' fluorosis, that is, hydro-telluric fluorosis, in areas where fluoride levels in water were high, is emphasised, but its effects are minimised (alterations in dental and skeletal fluorosis). Third, poisoning is similar to other industries. The most dangerous factories are the cryolite factories in Denmark, phosphate factories in North Africa, and fertiliser plants rich in phosphorus-fluorine in the United States. Fourth, because of the specific characteristics of smelters, their case is not considered comparable to the previous examples. The levels of fluorinated compounds in the air are, at this time, much lower. This position was supported by references to studies conducted in other countries.[57] Last but not least, France is very little concerned (only in the old factories) and harmful effects on health are limited.[58] The conclusion was definite: human cases of fluorosis in modern aluminium plants would be exceptional. For the environment, no evidence could be found of truly pathological damage that could be traced to a smelter and affect the surrounding population. The company should nevertheless continue its dual policy of medical surveillance and improved capture.

A year later, a new article by Dr Coulon to update information on this issue highlighted the collective work done by all the occupational health doctors working in the group's smelters. Radiological assessments were being made of the bone condition of personnel exposed for over six years. A dozen cases showed signs of fluoride impregnation 'with small bone apposition referring to the signs of banal osteoarthritis'. The percentage of osteoarthritis in those examined was identical to that of the population at large. The company also established a systematic analysis of fluoride ion levels in the urine of people exposed. Some cases of fluorosis were detected 'exceptionally' and the use of a protective mask was recommended for certain operations.

For the first time, occupational health doctors, under the supervision of Professor Fournier, Professor of Toxicology at the Fernand-Widal Hospital in Paris, made an oral survey of respiratory problems, in two smelters. The survey was followed by a series of medical auscultations (auscultation + spirometer to measure the total lung capacity and expiratory ventilation seconds). In his conclusion, Dr Coulon acknowledged that various respiratory problems had been found among workers in Saint-Jean (the oldest factory) but 'no more than in a population of Paris workers'. He used a study by Professor Kourilski, mainly on workers in the steel industry, as a reference. At Noguères, where there was smelter with a very recent capture system, the results were much better.

The two interviews, published a year apart, both minimised the risks of working in the smelters and the impact of disease. This attitude of the French company raises questions, and one can wonder about his intentions in this regard. The habit of not speaking publicly about occupational diseases refers to the practices of secrecy and compensation widely practised by the company. Comforted by the existence of a social and medical system that was established early in the life of the factories, the company probably minimised the social impact of its attitude. The emergence of this issue in the 1970s corresponds to the demands for transparency that are emerging throughout society. This company's attitude is especially strange in comparison with Canada, where the issue seems much better and clearly addressed by the Alcan Company.[59] The technology used in the smelters in Canada, the Söderberg anodes, was more harmful than that used in France, but the co-operation between university faculties of medicine, governmental services and industry was close, extensive and characterised by transparency and responsibility.[60]

Risky uses: the growth of the era of suspicion

Aluminium belongs to the 'commodities' category, and its use is widespread in all areas of industrial production. The post-Second World War period saw consumption skyrocketing and the emergence of many new products and practices. Food was particularly affected by changes in methods of preparation and preservation. Increasing urbanisation, greater use of refrigerators and freezers, and the development of gas stoves and electricity were all factors of social upheaval. Preservation techniques also underwent profound changes: canning, freeze drying, freezing, deep-freezing.[61] Food packaging became essential to these changes, and the physicochemical characteristics of aluminium (sealing, safety, stamping, rolling and so forth) were valuable assets. In addition to the traditional pots, foil invaded store shelves as wrapping for butter, cheese, cakes, dehydrated soup and other products.[62] In the kitchen, aluminium rolls changed culinary preparations with the appearance of aluminium envelopes for cooking, and new possibilities for food preservation and transportation. As this change took hold, the problem was that the prolonged contact of metal with food might cause contamination. The role of public institutions also grew during this period, from the national to the European level, subsequent to the Rome Treaty (1957).

From 1975, the crisis of the Denver dialysis patients in the United States had long-term effects on the consumer trust that had been built up in the previous decades. This crisis has also obliged the US aluminium companies to formulate a scientific monitoring strategy in this field. In 1975, a paper described the first case of fatal human encephalopathy.[63] Fine concretions were found in the brain of the deceased patient. The use of particle analytical microscopy revealed the presence of aluminium, combined with phosphorus. Thanks to the progress made in scientific instrumentation, two new methods were implemented to locate aluminium in the body: electron-probe microanalysis (Castaing electron microprobe) and ion microscopy.[64] As of 1976, new studies were made, including those by Allen Alfrey and William D. Keahny in the United States, which proved the connection between aluminium in the brain and clinical signs of encephalopathy in a group of patients with renal insufficiencies being treated by chronic dialysis. The origin of the intoxication was spotted in the therapeutic treatments: it was the aluminium salt given through the digestive tract to combat the patients' phosphoraemia. This work was also helped by progress made in quantifying aluminium in the human body since 1972. Indeed, Edwin Clarkson set the standard for the average person at 80 micrograms of aluminium per litre of blood. Faced with this crucial question of aluminium and health, US companies adopted a common strategy toward the public medical research community by having recourse to the expertise of a public university. Between 1955 and 1979, the Aluminum Association (AA) requested researchers at the Kettering Laboratory at the University of Cincinnati to make a desk study on aluminium and health. This strategic choice was relevant: Kettering Laboratory had been a pioneer in research on the problems of occupational and environmental health, especially in connection with General Motors. The Department of Environmental Health brought together a multidisciplinary team of scientists: physicians, analytical chemists, toxicologists, industrial hygienists and engineers. The research team systematically concluded that there was no need to worry about health problems coming from exposure to aluminium.[65]

But in the 1980s, a new rumour appeared: aluminium caused Alzheimer's disease. Why and how? Researchers working on Alzheimer's disease questioned the close relation between the symptoms of their patients' and the Denver patients. Here again aluminium was being suspected. Research was undertaken based on this working hypothesis. In February 1986, two British researchers announced their initial findings in *The Lancet*, a prestigious medical journal. One of the characteristic features of Alzheimer's, the 'senile plaques' in the brain of patients, was analysed using a microprobe analysis and a nuclear magnetic resonance system with very high resolution. The researchers found that aluminium and silicon had a similar distribution and were to be found in the same places. But they did not know how aluminium had reached the brain, and if it were the cause or the consequence of the disease. The rumour was out: aluminium was partly responsibility for Alzheimer's disease. The media, specialised or not, conveyed the information, in more or less sensational headlines. For the first time, France was forced to legislate specifically on aluminium in contact with foodstuffs, food products and beverages in 1987. The European Community followed France in 1988 with a more general guideline relating to materials and articles intended to come into contact with foodstuffs.[66] This crisis, in 1988, pushed the Royal Society of Chemistry, in London, to organise a symposium and to announce it under the title 'Aluminium in Food and the Environment'.[67] Twenty-two scientists were brought together to try to put the charges in the right perspective and to assess the state of knowledge. They concluded that aluminium was innocuous.

The influence of public opinion on health issues

In the 1990s, a radical change in the public debate occurred. Hitherto carefully differentiated, health problems related to occupational health and environment and those related to consumption were combined in the public debate. In France, many newspapers prepared feature files on this issue.[68] Manufacturers also had to adapt to this phenomenon. Two documents attest to this change; the question of health embraced the whole field of the workplace, the environment and materials as used in food. In 1992, Dr J.T. Hughes in the United Kingdom published *Aluminium and Health*.[69] The document was translated in 1997 into French by the French Aluminium Union and Aluminium Pechiney, and then completed by the addition of a new section called: 'Aluminium. Health and Environment. Questions and Answers.' These documents focused as much on aluminium as a material as on the risks associated with producing it and its use in food. It was up to the manufacturers to answer all questions/suspicions expressed in the media *via* the scientific expertise of a renowned professor of medicine. Two questions in the document sum up the conjunction of occupational disease and public health: 'Can we contract cancer in an aluminium plant?' and 'Is aluminium in contact with food a health hazard?'

The answer to the first question was argued as follows: 'The industrial history has shown that in a smelter, the old methods of production have proved potentially harmful to human health and could cause cancer. For this reason, in the early 1990s the French aluminium industry voluntarily announced it would exclusively use the new electrolysis technique called "prebake anodes."' But the wording was seen as a refutation of all previous statements. It effectively put an emphasis on an important technological choice, the prebaked anodes against the more polluting Söderberg system. For the second question, the answer was categorical: 'No. Aluminium in food does not create a health hazard.' No reference was made to scientific papers. The document, however, gave a large overview of Alzheimer's disease and the financial aid that the industry was giving to medical research.

In 1997, these issues had grown to an incredible size. The supranational World Health Organisation led an expert working group, under the International Programme on Chemical Safety (IPCS), which exonerated aluminium. Its conclusion was 'no evidence that aluminium is at the origin of Alzheimer's disease. Aluminium does not induce any pathology of the Alzheimer type *in vivo* in any species, including human beings.' In October 1997 an international conference, attended by some 40 researchers, was held in Montreal on 'Managing Health in the Aluminium Industry'. Remarkably, it was sponsored by all global producers of aluminium, headed by the British (International Primary Aluminium Institute, IPAI) and the Americans (the Aluminium Association, AA), in co-operation with the producers of South Africa, Norway, Australia, Europe, Japan and Quebec. The IPAI President was chairman of the Kaiser Aluminium Corporation. His opinion, stated at the outset of the report, shows the fundamental change of scale, from a national to an international then to a global approach: 'Safety and health issues are driven by global (not national) health, safety and environmental issues and economic competition,' and thus justify the transnational approach to issues of health and safety.[70] These words seemed especially fitting since the first paper, which was supposed to give an overview of the health question in the aluminium industry for the last 25 years, had made mention of the actions of the manufacturers in the field of research, in particular those of the AA. The difference with the situation in Europe during the same period of time was puzzling.

Conclusion

When aluminium is considered as a commodity over a long-term period, the issues of occupational health and public health in the aluminium industry are viewed very differently within geographical areas with fluctuating boundaries. At first these issues were limited to the confines of the smelters and to the domain of scientific research. The problems took place around each factory, and the actors were local. The debates had a national or international dimension only in the scientific domain. Public opinion seemed unconcerned by the health and environmental problems. After the Second World War, occupational health in the aluminium industry earned a position in the public debate at the national level.

The metal-safety problem, however, was brought up from the very beginning, first giving rise to studies and scientific controversy, then to – short-lived – public controversy in the late 1890s. This first period was symbolised by the premise that this new material was a metal that was vital to safe cooking. The debates occurred because the alloy purity was not well controlled. In the beginning, scientists in civil and military laboratories made chemical studies to confirm the innocuousness of aluminium. The end of this period was also characterised by the presence of independent experts funded by enterprises, both in France and the United States. When the harmlessness of aluminium was firmly ascertained, the debate ended.

A second period on the safety of aluminium started in the 1970s with the Denver dialysis patients and increased in the 1980s with Alzheimer's disease. First published in medical journals, the work and hypotheses of researchers were quickly taken up by the popular-science journals then consumer magazines and daily newspapers. The debate, stripped of its scientific rationality and objectivity, merely fed a collective fear.

In the 1990s, a third period started when the health issues included occupational disease and public health, and was treated transnationally by both industry and the supranational organisations. Throughout these years, we saw successive expert opinions, both public and private, being developed within and outside of laboratories. Manufacturers had to devise strategies to build up the trust of both their employees and their consumers. To convince each of them, the issue became definitively global, with a larger approach than at the beginning of the twentieth century.

Notes

1. Homburg, Travis, and Schröter, *The Chemical Industry in Europe, 1850–1914*; Bernhardt and Massard-Guilbaud, *Le démon moderne*; Moslet, *The Chimney of the World*; Uekoetter, *The Age of Smoke*; Massard-Guilbaud, *Histoire de la pollution industrielle*; Rosental and Omnès, "L'histoire des maladies professionnelles."
2. See Trentmann, *The Oxford Handbook of the History of Consumption*; De Grazia, *The Sex of Things*; Appadurai, *The Social Life of Things*; Chatriot, Chessel, and Hilton, *Au nom du consommateur*; Caron. "L'embellie parisienne à la Belle Epoque. L'invention d'un modèle de consommation"; Brewer and Porter, *Consumption and the World of Goods*; Fox and Lears, *Culture of Consumption*; Chauveau, "Consommer en masse"; Strasser, McGovern, and Judt, *Getting and Spending*; Frank, *The Conquest of Cool*; Scholliers, *Food, Drink and Identity*; Roche, *Histoire des choses banales*; Trentmann, *The Making of the Consumer*.
3. Hachez-Leroy, *L'Aluminium français*.
4. Bijker, Hughes, and Pinch, *The Social Construction of Technological Systems*.
5. Campbell, *Les enjeux de la bauxite*; Campbell and Ericsson, *Restructuring in Global Aluminium*; Campbell, *Mining in Africa: Regulation and Development*; Evenden, "Aluminum, Commodity Chains, and the Environmental History of the Second World War."
6. Geoffroy le Jeune, in 1728, identified alum as a part of clay; in 1754, Andreas Sigismund Marggraf showed that alum base formed an essential ingredient in the clays that Louis-Bernard Guyton de Morveau called *alumina*, a term taken for chemical nomenclature developed with Lavoisier in 1792. Thomson, *Système de chimie*, 409 ff.; Fourcroy and Duhamel, *Encyclopédie méthodique, Chimie, pharmacie et métallurgie*. 1786 and 1792. See Blanckaert et Porret, L'Encyclopédie méthodique (1782-1832), Des Lumières au Positivisme.
7. de Saussure, *Recherches chimiques sur la végétation*. Summary tables of experiences, p. 338 and seq. are particularly interesting.
8. His work followed that of three scientists since the early nineteenth century: Davy (1804), Œrsted (1825) and Wöhler (1827 and 1845). Wöhler was the first to give the light metal a physical form, albeit very imperfect, by obtaining a "grey powder" and sometimes "spongy masses."
9. Cf. For example, *Proceedings of the American Academy of Arts and Sciences*, Vol. 3 (May 1852–May 1857), Philadelphia, Meeting of 25 April 1854.
10. Sainte-Claire Deville mentioned the heavy pollution caused by aluminium production between 1855 and 1860 in the Paris region: "In April 1857, the small factory at La Glacière, located in a suburb of Paris, among houses and gardens, and pouring fumes charged with sodium and chlorine into the atmosphere, was obliged, as a result of public outcry, to stop its production of aluminium." Sainte-Claire Deville, "Recherches sur les métaux, et en particulier sur l'aluminium et sur une nouvelle forme du silicium."
11. Sainte-Claire Deville, "Recherches sur les métaux, et en particulier sur l'aluminium et sur une nouvelle forme du silicium."
12. Sainte-Claire Deville, "Mémoire sur la fabrication du sodium et de l'aluminium."
13. Two young scientists who had collaborated with Sainte-Claire Deville, the Tissier brothers, published a first book about aluminium in 1858. Their book is interesting because it is the first one on this issue since the introduction of the new technological process. But the two brothers referred to the Sainte-Claire Deville articles and results in most of the book. They failed to get their book accepted by the scientific community, which considered they had betrayed Sainte-Claire Deville's trust. Tissier and Tissier, *L'Aluminium et les métaux alcalins*.
14. This controversy was mentioned in a letter from H. Sainte-Claire Deville to Louis Le Châtelier in 1857 and published in *Revue de l'aluminium* 3 (1924).
15. *Revue de l'aluminium* 4 (1924), "Bulletin bibliographique," 29.
16. Cerfberr de Médelsheim, *Orfèvrerie religieuse en bronze d'aluminium*.
17. *Le temps*, 11 September 1864, 4.
18. Hément, *L'aluminium*.

19. Bijker, Wiebe E. "The Social Construction of Bakelite: Toward a Theory of Invention."
20. *Proceedings of the American Academy of Arts and Sciences* 3 (May 1852–May 1857), 223.
21. La Praz plant in the Maurienne Valley (Savoy) began to produce aluminium in 1893. Morel, *Histoire technique de la production d'aluminium.*
22. Board of Health of Savoy, 11 October 1902: "The fumes and smoke from the manufacture of these various products are not likely to affect public health and safety and that the health of surrounding populations can not be affected."
23. Gasche, *Le scandale Alusuisse: la guerre du fluor en Valais.*
24. These towers, in the La Praz plant, were ineffective and were soon removed.
25. Boullet, "Pechiney et l'environnement"; Mugnier, *Contribution à l'étude de l'évolution de la fluorose en Maurienne,* 63.
26. "The Maurienne is just entering an era of splendid industrial prosperity and I believe that by asking you rationally to respect the health of the workers I am assuring the protection of this industrial property. Instead of having to record an average working life, which currently is 10 years at the most, even in the opinion of those most concerned, we could raise that average. Wouldn't this be doing an invaluable service to one side and a highly valuable one to the other? In our survey, we heard from various representatives of the Saussaz, Saint-Jean-de-Maurienne and Venthon plants. It is obvious that none of these manufacturers will tell you that the health of their workers suffers from work at the plant. I will undoubtedly have to patiently wait for the results that these industrialists have to communicate to me on the state of their mutual aid fund. [. . .] No such document has been filed despite the promise. I still want to know the number of days each worker is on sick leave to find out about the ratio of health to sickness, a ratio that should give an idea about the functioning of the work force ... How can I officially collect the workers' complaints? And find out about those who have family responsibilities? [. . .] On the other hand, the factory workers have contracted a special type of diabetes due exclusively to the fumes of hydrofluoric acid. The population surrounding the plant complained of suffocating fumes that spread throughout the valley. "Rapport du Dr Hollande," 1907. Cited by Beaud, "La nature ne coûte rien, la détruire, ça rapporte," 74.
27. Massard-Guilbaud, *Histoire de la pollution industrielle.*
28. Rainhorn, "Le mouvement ouvrier contre la peinture au plomb."
29. Beaud, "La nature ne coûte rien."
30. Toussaint, *Historique de la Compagnie AFC,* volume 4. Typed document, archives Alcan-Rio Tinto, quoted by Georges, Tortil, and Voisin, *Cent ans d'évolution des métiers de l'électrolyse,* 45.
31. Ménégoz, "Protection de l'environnement autour des usines d'électrolyse"; Massard-Guilbaud, *Histoire de la pollution industrielle.*
32. Hachez-Leroy, "Du métal précieux au matériau invisible: la double vie de l'aluminium."
33. Balland, "Sur les ustensiles en aluminium"; Guichard, *Annales d'hygiène,* 42; Dr S. Camilla, "Sulla intaccabilità dell'alluminio dal punto di vista igienico," *Rivistà d'Igiene e Sanita pubblica,* 1 and 16 Dec. 1896, pp. 935 and 995, quoted in *Revue d'hygiène et de police sanitaire,* 19 (1897), "Revue des Journaux," 746; A. Khoklovsky, *Analyse chimique des marmites et des barillets en alliage d'aluminium, faisant partie de l'équipement des soldats.* Thèse de Saint-Pétersbourg, quoted in *Revue d'hygiène et de police sanitaire,* 21 (1899), "Revue des Journaux," 361; Leriche, "Ustensiles destinés aux aliments," *Revue d'hygiène et de police sanitaire.*
34. Graduate of the Imperial School of the Military Health Service in Strasbourg, Joseph-Felix-Antoine Balland (1845–1927) received his diploma for the profession of first-class pharmacist in August 1868. Balland carried out numerous analyses and worked to improve the conditions of food-product conservation.
35. Critical review published in *L'Union pharmaceutique,* 312.
36. Ditte, *Introduction à l'étude des métaux, Cours professés à la Faculté des sciences.*
37. Trillat, "Emploi de l'aluminium dans les industries de fermentation"; Trillat, "Sur les emplois de l'aluminium dans les industries d'alimentation."
38. In 1924, in a short article in the *Revue de l'Aluminium* entitled "The Safety of Aluminium in Food Use", Trillat took the defence of the lightweight metal by referring to his own work and also to the findings of the national public institutions.
39. Sparke, "Cookware to Cocktail Shakers"; Smith, *From Monopoly to Competition.*
40. Smith, *From Monopoly to Competition.*
41. Richards, *Aluminium: its History, Occurrence, Properties, Metallurgy & Applications, including its Alloys,* 485.

42. Hachez-Leroy, *L'Aluminium français*; Hachez-Leroy, "Le cartel international de l'aluminium du point de vue des sociétés françaises, 1901/1940."

43. Hachez-Leroy, *L'Aluminium français;* Hachez-Leroy, "Polémique autour d'un nouveau matériau: l'aluminium dans la cuisine XIXᵉ–XXᵉ siècles."

44. Truffert, "La teneur maximum admissible en aluminium des matières alimentaires."

45. Campbell, *Mission mondiale. Histoire d'Alcan.*

46. Smith, *From Monopoly to Competition.*

47. de Luigi, Meyer, and Saba. "La Società italiana dell'alluminio et son impact sur l'environnement dans la province de Trente (1928–1938)."

48. Cristiani, *Une nouvelle maladie. La Fluorose ou Cachexie fluorique*; Faes, *Les dommages causés aux agricultures par les usines électro-chimiques.*

49. Bureau international du Travail, "Notices d'information pour la déclaration des maladies professionnelles, Maladies dues au fluor et à ses composés."

50. The Vindt book evokes social conflicts in terms of salary, and mentions accidents but not occupational diseases. Vindt, *Les hommes de l'aluminium.*

51. Gasche, *Le scandale Alusuisse: la guerre du fluor en Valais.*

52. Bouchet, "Contribution à l'étude de la fluorose animale."

53. Boullet, *Entreprises et environnement en France de 1960 à 1990.*

54. Mazel, *Fluoruroses industrielles.*

55. Mazel, *Fluoruroses industrielles.*

56. Decree no. 63 865 of 3 August 1963. This decree made it compulsory for doctors to make declarations: Mazel, *Fluoruroses industrielles.*

57. In 1945, a study by the Medical Research Council of Fort William in Scotland, In 1972, a clarification made by the Canadian aluminium producer Alcan which affirmed not to have noted any industrial presence of fluorosis; in 1973, an investigation of the Institute of Medicine of Oslo.

58. "Bone densification… without pain or limitation of movement", and other instances of respiratory problems in the Pechiney smelters abroad.

59. Campbell, *Mission mondiale, histoire d'Alcan*, 1231–44.

60. Campbell, *Mission mondiale. Histoire d'Alcan*, Vol. III, chap. 30.

61. Flandrin and Montanari, *Histoire de l'alimentation*; Belasco and Scranton, *Food Nations.*

62. Hine, *The Total Package.*

63. Lapresle, "Documents cliniques, anatomiques et biophysiques dans une encéphalopathie avec présence de dépôts d'*aluminium.*"

64. Galle, "La toxicité de l'aluminium."

65. Kelly, "Overview of Health Issues for the Past Twenty-five Years in the Aluminium Industry," 6.

66. Arrêté du 27/08/87 relatif aux matériaux et objets en aluminium ou en alliage d'aluminium au contact des denrées, produits et boissons alimentaires. Directives 89–109 of the Council of European Communities of 21 December 1988 seek to increase similarity among the laws of Member States relating to materials and articles intended to come into contact with foodstuffs. (*La directive du Conseil des communautés européennes du 21 décembre 1988 vise au rapprochement des législations des Etats membres concernant les matériaux et objets destinés à entrer en contact avec des denrées alimentaires*).

67. Massey and Taylor, "Aluminium in Food and the Environment."

68. Galle, "La toxicité de l'aluminium"; "Les poêles: faites la différence!" *La santé dans l'assiette* 5 (1994); "Cuisson intolérable: l'aluminium", *Sciences et Avenir* (October 1996); "ALUMINIUM, ATTENTION, DANGER", France Soir, 16839 (1998); "Faut-il avoir peur de l'aluminium ?" *Que Choisir* 360 (1999); "Pollutions et santé," *Alternative Santé l'Impatient*, Hors série 25 (2001).

69. Hughes, *Aluminium and Your Health.*

70. Priest and O'Donnell, *Managing Health in the Aluminum Industry.*

Bibliography

"Aluminium, Attention, Danger." *France Soir*, 16839 (1998).

Appadurai, Arjun, ed. "The Social Life of Things. Commodities in Cultural Perpectives." Londres-New York: Cambridge University Press, 1986.

Balland, Joseph. "Sur les ustensiles en aluminium." *Compte-rendu des séances de l'Académie des Sciences* (26 August 1895): 381–3.

Beaud, Calliope. "La nature ne coûte rien, la détruire, ça rapporte." *Le Sauvage* July 74 (1975).

Belasco, Warren James, and Philip Scranton. *Food Nations, Selling Taste in Consumer Societies.* New York: Routledge, 2002.

Bernhardt, Christoph, and Geneviève Massard-Guilbaud, eds. *Le démon moderne. La pollution dans les sociétés urbaines et industrielles d'Europe.* Clermont-Ferrand: Presses universitaires Blaise Pascal, 2002.

Bijker, Wiebe E. "The Social Construction of Bakelite: Toward a Theory of Invention." In *The Social Construction of Technological Systems*, edited by Wiebe E. Bijker, Thomas P. Hughes, and Trevor Pinch, 17–50, 1989.

Bijker, Wiebe E., Thomas P. Hughes, and Trevor Pinch. *The Social Construction of Technological Systems.* Cambridge: The MIT Press, 1989.

Blanckaert, Claude, and Michel Porret. *L'Encyclopédie méthodique (1782–1832), Des Lumières au Positivisme.* Genève: Droz, 2006.

Bouchet, Jean. "Contribution à l'étude de la fluorose animale." Thèse pour le doctorat vétérinaire, Ecole vétérinaire d'Alfort, 10–36, 1949.

Boullet, Daniel. "Pechiney et l'environnement." *Cahiers d'histoire de l'aluminium* 26 (2000).

Boullet, Daniel. *Entreprises et environnement en France de 1960 à 1990: les chemins d'une prise de conscience.* Geneva: Droz, 2006.

Brewer, John, and Roy Porter, eds. "Consumption and the World of Goods." New York: Routledge, 1993.

Bureau international du Travail, "Notices d'information pour la déclaration des maladies professionnelles, Maladies dues au fluor et à ses composés." *Sécurité, Hygiène, Travail* (1955): 191–2.

Camilla, S. Dr. "Sulla intaccabilita dell'aluminio dal punto di vista igienico." *Rivista d'Iyene e Sanita pubblica* (1896): 935–95.

Campbell, Bonnie. *Mining in Africa: Regulation and Development.* London: Pluto, 1999.

Campbell, Bonnie. *Les enjeux de la bauxite. La Guinée face aux multinationales de l'aluminium.* Montreal: Presses de l'Université de Montréal, 1983.

Campbell, Bonnie, and Magnus Ericsson, eds. *Restructuring in Global Aluminium.* London: Mining Journal Books, 1996.

Campbell, Duncan C. *Mission Mondiale. Histoire d'Alcan*, 3 vols, Montréal: Publication privée, 1990.

Campbell, Duncan C. *Mission Mondiale, histoire d'Alcan*, 3 vols, Ottawa: Ontario Publishing Company Ltd, 1991.

Caron, François. "L'embellie parisienne à la Belle Epoque. L'invention d'un modèle de consommation." *Vingtième siècle. Revue d'histoire* (1995): 42–57.

Cerfberr de Médelsheim, Alphonse. *Orfèvrerie religieuse en bronze d'aluminium.* Paris: Société des livres utiles, 1869.

Chatriot, Alain, Marie-Emmanuelle Chessel, and Matthew Hilton, eds. *Au nom du consommateur. Consommation et politique en Europe et aux Etats-Unis au XXe siècle.* Paris: La Découverte, 2004.

Chauveau, Sophie. ed. "Consommer en masse." *Vingtième siècle. Revue d'histoire* (2006) 91:204.

Cristiani, Hector. *Une nouvelle maladie. La Fluorose ou Cachexie fluorique*. Paris: Masson et Cie, libr.-éditeurs, 1926.

"Cuisson intolérable: l'aluminium." *Sciences et Avenir*, October 1996.

De Grazia, Victoria, and Ellen Furlough, eds. "The Sex of Things. Gender and Consumption in Historical Perspective." Berkeley: University of California Press, 1996.

de Saussure, Théodore. *Recherches chimiques sur la vegetation*. Paris: Vve Nyon Libraire, 1804.

Ditte, Alfred. *Introduction à l'étude des métaux, Cours professés à la Faculté des sciences*. Paris: Société des Editions scientifiques, 1902.

Evenden, Matthew. "Aluminum, Commodity Chains, and the Environmental History of the Second World War." *Environmental History* 16 (2011): 69–93.

Faes, Henry. *Les dommages causés aux agricultures par les usines électro-chimiques*. Paris: Payot, 1921.

"Faut-il avoir peur de l'aluminium?" *Que Choisir*, 360 (1999).

Flandrin, Jean-Louis, and Massimo Montanari. *Histoire de l'alimentation*. Paris: Fayard, 1996.

Fourcroy, Antoine Françoisde, Hugues Maret, and Jean-Pierre Guillot Duhamel, (dir). *Encyclopedie méthodique, Chimie, pharmacie et métallurgie*, Vol. Tome second, Paris: Panckoucke Libraire, 1792.

Fox, Richard Wightam, and T. J. Jackson Lears. *Culture of Consumption: Critical Essays in American History, 1880–1980*. New York: Pantheon Books, 1983.

Frank, Thomas. *The Conquest of Cool: Business Culture, Counterculture, and the Rise of Hip Consumerism*. Chicago: University of Chicago Press, 1997.

Galle, Pierre. "La toxicité de l'aluminium." *La Recherche* 178 (1986): 766 75.

Gasche, Urs P. *Le scandale Alusuisse: la guerre du fluor en Valais*. Lausanne: Éditions d'en bas, 1982.

Guichard, Marcel. *Annales d'hygiène*, July (1896), 42.

Hachez-Leroy, Florence. "Le cartel international de l'aluminium du point de vue des sociétés françaises, 1901/1940." In *International Cartel revisited — Vues nouvelles sur les cartels internationaux (1880 – 1980)*, edited by Dominique Barjot, 153–62. Caen: Éditions - Diffusion du Lys, 1994.

Hachez-Leroy, Florence. *L'Aluminium français, l'invention d'un marché, 1911–1983*. Paris: CNRS Editions, 1999.

Hachez-Leroy, Florence. "Du métal précieux au matériau invisible: la double vie de l'aluminium." In *Les chemins de la nouveauté. Innover, inventer au regard de l'histoire*, edited by Anne-Françoise Garçon and Liliane Hilaire-Perez, 431–442, Paris: CTHS, 2003.

Hachez-Leroy, Florence. "Polémique autour d'un nouveau matériau: l'aluminium dans la cuisine XIXe–XXe siècles." In *Histoire des innovations alimentaires (XIXe et XXe siècles)*, edited by Alain Drouard and Jean-Pierre Williot, 149–161, Paris: L'Harmattan, 2007.

Hément, Félix. *L'aluminium*. Paris: Lib. Hachette, 1868.

Hine, Thomas. *The Total Package: The Evolution and Secret Meanings of Boxes, Bottles, Cans and Tubes*. Upland: Diane Publishing Co, 2001.

Homburg, Ernst, Anthony S. Travis, and Harm G. Schröter, eds. *The Chemical Industry in Europe, 1850–1914: Industrial Growth, Pollution and Professionalization*. Dordrecht: Kluwer, 1998.

Hughes, John T. Dr. *Aluminium and Your Health*. London: Rime House Publisher, 1992.

Kelly, John W. "Overview of Health Issues for the Past Twenty-Five Years in the Aluminium Industry." In *Managing Health in the Aluminum Industry*, edited by Nicholas D. Priest and Thomas V. O'Donnell, 1–7, London: Middlesex University Press, 1997.

Lapresle, Jean et al., "Documents cliniques, anatomiques et biophysiques dans une encéphalopathie avec présence de dépôts d'aluminium." *Compte Rendu de la Société de biologie et de ses filiales* (1975): 282–5.

Leriche, Alfred. "Ustensiles destinés aux aliments." *Revue d'hygiène et de police sanitaire* 22 (1900): 704–26.

"Les poêles: faites la différence !" *La santé dans l'assiette*, 5 (1994).

Luigi, Guidode, Edgar Meyer, and Andrea F. Saba. "La società italiana dell'alluminiuo et son impact sur l'environnement dans la province de Trente (1928–1938)." *Cahiers d'histoire de l'aluminium* (1994): 38–53.

"L'Union pharmaceutique." 1903.

Massard-Guilbaud, Geneviève. *Histoire de la pollution industrielle, France, 1789–1914*. Paris: Editions de l'EHESS, 2010.

Massey, Robert C., and D. Taylor. "Aluminium in Food and the Environment." *Proceedings of a Symposium organised by the Environment and Food Chemistry Groups of the Industrial Division of the Royal Society of Chemistry*. London: The Royal Society, 1989.

Mazel, André. *Fluoruroses industrielles*. 2e édition Toulouse: Imprimerie ouvrière, 1958.

Ménégoz, Daniel C. "Protection de l'environnement autour des usines d'électrolyse." In *Histoire technique de la production d'aluminium*, edited by Paul Morel. 131–174, Presses universitaires de Grenoble, 1991.

Morel, Paul, ed. *Histoire technique de la production d'aluminium*. Grenoble: Presses universitaires de Grenoble, 1991.

Moslet, Steven. *The Chimney of the World. A History of Smoke Pollution in Victorian and Edwardian Manchester*. London: Routlege, 2008.

Mugnier, Xavier-Laurent. "Contribution à l'étude de l'évolution de la fluorose en Maurienne." Thèse de l'Ecole vétérinaire de Lyon. Université Claude-Bernard Lyon 1, 2002.

"Pollutions et santé." *Alternative Santé l'Impatient*, Hors série 25 (2001).

Priest, Nicholas D., and Thomas V. O'Donnell, eds. *Managing Health in the Aluminum Industry*. London: Middlesex University Press, 1997.

Proceedings of the American Academy of Arts and Sciences, May 1852–May 1857.

Rainhorn, Judith. "Le mouvement ouvrier contre la peinture au plomb: stratégie syndicale, expérience locale et transgression du discours dominant au début du XXe siècle." *Politix* (2010): 9–26.

Revue d'hygiène et de police sanitaire, 1899.

Revue d'hygiène et de police sanitaire, 1897.

Richards, Joseph W. *Aluminium: its History, Occurrence, Properties, Metallurgy and Applications, Including its Alloys*. Third Edition Philadelphia: Henry Carey Baird & Co, 1896.

Roche, Daniel. *Histoire des choses banales. Naissance de la consommation dans les sociétés traditionnelles (XVIIe–XIXe)*. Paris: Fayard, 1997.

Rosental, Paul-André, and Catherine Omnès. "L'histoire des maladies professionnelles, au fondement des politiques de 'santé au travail.'." *Revue d'histoire moderne et contemporaine* 56, no. 1 (2009): 5–11.

Sainte-Claire Deville, Henri. "Recherches sur les métaux, et en particulier sur l'aluminium et sur une nouvelle forme du silicium. Mémoire présenté à l'Académie des sciences, le 14 août 1854." *Annales de Chimie et de physique*, 3e série, t. XLIII (1855): 5–33.

Sainte-Claire Deville, Henri. *De l'aluminium*. Paris: Mallet-Bachelier Imprimeur-Librairie, 1859.

Sainte-Claire Deville, Henri. "Mémoire sur la fabrication du sodium et de l'aluminium." *Annales de Chimie et de physique* 3e série, t. XLVI. Paris: Victor Masson Libraire, 1856.

Scholliers, Peter, ed. *Food, Drink and Identity: Cooking, Eating and Drinking in Europe since the Middle Age*. Oxford: Berg, 2001.

Smith, George David. *From Monopoly to Competition: The Transformation of Alcoa, 1888–1986*. Cambridge: Cambridge University Press, 1988.

Sparke, Penny. "Cookware to Cocktail Shakers: The Domestication of Aluminium in the United States, 1900–1939." In *Aluminum by Design*, edited by Sarah Nichols. 112–139, Pittsburgh: Carnegie Museum of Art, 2000.

Strasser, Susan, Charles McGovern, and Matthias Judt, eds. *Getting and Spending: European and American Consumer Societies in the Twentieth Century*. Cambridge: Cambridge University Press, 1999.

Thomson, Thomas. *Système de chimie*. Paris: Méquignon-Marvis Libraire, 1818.

Tissier, Charles, and Alexandre Tissier. *L'aluminium et les métaux alcalins. Recherches historiques et techniques sur leurs propriétés, leurs procédés d'extraction et leurs usages*. Paris: Eugène Lacroix, Imprimeur-Editeur, 1858.

Toussaint, Paul. *Historique de la Compagnie AFC*, Archives Rio Tinto-Alcan.

Trentmann, Frank, ed. *The Making of the Consumer. Knowledge, Power and Identity in the Modern World*. Oxford: Berg, 2006.

Trentmann, Franck, ed. *The Oxford Handbook of the History of Consumption*. Oxford: Oxford University Press, 2012.

Trillat, Auguste. "Emploi de l'aluminium dans les industries de fermentation." *Bulletin de la société d'encouragement à l'Industrie nationale*, May–June (1915).

Trillat, Auguste. "Sur les emplois de l'aluminium dans les industries d'alimentation." *Bulletin de la Société d'encouragement*, October (1921).

Truffert, Louis. "La teneur maximum admissible en aluminium des matières alimentaires." *Annales de falsifications et fraudes* (1950): 502–4.

Uekoetter, Frank. *The Age of Smoke. Environmental Policy in Germany and the United States, 1880–1970.* Pittsburgh: University of Pittsburgh Press, 2009.

Vindt, Gérard. *Les hommes de l'aluminium. Histoire sociale de Pechiney 1921–1973.* Paris: Les Editions de l'Atelier, 2006.

Yelnik, Georges, Pierre Tortil, and Philippe Voisin. "Cent ans d'évolution des métiers de l'électrolyse." Paris: Institut pour l'histoire de l'aluminium, 1997.

Fiddling, drinking and stealing: moral code in the Soviet Estonian mining industry

Eeva Kesküla

Anthropology, Goldsmiths, University of London, London, UK

This article explores workplace cheating taking place in the oil-shale mines in the north-eastern part of Soviet Estonia from the 1950s to 1980s. The author focuses on four different types of workplace cheating and misbehaviour: fiddling with production numbers; fiddling with health and safety; drinking and absenteeism; and stealing. These were not the only types of cheating taking place, but were more significant in the mining area and most prevalent in the memoirs and oral histories recorded or published in the 2000s. Analysing these four types, the author carves out the moral code of workplace cheating, as well as the acceptable levels of each of these activities. She also emphasises that this type of cheating was closely tied to the overall logic of the Soviet system in which fiddling required co-operation with colleagues, often between workers and managers, while also looking out for individual interests. Further, the author shows that due to the similar shared experiences of workers and engineers/managers, their overall class experience and consciousness, including their moral code regarding cheating at the workplace, was very similar.

[The mine's chief engineer] Parma took things the way they were: if they did not meet the production target, then that was the way it was. [. . .] First the snow filled the trench and flooded the mine. They had to work with a bulldozer for several days. Then the health and safety inspector closed the first production department because of the condition of the driveways [. . .]

[The mine director] Laane was much more dissatisfied. First he was restlessly walking about in his office, and then he came to sound out Parma. Laane sat in the armchair, smoked his pipe, and hesitated over where to begin. [. . .] Looking at the chief engineer, he was thinking, 'What a guy, so inflexible. Working in a managerial position, it is necessary to think flexibly, to pluck solutions out of thin air.' [. . .]

'There is nothing to be ashamed of. We did what we could,' Parma said.

'In a sense, we did. But there are ways of doing things differently [. . .] The measuring of the oil shale in storage has not finished yet. The mine surveyor can measure in different ways. We cannot expect absolute precision in measuring the storage. You know it yourself, even a six per cent error is allowed by the law.'

'We must measure as precisely as possible.'

'Everyone can make a mistake. Even our mine surveyor. You would not be very angry with your sister if something like this happened to her. We will measure the exact amount that the plan demanded in storage. In January we will exceed the plan for sure, then we can adjust again … The state will not suffer one bit. Only a small production manoeuvre.'

Raimond Kaugver's novel, *In West Seven*[1]

Introduction

This conversation between the chief engineer and the director of an underground oil-shale mine in the north-eastern part of Soviet Estonia takes place in the novel of Estonian writer Raimond Kaugver. His socialist realist novel talks about everyday life and work in the mine, the moral dilemmas of the workers and engineers, their doubts about work, building Communism and even finding love. Kaugver spent several months working in the mine as a labourer in the early 1960s and encountered the everyday problems of a Soviet mine, including the common ways of cheating the system and misbehaviour of the miners, such as in the dialogue above. This is the focus of this article.

Estonia was incorporated into the Soviet Union in 1940. Oil-shale mines had already been operating in north-east Estonia since 1916 due to fuel shortages during the First World War, and continued throughout the period of the first Estonian Republic under private and national ownership.[2] Under Soviet rule, the mines were incorporated into one state-owned company, and new mines were opened to increase production significantly, mostly for producing household gas and electricity in the western part of Soviet Russia.[3] Migrant labour from across the Soviet Union, particularly from Ukraine, Belarus and Russia, was sent to Estonia to work in the mines.[4] Among the workers, there were people who had fought on both sides of the war and later came to work in the mines, often under a new name. Miners' backgrounds were not checked very thoroughly if they were good workers, but those with suspicious backgrounds were not given any public recognition or honours for their work.[5]

In the late 1940s, mining engineering started to be taught at the Tallinn Polytechnic University. It mostly attracted young men and women from poor Estonian peasant families, since the stipend for mining students was higher than for other specialities. Additionally, students who would not have been accepted by other universities or faculties, because of the suspicious background of their parents, were accepted in mining where a lot of new skills were needed. The new working class and engineers of the post-war period differed significantly from the pre-war demographics of foreign-trained engineers and local Estonian peasants who had become miners. The new crowd was characterised by ethnic diversity as well as diversity of backgrounds and attitudes towards work, including how one should behave at the workplace. Within this mix, a new moral code, including workplace fiddling and misbehaviour, was also created, with its moral doubts and questions along the way. The moral code defined what was considered acceptable at the workplace, and what the dominant values and moral boundaries of acceptable behaviour were, including shared ideas of entitlement that did not cause condemnation of others in the community.

Looking at worker–state relations in the Soviet Union, Sarah Ashwin[6] distinguishes three main explanations for worker compliance. Firstly, an implicit social contract existed between the working class and the regime: the workers complied with the regime and the general rules of the game in exchange for labour security, social benefits and relative individual freedom as consumers.[7] Secondly, other authors have instead emphasised the regime-sponsored atomisation of the working class. Authors like Don Filtzer emphasise that the individualisation of incentives of the labour process prevented the emergence of workers' solidarity, and left workers with only individual forms of resistance like absenteeism or drunkenness.[8] Furthermore, the workers were unable to organise because the secret police prevented any kind of independent organisation and therefore the workers lacked any kind of political voice.[9] A third explanation, used mostly in poststructuralist social histories of the Stalinist era, focused on the discursive role of class language in the formation of class consciousness,[10] which as Ashwin points out, came at the expense of other forms of resistance. According to those interpretations, the state had monopolised the language of class and the workers could not express their interests in class terms, which prevented them from forming an effective opposition to the regime, being constrained by the lack of autonomous language.

I believe that there are elements of truth in all those explanations.[11] Although state monopolisation of workers' language and of representative organisations like the trade unions prevented political expressions of class, other ways of expressing it collectively remained. The workplace served as a moral community, binding workers together emotionally. The labour collective, backed up by relative affluence in the case of miners, helped to form a common moral community and blur the lines between workers and engineers. Although workers were doing mostly manual unskilled and skilled labour, while engineers had spent five years in an institute studying mining engineering, the structural conditions of the mine and their similar background helped to form a common experience of work and life. It created a common moral code of what was acceptable in workplace cheating and misbehaviour. A lot of the fiddling that I show below was actually done for the benefit of the whole company rather than the individual worker. Nevertheless, the atomisation thesis is also partially true, as the need for personal relationships to gain material goods or the piece-rate pay system made workers compete with each other. This contributed to the development of a particular culture of cheating in a different way and is expressed in the more individual forms of misbehaviour like stealing.

In Gerald Mars' classical study about workplace crime[12] he distinguishes between wolf, donkey, vulture and hawk jobs based on their level of control and the nature of the group. According to his characterisation, miners doing a traditional working-class job would belong to the group of wolves, with low autonomy and strong mutuality and reciprocity in the group. The type of cheating that wolves can undertake depends on them sticking together and looking out for each other. For example, the dockworkers that Mars studied could steal cargo only by working together and looking out for each other. Managers, on the other hand, are hawks with strong autonomy and individuality, doing jobs where innovation as well as maintaining the rules is needed. Mars points out that the archetypical hawks are precisely Soviet managers who need to push for the transgression of bureaucracy in order to fulfil the plan. It seems that in the Soviet mines that I studied, everyone needed to be a hawk. This was needed in order to gain access to goods and services and to creatively nurture beneficial relationships in a situation in which incentives were individualised and official bureaucracy hindered everyday life. At the same time, both managers and workers needed to form a wolf pack maintaining strong relations of generalised reciprocity, or *blat* relations (informal relations helping with access to goods and services),[13] looking out for one's team within the system of strong ideology of work collectives, culture of blame and collective responsibility.

Looking at different ways of cheating and resisting in a Soviet workplace, my research follows on from the labour-process debate and the questions of control at the workplace. Both the deskilling approach to the labour process[14] and research following the Foucauldian tradition[15] can be criticised on the basis that the agent and any subjectivity of labour is removed from the analysis. 'Too often the language of Foucauldian-influenced researchers is of the "good" or docile worker who adjusts to the techniques propounded by those who would engineer our souls [...]. More often, the voice of labour is not accessed but constituted with the managerial discourse.'[16] Such approaches do not distinguish between managerial intents and outcomes, and either make worker resistance futile or tend to see resistance in everything. Besides understanding the general moral code of the Soviet workplace and the motivations and logic of fiddling and misbehaviour, I also want to emphasise the moral dilemmas and agency of particular individuals in this socio-historic context.

I have chosen particular topics that are covered by the umbrella term 'workplace cheating', which include fiddling with production numbers, fiddling with health and safety, drinking and absenteeism, and stealing. My aim here is to show different aspects of cheating and misbehaviour at a Soviet workplace. These are in no way the only ways of cheating. Nevertheless, I chose these particular ones because they occurred most frequently in the oral histories of retired miners that I collected during my fieldwork in 2008 and 2009,[17] as well as in the written memoirs of mining engineers that were collected and published by retired mine directors and engineers for the 90th anniversary of oil-shale mining in Estonia.[18] Secondly, these four ways of disobeying the state are intimately linked to the political economy of the Soviet socialist system. They are also somewhat specific to the profession of mining, especially the questions of health and safety that are more central to this profession than to others. Thirdly, the four types show the more collective as well as individual forms of fiddling and misbehaviour. Finally, I chose these four types because they are characteristic of both workers and managers.

In this paper, I argue that during the Soviet period, a particular moral code of cheating and misbehaviour at the workplace was created in the Soviet Estonian mines. I also argue that in general this moral code, which included fiddling with statistics, hiding workplace accidents, drinking alcohol, absenteeism and stealing, was shared by both workers and engineers. Furthermore, I show how the different ways of cheating required acting both as a collective and as an independent entrepreneur, a hawk and a wolf. To trace these trends, I will look at the different ways of cheating from the perspective of managers and workers, and highlight the moral dilemmas and consensus that surrounded these activities.

The moral doubts of cheating with production

One of the main characteristics of the Soviet production system was extremely centralised planning with centrally assigned production norms that were often hard to fulfil due to shortages of labour, machinery and materials.[19] Deliberately creating errors in measuring the monthly production, like in the story of Parma and Laane at the beginning of the article, was one common way of fiddling with statistics and showing the completion of norms. As the mine director was suggesting to the chief engineer, the mine surveyor could 'accidentally' measure a slightly higher number of oil shale than was actually mined, to show that the mine had fulfilled the plan. There were also other ways of cheating with production numbers both at the managerial level and at the level of the miners' team, a brigade. Just as there were clashing moralities in the dialogue of the fiddling-prone mine director and the principle-led chief engineer in the fictional story, there were also different moral codes relating to cheating with production numbers in real-world situations. One of the most common ways of fiddling production numbers was related to the quality of oil shale. It demanded the co-operation of mine surveyors, like in the story above, or other workers and engineers such as quality controllers. In order to understand the circumstances in the mine, I will briefly explain the technology of oil-shale mining.

Oil shale, a three-metre-high seam of light brown sedimentary rock, is situated five to 75 metres deep in Estonia. Within this three-metre seam, there are thinner seams of white limestone, making the mineshaft look like a layer cake. Before the mechanisation of most mining in the 1970s, miners had to separate the oil shale and limestone underground and send only the brown energy-rich stone to the surface to be used in power plants or the chemical industry. The white limestone was supposed to be placed in piles underground that helped to hold up the mine ceiling and stop the earth from sinking where the mines were shallow. Separating the two stones was, however, hard work, and slowed down the miners who were paid a piece rate per each tonne of oil shale that they shovelled onto the cart or conveyer belt. If the quality-control department discovered that the percentage of limestone was higher than allowed, the miners lost their bonuses. However, miners were cheating and trying to get away with shovelling both oil shale and limestone. It was important for them to have good relations with the quality-control department who measured the percentage of limestone in oil shale. This included filling some carts with particularly clean oil shale and marking those carts with chalk to let the quality controllers know which carts to check.

Nevertheless, not all quality controllers agreed to do favours for the miners. The ones who did were usually friends or family of the miners or were receiving some goods and services from the miners in return. Others had stronger principles against helping the miners. Aili Kogerman[20] writes about her experience as a young female engineer and the head of the quality-control service in one of the mines in the late 1950s. She remembers how she managed to ruin her relationship with the miners. As she recalls, there was no great class difference between the young workers and engineers of the mine, and the youth spent time together regardless of the job they did; there was friendly teasing and pranks were played between her and the young miners. The serious conflict only emerged later when she became opposed to the slack quality control in the mine. She recalls how, during her time as the quality-control manager, she became acquainted with some gas safety control inspectors, who strongly impressed her with their serious attitude towards their work and their stories about how well organised and strict the institution of gas-control inspection had been during the first Estonian Republic, before the Soviet occupation. This made the young engineer feel guilty about how she fulfilled her duties and how she had accepted cheating with numbers. Discussions with the director and the chief engineer of the mine did not lead to a change in the system. The managers said that they were aware of the fiddling with quality statistics and that they were responsible for it; the young engineer should not worry.

Writing her memoirs in the 2000s, she admits that this is how she should have left the case and there was no need for her to start hassling the miners. But after learning that a particular brigade's carts were half-filled with limestone, she ordered that every one of them be checked, and disqualified the carts that contained 30% limestone instead of the 7% that was allowed. This meant that the miners were left without their monthly bonus, a significant part of their salary in the Soviet system. She recalls the revenge of the miners of that brigade, who came to her office and smashed her desk with a pickaxe, compelling her to walk home with bodyguards.[21] Kogerman ends the narrative by telling how the miners took the case to court, where the judge blamed her for hating Russians and members of the Communist Party.

There are several interesting points in this story. Kogerman, a young Estonian-speaking engineer, is sent to the mainly Russian-speaking mining area. It is not the fact that she is young and with strong principles, but that the gas inspectors who tell her stories of a bygone era leave a very strong impression on her and make her rethink how she should do her work. In her memoirs, she does not describe any ethnic tensions between Estonians and Russians other than in the remark by the judge. But for her, the First Estonian Republic signified honesty and strict rules, while her own working life was full of fiddling on the behalf of managers as well as workers.

Secondly, writing the memoirs at the end of her working life, she regrets punishing the miners and admits that this did not correspond to the general moral norms of the mine and expectations of how quality control should be done. This is because of the dominant moral code concerning the quality control of oil shale in the mining region. A former underground foreman from a nearby mine confirmed that, although an underground foreman had the right to stop the miner if he was throwing limestone on the conveyer belt, this was not done too strictly. Everyone understood that shovelling by hand was very hard work and this 'made people closer and look out for each other', like Mars' wolf pack. Some foremen were stricter than others, each acted according to their conscience, but the general rule was that miners were not punished if there was no good reason for it. This explains why the miners saw young Kogerman's behaviour as unreasonable.

From the perspective of the miners, the stories appear differently, as some of them complained in interviews that the quality-control managers recorded the percentage of limestone production as being higher than it actually was because the management did not want to pay bonuses. 'Especially on the final days of the month when the plan had already been fulfilled, we were trying to do a very clean job, one miner was shovelling and the other was picking out limestone pieces to get the overall limestone percentage down. But they were raising the percentage artificially for some and ignoring it for some brigades; there was a lot of fiddling and nepotism,' said Artur, a miner and Hero of Socialist Labour who complained about his days before mechanised mining in the 1970s. The example of quality control shows how conflicts between workers and managers were possible but were usually avoided in one workplace. If they did occur, this was usually due to the importance of special ties formed between particular managers and brigades or workers, expressing the atomising power at the Soviet workplace that was in operation alongside the uniting one.

Nevertheless, it is important to emphasise that, similarly to the issues of quality control, there were men who were not interested in the rewards that came along with fiddling production statistics, or at least they present themselves in such a way now. Leo Torn, who was the director of mine No. 4 from 1963–86, remembers how the initiatives of Heroes of Socialist Labour become very fashionable in the 1960s. In Donbass, a tunnelling campaign of 'five days' work in four days' was launched. One day, the town's Party official came to him and suggested finding a brigade that supported this initiative. Torn replied that his men were already doing five days' work in three days. The Party official explained that the Donbass initiative had been approved at the highest level of the Party Central Committee and that it was not good to rush ahead of that. Torn did not agree to take a pledge that was smaller than the actual achievements, and the Party official left angry. There is some bitterness as well as pride in Torn's words when he writes about those who accepted the challenge and were rewarded: 'But the Randalu and Pärtel from mine No. 2 were smarter and signed the initiative. This does not mean that they started working better or worse; everything continued as usual but brigade leader Pärtel became a Hero of Socialist Labour and Randalu was given Lenin's Order.'[22] He indicates that the initiatives of creating heroes were not objectively based on how hard someone worked but on how able they were to play politically.[23] Torn also emphasises that there was plenty of hard work done that did not always include fiddling with statistics or quality. Although it is not explicit in his narrative, there is some idea of 'Estonian honesty and simple-mindedness' in his memoirs which I encountered also in Aili Kogerman's narrative. Retired mine directors were also talking about using honesty rather than fiddling to receive extra benefits from Moscow from the Ministry of Coal Industry. This can be interpreted as a way Estonian speakers distinguished themselves from what they saw as Soviet or Russian 'mentality', emphasising their difference and different moral values. This distinction is modest, understated and implicit, but nevertheless present and lingering in many of the stories of Estonian-speaking engineers and workers. Nevertheless, these stories only emphasise the general expectations to fiddle and to support others in their fiddling activities.

Fiddling health and safety

Cheating with health and safety was mainly done in two ways: ignoring health and safety measures and hiding injury statistics. Similarly to improving production numbers, changing health and safety statistics was important for keeping workers' bonuses. As the brigade with too many workplace accidents was in danger of losing their bonus, smaller accidents were usually not reported. In the hope of keeping the brigade's good reputation, getting bonuses or ensuring passes for tourist trips all across the Soviet Union, miners never reported the accidents as having happened at the workplace. In the interviews, former miners spoke about broken fingers or toes injured due to pieces of rock falling, as if it had been nothing. These accidents, if they needed the attention of the doctor, were reported as happening on the way to work or on the way from work to home. This way, miners were entitled to the same benefits as a workplace accident but without the penalties. Usually, rather than going to the first-aid point in the mine, the miner would go to the Accident and Emergency department in the public hospital of the town and tell a story that would usually involve a minor accident with public transport, for example a bus driving over a toe, or possibly an accident that happened at the garage at home, with one's personal tools. For example, here is the story of Artur, the Hero of Socialist Labour, the head of a successful mining brigade. He was talking about an accident that could potentially be very serious. He was drilling the ceiling when a loose layer of rock fell from it. Artur fell and badly bruised his knee. He describes the aftermath of the accident:

> Then I called the underground locomotive, drove upstairs to the manager's office and told him what had happened. He asked whether I thought something was broken. I said that it was certainly not broken but badly bruised. He told me I should decide for myself whether to go to the first aid point at the mine or pretend that it happened on the way from work to home. And I thought, if the number of injuries is too high, the brigade might lose its bonus – I will not go to the first aid point in the mine. Then I somehow limped to the Accident and Emergency in town; my brigade mate was helping me. The doctor asked what had happened and I said it had all been very simple, I had started exiting the bus, stumbled and fallen with my knee against the paving stone. The doctor did not believe me and said that some people say that their hand got stuck in a ventilator on the way from home to work. They knew that everyone was cheating but sent me to do an X-ray anyway. I spent a few weeks at home because it was quite serious. But other than that nothing happened to me, some broken fingers and toes but no one even notices those.

Miners hid accidents not only for fear of losing their own bonuses; due to the rule of collective responsibility, one man's accident also meant that the whole brigade's bonus, including that of the head of the department, was withheld. Therefore, men like Artur in the story above felt enormous pressure from their colleagues and managers to hide their accidents. This pressure was especially high for successful brigades and brigade leaders who felt they had to look after their team. The moral code in this case was definitely read in one way: if this was not a major accident, you hid it for the sake of everyone. Here, Artur had to act like a hawk to defend his wolf pack. The Soviet system was built on the one hand on the idea of the labour collective, and hence collective responsibility, but on the other, the responsibility of the individual in deciding whether to report the accident, and being blamed as an individual by the brigade if everyone lost their bonuses. No doubt, besides fiddling to keep the benefits and the honour of the brigade, it was also related to the macho culture of the miners: hiding accidents was a heroic deed, showing comradeship with brigade mates.[24] It is shown in the way Artur talks about broken fingers or toes, as if they were nothing, although they must have certainly been painful and disturbed work and everyday activities.

If it had been an unfortunate month with serious accidents that miners themselves had been unable to hide, then fiddling with statistics became helpful again. Mining engineers Kaup and Nugis[25] write in their memoirs how the number of workplace accidents was always compared to the number the previous year. If the number increased, it was unfortunate because the brigade could lose the bonus. If it decreased it was also not good because then they had to worry about the solutions if the number rose again the following year.[26] A wise engineer, as a retired health and safety inspector explained to me, always kept the number of accidents at the same level. A foolish one would decrease them to the point of absurdity, where they could not decrease anymore, and then there would be a big jump in accidents and he would lose his position. The truth was that the numbers on paper rarely corresponded to the real situation in a system that was built on the desire for constant improvement, which could in real life rarely be achieved.

The second option for fiddling with health and safety in order to meet the targets was not to follow the health and safety regulations strictly. The official regulations about *tekhnika besopasnosti*, or health and safety technology as it was called, were rather strict, and following the rules line by line would have slowed down miners' work significantly, therefore endangering fulfilling the plan and miners' bonuses. Ignoring some of the rules meant that co-operation with the health and safety inspector was needed. This was particularly important for the record-breaking brigades. The 'fast-tunnelling brigades', those tunnelling more than 140 metres of new tunnels a month, had an agreement with the health and safety inspector that on the record-breaking months the inspector would not visit them. 'At this kind of tempo, it was impossible to follow the health and safety rules,' wrote one of the staff of the Sompa mine.[27] 'There was even a quiet agreement that on this month the inspector would not visit the brigade of Rooden. Nevertheless, 545 metres was tunnelled without accidents. People worked on the borderline of risk and clearly sensed the border that they could not cross. There was a lot in the health and safety regulations that was fulfilled only when the inspector was present.'[28]

Since fulfilling the plan and getting a bonus was a common aim for both workers and engineers, this risk-taking took place with the full knowledge of management and inspectors, and the moral code was quite straightforward: it was acceptable not to follow the safety rules when men were after records, bonuses or high-prestige awards like 'Honour of the Miner' or 'Hero of Socialist Labour'. Nevertheless, miners' work was dangerous and there were also inspectors or engineers who would not allow work to continue if the threats to health and safety were not removed. This had become an obstacle to meeting the target in the case of Parma and Laane in the fictional mine. On the one hand, mine managers felt the pressure to meet the target and guarantee good bonuses for themselves and their workers. On the other hand, if a serious injury or death occurred in the mine, it was higher-up managers who were punished; they were forced to leave their position and even imprisoned. In an interview with a former head of a mining production department, my interviewee told me that he was forced to leave the mine because there were serious accidents. He had not collected a signature from a worker about having read the health and safety instructions, and the worker was injured. Therefore, for both workers and the engineers-managers, ignoring the health and safety rules meant careful balancing of the abundant bonuses and honour or risking one's life or position. The general consensus was that breaking certain rules was acceptable, but this had to be done without seriously endangering lives. If an accident happened in a brigade that the health and safety inspector had not visited due to a mutual agreement, the accident would be the inspector's fault. The former inspectors that I interviewed now preferred to give an impression of themselves as strict men who were respected in the mines and who applied real sanctions if things were not in order. In reality, in a place where inspectors and mine directors had often studied together, worked together or were neighbours, mutual understanding was quite common. Inspectors knew that mines had to fulfil the plan and were possibly less strict about minor offences, while engineers and managers agreed to clean up the really dangerous issues if needed. The personal connections and *blat* relations were also always a part of the workplace.

In general, the main ways of cheating with health and safety both involved risk and decision-making: whether to report an accident that had already happened, at the cost of bonuses, and whether to ignore health and safety rules, hoping that no accident would happen, to ensure bonuses and honour. In both of these cases, both workers and managers had to be involved and both of them faced risks if the fiddling did not succeed in the way they had intended.

Alcoholism and absenteeism

Common aspects of the Soviet workplace were heavy drinking and absenteeism as a result of drinking. Drinking was also a major problem in the mining region of Soviet Estonia. As many former miners told me, the work was so hard and so boring that one had to drink to stay sane. It was also believed that those who were heavy drinkers were also hard workers. I heard a story about the mine director who hired a worker after two questions: are you a hard worker, and do you drink? After the worker said that he was a hard worker and asked whether the director had any vodka to offer, the director was pleased. Apparently, true workers had to both work and play hard. A miner who now works as a guide in the Kohtla mining museum told how some men managed to tour all 12 mines of the area in one year. After every payday the worker would start drinking, and not show up at work for 10 days. He then got fired and, as there was a constant shortage of workers in the mining area, he would immediately be hired by the next mine, again to work hard for a month and then go on a drinking spree.

In many mines, vodka was sold even in the cafeterias. Miners' high salaries and the availability of vodka encouraged drinking, as well as the nature of the work and the ease of finding a new job in a situation of constant labour shortage in the industry. Although men were also drinking at the workplace or coming to work drunk, this was not regarded highly by other miners. Before mechanised mining, when miners worked in pairs throwing oil shale on the conveyer belt, a miner would be quite angry if his colleague showed up at work drunk or badly hung-over, because then he would not be able to do the work at the necessary speed. Therefore, miners decided instead to stay home and have a rest after heavy drinking; drinking and absenteeism could not be viewed as separate. Most cases of absenteeism in the mining region seemed to be caused by heavy drinking.[29] For managers and engineers this posed a significant problem. Vladimir Ivanov, who worked in the processing plant of a mine on the surface in the 1970s, remembers:

> One of my duties was to compile the number of workers for each shift. This was a real challenge because oil shale loaders, bulldozer drivers and mechanics were big consumers of alcohol. They could drink before work, during work or not show up at work at all. In this case I had to go to the village and find a replacement man. The only good thing was that the village was just a few kilometres away, I could get there quickly.[30]

Besides the punishment of workers by firing, other means were tried to control miners' drinking. A miner remembers an All-Soviet official letter (probably from the 1950s) that obliged the managers of the mine to organise drinking sessions together with workers, as things tended to get out of control when workers were drinking by themselves:

> To celebrate International Women's Day, a big party was organised in Sompa Club. Announcements were put up that everyone was welcome to attend, that men had to pay five roubles and women three roubles to get in. It was a lot of money at that time. Some women from the office were excused from work to prepare food. Big dishes with beetroot salad were carried to the club. Charly and I carried many boxes of alcohol from the shop. We made the hall lighting very cosy with colourful paper. For music, a tape player and tapes were brought from the dormitory. Everyone liked the party. Besides managerial employees there were a lot of workers. Later more such parties were organised. But then after a while another All-Soviet official letter appeared in which the order was given to stop the drinking altogether. If people reacted to the first letter quickly, things did not go as smoothly with the second one. A silent era started, when we continued in the old way but in a quieter manner and separately.[31]

This example shows that drinking was not reserved only for workers but also appreciated and practised by engineers and managers. It was a way of establishing the unity of the collective as well as something that provided consolation to both engineers and miners who were fighting the hard conditions of the underground. Another engineer, who presents himself as a pro-Estonia anti-Soviet character in his memoirs published in 2008, points out that the workers who were secretly Communists during the First Republic, and who assumed high positions in the mine after the Soviet takeover, were all serious alcoholics.[32] The engineer finds it important also to underline that he himself never touched alcohol, equating being a socialist with being a drinker, and implicitly also with being Russian. In the 1980s, besides punishments like firing, public shaming and comrades' courts, the doctors of the mines started treating alcoholics. More radical measures were implemented by a mine director who lobbied to close the only bar in the village to limit drinking. The bar had been the place to look for engineers and specialists if they had been missing work for several days due to a drinking binge and their colleagues needed the skilled men to return to work. The director of the mine, using the influence of miners' wives, closed the bar, also eliminating a space where community issues were discussed.

Closing the bar might have changed community life in the village, but it did little to stop the men from drinking. One of the least effective ways to decrease drinking was the abstinence propaganda. Veera, a woman from the mine's lamp station, who gave me a thorough overview of her career that had consisted of fiddling and cheating, recalled an event during the Gorbachev abstinence campaigns in the late 1980s. A high official from Moscow, who was visiting the mine, saw a list of names of men who had been to the sobering-up station on the wall in the mine office. He demanded that these men be gathered together so that he could give them a lecture about drinking. Veera was asked to find the men and gather them in a hall, but the task was impossible since some men were underground and some worked on different shifts. Veera and her colleague started gathering anyone they could find into the hall: engineers, mechanics, workers, those who were still drunk that morning and those who never touched alcohol. The official from Moscow and the director of the mine were very satisfied that they could deliver the lecture, not realising that it was a different audience. However, it is doubtful whether anyone started drinking less because of it. Since it was difficult to reduce real drinking, it had to be done at least in statistics, similar to fiddling the numbers of injuries.

The main moral norm was that everyone drank, both workers and engineers. Higher-level managers worried about fulfilling plans due to absenteeism, and tried to limit workers' drinking. Nevertheless, it seems that measures to reduce drinking had no consequences since jobs were widely available and drinking was generally seen as acceptable. This left the option of fiddling with statistics on absenteeism and drinking. It was more acceptable to skip work rather than come to work drunk, especially for miners who worked piece rate. Drinking was the affirmation of the wolf pack, and was used as proof of being a good worker as well as for creating special ties with managers in the manner of an individualist hawk.

Stealing

Stealing was another aspect of workplace dishonesty that was very widespread in the mines. It seems to have been especially common among ex-prisoners who had been released through the amnesty after Stalin's death. Veera from the lamp station remembers having to train new miners with a prison background who subsequently disappeared after having stolen and eaten a pig from the nearby *kolkhoz*. Stealing from the workplace was very common too and usually started with stealing building materials when the mines were still being constructed. Mostly, miners stole materials and tools from the workplace for their own private use. For example, Kaup and Nugis write about the end of the 1960s:

> By then the former wealthy miners' salaries had dropped significantly and, facing poverty, the more entrepreneurial miners started building sheds for keeping animals in the nearby pine forest. This took place in secret and the first signs of it were the timber, ventilation pipes and pieces of the conveyor belt that started disappearing from the mine.[33]

Miners were taking material for their own houses, allotments and greenhouses, and also sharing the materials with their neighbours for a bottle of vodka or some cash. Tools in the mine were also used for personal purposes. Stealing seemed to become especially widespread in the late 1980s when an article published in the *Estonian Miner* described how, from the building site of the new sanatorium for miners, one could remove anything one might wish for. Although a checkpoint was set up for entering and leaving the site, this had no significant effects. The article also pointed out that employees' personal things were stolen from the cloakrooms of the workplaces. The management of the mines, however, did not even call the police, but simply paid compensation for the things stolen. 'This situation is abnormal and we have to fight against it with all our might, and not count only on the employees of the control and revision department.'[34]

The serious threat of theft can be seen in the description of the 'Estonia' mine written by its long-time engineer, Nurklik.[35] He describes an area where all the production departments (those involved in mining) did their key repair work. Each department had a room that was locked up in a thief-proof manner with tools, a welding machine, and spare parts in shortage. In this room, the best mechanics of the department were rebuilding agricultural tractors into mining machinery. He describes the rebuilding process, adding that parts which could 'dissolve', that is, be stolen, while the tractor was in the room, were taken off and hidden, temporarily fixed by welding them in place, or covered with metal plates welded onto the precious machine parts. Workers were stealing anything necessary and unnecessary from the mine and from each other, he concluded.

The locks indicated that it was acceptable to steal anything, and these locks would have protected against the workers of other production departments in the mines. One would not however steal large items from one's own department since it would disrupt work and the making of money. The moral boundaries seemed to depend not only on whether the worker stole from his own workplace but on which department he stole from. The height of stealing from the mines was reached in the 1990s when rising unemployment pushed many people to steal metal. Nikolai[36] writes that all unguarded electric wires were stolen from the territory of the mine. Workers constantly had to invent new signal systems. Weekends when the mine was not in operation were the most dangerous, when external intruders even managed to find their way underground. 'The processing plant that contained a lot of thick copper cables had to be guarded like a defence building in a war situation.'[37] In the more shallow mines, cables were attached to tractors on the surface and then pulled up from the mines.

In a Polish study of stealing and informal economies at the workplace, Firlit and Chłopecki[38] distinguish between theft, lifting, arranging to remove things, doing favours for no payment, exchanging services, *handel* or barter, side jobs and bribery, all of which were taking place in Polish factories in the late socialist period. They claim that the workers involved in these activities hardly ever used the word 'theft'. Lifting seemed to be justified if the items did not belong to anyone in particular: it was acceptable to lift materials from the factory, but not acceptable to steal them if they were already sold to a particular client or lifted and put aside by someone else. Their main argument is that these activities of the informal economy do not somehow stand separately from the formal economy, but support it, and are intertwined and linked with it. In Polish society, the authors claim, stealing was looked upon very negatively, while lifting public property from one's own workplace was considered acceptable.

From the materials and stories available, it seems that in Soviet Estonia, just as in Poland, petty theft from the workplace to supply items to private household economies was acceptable. The materials and tools of one's own workplace, in miners' minds, seemed to belong to them anyway and could be taken and put to better use elsewhere. Besides that, there was stealing larger items that were stolen from one's own workplace but not from one's own department. Thirdly, there was stealing from someone else's workplace, or someone's private property, like things left in coat pockets in the cloakroom.

Since people still do not like to talk about stealing and the newspapers condemned all these forms of stealing equally, I have to rely on my fieldwork in 2008 to propose the typology and moral code for stealing. Currently, it is acceptable to lift small items from one's own department because miners have a good overview of what the department can live without and what can easily be replaced. Most workers are not engaged in what they consider stealing, involving other departments or other people's property, but everything is kept locked up because there is a real danger that if someone from another department happens to wander in, they might lift something they like, even quite a small thing, like a very good screwdriver that they see lying around. This type of lifting is not morally condemned, but rather accepted as natural, and the best way to protect oneself is to keep an eye on things. The checkpoints that were mentioned in relation to building the sanatorium 20 years ago are now operating in the mines, and often, when leaving work, miners and engineers have to open their car boot to show that they have not stolen anything. The mine management can punish those caught stealing, but cannot change the moral code that indicates that it is acceptable to steal things that are not well safeguarded, especially small things that can be easily replaced. Again, there is no significant difference between workers and lower-level engineers. The higher-level managers would be involved in other types of swindling and stealing, the nature of which, I believe, has changed more significantly after the end of socialism. The petty lifting, however, although not as widespread as in the Soviet period and especially the 1990s, has remained acceptable regarding smaller items. Lifting larger items means teaming up with someone, possibly from one's own department, and lifting from someone else's, in which case both the wolf pack and the atomisation of workers are in effect. Lifting smaller items might be a more individual enterprise but requires tolerance and the wolf pack, including the managers, turning a blind eye in one's own department.

Conclusion

Stealing, drinking and absenteeism, along with fiddling with statistics to hide injuries and to show higher production numbers, were part of the everyday workplace culture in the mines of Soviet Estonia. With the constant pressure to improve, increase and build a better society came the demand to constantly show results. In the mine, besides all the technical and human-related mishaps, the natural environment and geology also sometimes failed even the greatest efforts and hard work put into meeting the target. This posed serious moral dilemmas for the mine employees – whether to show the production numbers as slightly higher than they actually were, whether to punish the miners for sending up poor-quality oil shale. This seemed especially hard for those who believed in some other moral principles that were not dominant in the wider community. For others, there were particular boundaries that were mostly accepted – to control the quality of oil shale but not to be too strict, to report bigger accidents in the mine but to hide broken fingers and toes, to drink but not to show up at work drunk too often, to steal but not from one's own department.

The moral code of the mining region resonated with the broader moral code of the Soviet workplaces expressed in the six paradoxes of socialism, widely known in Soviet folklore. The first two were particularly relevant in the realm of the workplace:

No unemployment but nobody works. [Absenteeism]

Nobody works but productivity increases. [False reporting]

Productivity increases but the shops are empty. [Shortages]

The shops are empty but fridges are full. [*Blat*]

Fridges are full but nobody is satisfied. [Privileges of others]

Nobody is satisfied but all vote unanimously. [Cynicism][39]

The Soviet political economy, which was based on full employment, shortage of consumer goods and the propaganda of ever-increasing production numbers and achievements in the context of the Cold War, created conditions for particular types of workplace cheating. Full employment allowed drinking, stealing and absenteeism. Production propaganda, as well as socialist competitions that were supposed to motivate an increase in productivity, encouraged fiddling with statistics. What was particularly socialist about this workplace culture? This can be answered when comparing the socialist mine with the capitalist one where I did my fieldwork in 2009–10. When full employment has been replaced with 20% unemployment in the region, workers are not so keen to drink and be absent anymore. In the situation where socialist competitions have been abolished and the mine produces a specific amount of oil shale ordered by clients, fiddling with statistics is no longer necessary nor possible. Some aspects of shop-floor culture are however not as dependent on the political economy. Miners still look out for opportunities for petty stealing and, since the health and safety regulations have changed very little, accidents still happen only on the way to work or are not reported at all. Since new miners are trained up by the old ones, those aspects of the previous moral code that are still available are transmitted to the younger generation.

Analysis of small-scale cheating and misbehaviour at the workplace can show the structural conditions of a particular regime and what type of workplace fiddling it allows. Rather than focusing on the issues of surveillance and control (which did exist in the mines as in other Soviet workplaces), I chose to pay attention to the freedoms and opportunities to disregard the rules that Soviet workers had. In a country where workers' political rights through Party politics or workers' organisations were taken over by the state, the ways of not obeying the system were placed much more on the everyday, micro level of practices. The small-scale fiddling, cheating, drinking and stealing mostly required co-operation from others. So although certain cheating was happening due to individual selfish motives, the nature of the workplace bound the employees together. The common experience was confirmed by common cultural understandings of acceptable practices at the workplace and lessened the social distance between engineers and workers. These forms of disobedience should not necessarily be framed as heroic resistance or weapons of the weak,[40] but instead seen in their particular context, where they were acceptable, beneficial or necessary for survival and explained in their own cultural terms bound together by a specific moral code.

Nevertheless, moral doubts occurred along the way, and in the stories of Estonian-speaking engineers and workers, they were often related to ethnic or national categories. Often, like in the story of the young female engineer, this referred to the idea that there was less cheating in the period of the Estonian Republic, that the 'Estonian' and 'Soviet' or 'Russian' moral codes were somehow different. In these narratives the concepts of Soviet and Russian are often used interchangeably with the connotation that they include more cheating or fiddling, and that this is somehow not naturally characteristic to Estonians, who are faced with huge moral dilemmas or still try to do things honestly, leading to two possible results: (1) they achieve what they need to because Russians know that Estonians cannot lie and therefore fulfil their duties (for example Estonians have asked for the precise amount of money they needed for a particular project, not more, as Russians would have done); or (2) they lose out on the honour, glory and benefits because they cannot fiddle, but they still talk about it because they can display the honesty that they are so proud of. Nevertheless, these themes in the narratives that have surfaced in the 2000s, when most of my stories were collected, might not have been stressed as much in the Soviet period. Furthermore, this did not divide the mining community into two camps with different moral norms. Generally, playing the system prevailed among both Estonian and Russian speakers, and the co-operation of workers and managers was needed for a successful fiddle. Playing the system required both managers and workers to co-operate and stick together as a wolf pack, confirming the importance of the labour collective and at the same time behave like innovative, individual competitive hawks to achieve individual benefits or advantages for the brigade. The conditions of co-existing incorporation and atomisation among Soviet workers, as well as the particular ethnic makeup and specifics of the mining profession, together created a particular moral code of the Soviet Estonian mine.

Acknowledgements

I would like to thank Frances Pine, Mao Mollona, David Pepper and the two anonymous reviewers for feedback on this article. This research would not have been possible without the retired miners' and mine engineers' warm reception and willingness to share their stories. My doctoral research was funded by the Estonian Archimedes Foundation's programme 'Kristjan Jaak's doctoral studies abroad'.

Notes

1. Kaugver, *Seitsmendas Läänes* [In West Seven], 184–5.
2. Crowe, "The History of the Oil Industry in Independent Estonia"; Metsaots, Sepp and Roose, "Evaluation of Oil Shale Mining Heritage in Estonia."
3. Holmberg, "Survival of the Unfit: Path Dependence and the Estonian Oil Shale Industry," 134, 176.
4. Printsmann, "Public and Private Shaping of Soviet Mining City: Contested History?"; Vseviov, *Kirde-Eesti urbaanse anomaalia kujunemine ning struktuur pärast Teist maailmasõda* [The Formation and Structure of the Urban Anomaly in Northeast Estonia after WWII].
5. Käosaar, "Mälestused" [Memoirs], 649, Nurklik, "Estonia Kaevandus" ["Estonia" Mine].
6. Ashwin, *Russian Workers: The Anatomy of Patience*, 3–4.
7. Cook, *The Soviet Social Contract and Why it Failed.*
8. Filtzer, *Soviet Workers and De-Stalinization.*
9. Studies like that by Baron about the brutal suppression and violence used against the worker protest in Novocherkassk in 1962 support this view. See Baron, *Bloody Saturday in the Soviet Union.*
10. Kotkin, "Coercion and Identity: Workers' Lives in Stalin's Showcase City"; Kotkin, *Magnetic Mountain: Stalinism as a Civilization*; Siegelbaum and Suny, *Making Workers Soviet: Power, Class, and Identity.*
11. A similar argument is presented by Sarah Ashwin (*Russian Workers: The Anatomy of Patience*, 3–16) who believes that in order to understand the quiescence of Russian workers after socialism, it is necessary to understand the particularities of the Soviet workplace structure. She argues that Soviet workers were incorporated into society through the labour collective that they genuinely appreciated, but at the same time were atomised by the need to approach management individually and by direct competition with other workers for privileges. Ashwin, *Russian Workers: The Anatomy of Patience*, 3–4.
12. Mars, *Cheats at Work: An Anthropology of Workplace Crime.*
13. Ledeneva, *Russia's Economy of Favours;* Ledeneva, Lovell and Rogachevskii, *Bribery and Blat in Russia.*
14. Braverman, *Labor and Monopoly Capital.*
15. cf. Sewell and Wilkinson, *Empowerment or Emasculation?*; Sewell and Wilkinson, "Someone to Watch Over Me."
16. Smith and Thompson, "Re-evaluating the Labour Process Debate," 215.
17. I have changed the names of the informants who gave me oral-history interviews, to protect their identities. I have referred to the authors of the published memoirs by their real names.
18. Suuroja, *90 aastat põlevkivi kaevandamist Eestis.*
19. Burawoy and Lukács, *The Radiant Past: Ideology and Reality in Hungary's Road to Capitalism*; Filtzer, *Soviet workers and De-Stalinization*; Verdery, *What Was Socialism, and What Comes Next?*
20. Kogerman, "Noore naisinsenerina Eesti põlevkivitööstuses" [In the Estonian Oil Shale Industry as a Young Female Engineer].
21. Memoirs from another mine nearby present a story of Maria Malm, a tall and strong quality controller. Two miners decided to seek revenge for losing their bonus. When the drunk miners encountered her on her way home from work and wanted to punish her for overly strict control work, she grabbed them by their collars, banged their heads together and threw them into a ditch, frightening off the revenge seekers for a long time. Kaup and Nugis, "Kaevandus nr 4" [Mine no 4].
22. Ibid., 232.
23. The requirements for a Hero of Socialist Labour, the highest award a miner could receive, were good work results, being a member of the Communist Party, having at least two children, and

not having problems with alcohol. On alternate years, the hero had to have an either Estonian or Russian surname.

24. A similar account of sacrificing health over money and comradeship in the British mines is given in McIvor and Johnston, *Miners' Lung: A History of Dust Disease in British Coal Mining*, 237–71.
25. Kaup and Nugis, "Kaevandus nr 4" [Mine no 4].
26. Ibid., 249.
27. Ibid.
28. Ibid.
29. Nevertheless, there were also other cases for absenteeism: for example, queuing up for provisions that were in short supply could take a whole work day.
30. Kaup and Nugis, "Kaevandus nr 4" [Mine no. 4], 238.
31. Ibid., 248.
32. Kiristaja and Rannus, "Kohtla kaevandus" [Kohtla Mine], 126.
33. Kaup and Nugis, "Kaevandus nr 4" [Mine no 4], 250.
34. Sevin, "Rahaasjad laokil" [Disorganised Finances], 2.
35. Nurklik, "Estonia Kaevandus" ["Estonia" Mine].
36. Nikolai, "Ahtme Kaevandus" [Ahtme Mine].
37. Ibid., 199–200.
38. Firlit and Chłopecki, "When Theft is Not Theft."
39. Ledeneva, "Blat Lessons: Networks, Institutions, Unwritten Rules," 122.
40. Scott, *Weapons of the Weak*.

Bibliography

Ashwin, S. *Russian Workers: The Anatomy of Patience*. Manchester: Manchester University Press, 1999.

Baron, S. H. *Bloody Saturday in the Soviet Union: Novocherkassk, 1962*. Stanford: Stanford University Press, 2001.

Braverman, H. *Labor and Monopoly Capital: The Degradation of Work in the Twentieth Century*. New York: Monthly Review Press, 1974.

Burawoy, M., and J. Lukács. *The Radiant Past: Ideology and Reality in Hungary's Road to Capitalism*. Chicago: University of Chicago Press, 1992.

Cook, L. J. *The Soviet Social Contract and Why it Failed: Welfare Policy and Workers' Politics from Brezhnev to Yeltsin*. Cambridge, MA: Harvard University Press, 1993.

Crowe, D. M. "The History of the Oil Industry in Independent Estonia." *Nationalities Papers: The Journal of Nationalism and Ethnicity* (1978), 9–17.

Filtzer, D. *Soviet Workers and De-Stalinization: The Consolidation of the Modern System of Soviet Production Relations, 1953–1964*. Cambridge: Cambridge University Press, 1992.

Firlit, E., and J. Chłopecki. "When Theft is Not Theft." In *The Unplanned Society: Poland During and After Communism*, edited by J. R. Wedel, 95–109. New York: Columbia University Press, 1992.

Holmberg, R. "Survival of the Unfit: Path Dependence and the Estonian Oil Shale Industry." *Department of Technology and Social Change*. Linköping: Linköping University, 2008.

Käosaar, M. "Mälestused." [Memoirs]. In *90 aastat põlevkivi kaevandamist Eestis: Tehnoloogia ja inimesed* [90 Years of Mining Oil Shale in Estonia], edited by Ü. Tambet, 636–656. Tallinn: Geotraik KS, 2008.

Kaugver, R. *Seitsmendas Läänes* [In West Seven]. Tallinn: Eesti Raamat, 1965.

Kaup, E., and K. Nugis. "Kaevandus nr 4." [Mine no 4]. In *90 aastat põlevkivi kaevandamist Eestis: Tehnoloogia ja inimesed* [90 Years of Mining Oil Shale in Estonia], edited by Ü. Tambet and N. Varb, 250–278. Tallinn: GeoTrail KS, 2008.

Kiristaja, R., and M. Rannus. "Kohtla kaevandus." [Kohtla Mine]. In *90 aastat põlevkivi kaevandamist Eestis: tehnoloogia ja inimesed* [90 Years of Mining Oil Shale in Estonia], edited by Ü. Tambetand and N. Varb, 96–102. Tallinn: GeoTrail KS, 2008.

Kogerman, A. "Noore naisinsenerina Eesti põlevkivitööstuses." [In the Estonian Oil Shale Industry as a Young Female Engineer]. In *Inseneri elutöö Eesti Põlevkivitööstuses* [Engineer's Life Work in the Estonian Oil Shale Industry], edited by J. Tomberg, 137–146. Tallinn: Teaduste Akadeemia Kirjastus, 2002.

Kotkin, S. "Coercion and Identity: Workers' Lives in Stalin's Showcase City." In *Making Workers Soviet*, edited by L. Siegelbaum and R. Suny, 274–310. London: Cornell University Press, 1995.

Kotkin, S. *Magnetic Mountain: Stalinism as a Civilization*. Berkeley: University of California Press, 1997.

Ledeneva, A. *Russia's Economy of Favours: Blat, Networking, and Informal Exchanges*. New York: Cambridge University Press, 1998.

Ledeneva, A. "Blat Lessons: Networks, Institutions, Unwritten Rules." In *The Legacy of the Soviet Union*, edited by W. Slater and A. Wilson, 122–143. London: Palgrave Macmillan, 2004.

Ledeneva, A. V., S. Lovell, and A. B. Rogachevskii. *Bribery and Blat in Russia: Negotiating Reciprocity from the Middle Ages to the 1990s*. Basingstoke: Macmillan, 2000.

Mars, G. *Cheats at Work: An Anthropology of Workplace Crime*. Reprinted edition London: Dartmouth Publishing Co., 1994.

McIvor, A., and R. Johnston. *Miners' Lung: A History of Dust Disease in British Coal Mining*. Aldershot: Ashgate, 2007.

Metsaots, K., K. Sepp, and A. Roose. "Evaluation of Oil Shale Mining Heritage in Estonia." In *Sustainable Development and Planning V*, edited by C. A. Brebbia and E. Beriatos, 453–468. WIT Press, 2011.

Nikolai, V. "Ahtme kaevandus." [Ahtme mine]. In *90 aastat põlevkivi kaevandamist Eestis: Tehnoloogia ja inimesed* [90 Years of Mining Oil Shale in Estonia], edited by Ü. Tambet and N. Varb, 456–465. Tallinn: GeoTrail KS, 2008.

Nurklik, T. "Estonia Kaevandus." ["Estonia" Mine]. In *90 aastat põlevkivi kaevandamist Eestis: Tehnoloogia ja inimesed* [90 Years of Mining Oil Shale in Estonia], edited by Ü. Tambet and N. Varb, 224–256. Tallinn: GeoTrail KS, 2008.

Printsmann, A. "Public and Private Shaping of Soviet Mining City: Contested History?" *European Countryside* (2010), vol.2, pp 132–150.

Scott, J. C. *Weapons of the Weak: Everyday Forms of Peasant Resistance*. New Haven: Yale University Press, 1985.

Sevin, S. "Rahaasjad laokil." [Disorganised Finances] *Eesti Kaevur* Kohtla-Järve, Kohtla Järve: Kirjastus Koit, 1989.

Sewell, G., and B. Wilkinson. "Empowerment or Emasculation? Shopfloor Surveillance in a Total Quality Organisation." In *Re-Assessing Human Resource Management*, edited by P. Blyton and P. Turnbull, 97–115. London: Sage, 1992.

Sewell, G., and B. Wilkinson. "Someone to Watch Over Me: Surveillance, Discipline and the Just-in-Time Labour Process." *Sociology* (1992), 26(2): 271–289.

Siegelbaum, L. H., and R. Suny. *Making Workers Soviet: Power, Class, and Identity*. Ithaca: Cornell University Press, 1994.

Smith, C., and P. Thompson. "Re-evaluating the Labour Process Debate." In *Rethinking the Labour Process*, edited by M. Wardell, T. L. Steiger, and P. Meiksins, 205–263. New York: State University of New York Press, 1999.

Suuroja, K., ed. *90 aastat põlevkivi kaevandamist Eestis: Tehnoloogia ja inimesed*. Tallinn: GeoTrail KS, 2008.

Verdery, K. *What Was Socialism, and What Comes Next?* Princeton, NJ: Princeton University Press, 1996.

Vseviov, D. "Kirde-Eesti urbaanse anomaalia kujunemine ning struktuur pärast Teist maailmasõda." [The Formation and Structure of the Urban Anomaly in Northeast Estonia after WWII] *Tallinn Pedagogical University Dissertations on Humanities*. Tallinn: Tallinn Pedagogical University, 2002.

Hygienists, workers' bodies and machines in nineteenth-century France

Thomas Le Roux

Centre de Recherches Historiques CNRS/EHESS, Paris, France; Maison Française d'Oxford, Oxford, UK

The new machines introduced by industrialisation subjected workers' bodies to a new pace of work, new tasks and hitherto unknown risks. While the hygienist community in France contributed enormously to the emergence of public health in Europe, it focused only belatedly on the dangers of machines for the physical integrity of workers. This article seeks to explain why there was so little interest in this issue during the first phase of French industrialisation (1800–70). Industrial work was perceived by public-health advocates as a step forward compared to former crafts, often carried out in unhealthy workshops. For them, machines helped rationalise production tasks, ventilate workspaces, relieve workers' suffering and replace men for the most laborious and dangerous tasks. Because of these many advantages, they forgot about the drawbacks of industrial mechanisation. As the decades went by, accidents due to machines maimed and killed more and more workers. Despite the warnings issued by some doctors, it was not until the 1860s that hygienists started to question the benefits of machines. However, engineers rather than doctors took over the responsibility of safety at work, followed by lawmakers who dealt with this issue at the end of the nineteenth century.

Introduction

With the industrial era and the radical technological changes that ensued, the relationship between the human body and its environment changed, especially in workshops and factories where the introduction of mechanisation drastically transformed production processes, the organisation of work and the control of tools and the body. While machines certainly brought relief to craftsmen' and workers' bodies for certain tasks and spared them from some toxic substances, these machines also brutally subjected them to a hellish pace, deafening din and new risks. The number of industrial accidents increased so greatly throughout the nineteenth century that in 1898, after much heated debate, a law was eventually passed in France which introduced the first accident-insurance scheme within a European context of much-needed legislation on this issue.

The history of representations of the body and a renewed interest in the history of occupational health have recently provided substantial insights into the framework of medical conceptions of injuries and disabilities in the workplace. Both in Britain and France, a general synthesis on the history of the human body from the early-modern period to today is now available with specific volumes on the nineteenth century, the age of empire and the age of industry. But their cultural approaches do not allow for much focus on bodies at work.[1] Working-environment and occupational diseases have been topics of research for a long time, especially in the United States and Great Britain, and we know a great deal about the legal policies that tackled safety problems and cultural responses to the emergence of workplace accidents.[2] More recently, this field of research has boosted several studies on medical knowledge, gender and transnational transfers, knowledge and laws about safety and disease at work.[3] Concerning the relationship between bodies and injuries at work, special attention has been devoted to the case of children. Among the literature, a recent PhD dissertation by Niels van Manen brings special attention to the various ways of attempting to replace chimneysweepers with machines in England, and Peter Kirby adds occupational hazards into his studies on childhood at work.[4]

Unlike in Britain, the history of work-related accidents and related regulations in France has been relatively undocumented. Recent publications highlight the social question of occupational health and the cultural framework of the emergence of machinery, but not the importance of the public-health movement in defining the new acceptable workplace environment – with the exception of a wonderful book by Caroline Moriceau on industrial hygiene.[5] In this article, we aim to extend those topics and deal with the question of the relationship between bodies and machines in factories in more depth by examining the thoughts and practices of hygienists.[6] In her important review of the hygienist community, Ann La Berge does not refer to any research on this topic by the hygienists, and similarly, the lack of in-depth thinking by hygienists on the body/machine relationship is striking in a more recent article.[7] With our contribution, we would like to revisit this statement and understand why, despite being an influential community whose research was highly regarded in nineteenth-century Europe, French hygienists were not immediately interested in the impact of the accidents and daily wear on workers, and why a law to regulate these matters was not considered before the 1870s. In so doing, we would like to connect their action to economics and politics, and present how their very influential doctrine shaped the regulation or absence of regulation from the authorities. Following the works of several scholars, the issue of governing the workplace in both discipline and economics guides our arguments.[8]

Our main argument is that the hygienists justified the dispossession of work tools by machines and the forced submission to a technocratic order that accompanied the advent of mechanisation and its consequences on workers' bodies.[9] Working to promote industrial adjustment in society, French public-health advocates actually perceived machines as intrinsically tied to progress. Rather than challenge mechanisation, they instead sought to mitigate its disadvantages through various means. Their attitude and recommendations on the subject deserve to be thoroughly examined and help shed light on the slow progress towards a law aimed at making changes in the workplace. This article thus seeks to illustrate a few key stages in the mind-set and action of French hygienists with regard to the body/machine relationship – and especially the issue of accidents – during the initial industrialisation of society between 1800 and 1870 when the novelty of machines was disrupting society in unprecedented ways. During these crucial decades, the work of Dr Louis René Villermé, completed in 1840, became the seminal backbone of the hygienist movement. It was forged by the activities and precepts of the Paris Health Council founded in 1802 and it substantially contributed to shaping thought about public health for another generation to come. Its origins and legacy are testament to the fundamental pact between industry and public health in France.

Origin and justification of the body as a component (1800–40)

Scientific progress, standardisation and economic rationalisation turned workers into components in the production process; they became another element subject to statistics and the universal ordering of the world.

Unlike craftsmen, who controlled their work tools, had relatively secret working processes and dictated their own production rates, workers had to conform to the requirements of their production sector and became a measurable and controllable variable of managerial rationality.[10] In this respect, workers' bodies needed to be disciplined. This utilitarian vision of work and that of the doctors and chemists who were to found the hygienist movement converged very quickly in France. A former doctor turned chemist and entrepreneur, Jean-Antoine Chaptal, embodied this convergence. During his tenure as Interior Minister (1800–4), he founded the cradle of the French public-health movement: the Paris Health Council. In 1798, Chaptal opened a large sulphuric-acid factory in Paris; the following year, he published *L'essai sur le perfectionnement des arts chimiques* (Essay on the Method of Perfecting the Chemical Arts) which can be regarded as a true programme of economic governance written 20 years prior to his great work, *De l'industrie française*[11] (About French Industry). In his essay, Chaptal discussed ways to optimise industrial production using the favourable context created by new, post-revolutionary institutions. With regard to labour issues, he noted: 'The various tasks in a workshop are not all easy or pleasant; and since young men are all too often inclined to refuse difficult or repulsive tasks, a coercive force is needed to compel them to carry out these tasks, and this force can only be found in the ties that bind them to the workshop and keep them at the disposal of their superiors.'[12] Thus for Chaptal, workers' bodies had to be disciplined and the issue of working conditions was strictly a private matter between authoritative entrepreneurs and their totally subservient employees. The initial connection with the first hygienists came about with the issue of industrial pollution. At the turn of the century, proceedings were instituted against Chaptal following accusations by neighbours that his sulphuric-acid factory was polluting the surrounding properties. On a more general level, as the Minister in charge of industrial regulation, he was routinely summoned by Prefects to palliate the lack of effective nuisance regulations. Between 1802 and 1804, while ordering his own trial to be halted, Chaptal referred the whole matter to a committee of medical and scientific experts, over which he personally ensured control. He began by founding the Paris Health Council, which he helped turn into a body ruled by chemists with a soft spot for industry. Amongst its first four members were his pharmacist and chemist colleagues from the Academy of Sciences and the Society for the Encouragement of National Industry, Cadet de Gassicourt, Deyeux and Parmentier, who shared similar ideas about worker discipline. Later, the industrialist Darcet assumed leadership of the Council despite being one of the biggest polluters in Paris. In 1816, he became associated with Chaptal's interests when he was named director of the latter's sulphuric-acid factory. Similarly, Dr Marc was also a chemical manufacturer; as for Bérard, Vice-Chairman of the Council from 1817, he was Chaptal's partner in a number of ventures including lighting-gas companies. Even outside the Council, which overtly bound industrial investment to hygienism, Chaptal sought to provide the government with arguments disputing the harmfulness of industry on the public sphere. Together with Guyton de Morveau, Chaptal wrote an Academy of Science report in 1804 on unhealthy industrial enterprises which lay the foundations for administered and industrialist regulation. The chemical industry was presented as harmless and the report further refused to list work-related illnesses and hazards as government prerogatives. Workers had to accept occupational hazards and bear the consequences by virtue of the contract binding them to their employer.[13] Chaptal thus created an economic policy based on a reinforced state, administrative rationality and physical submission in what Michel Foucault has referred to as the creation of a biopower.[14] It is therefore not surprising that hygienists and, in particular the Health Council – despite being the major French health institution – did not do much to protect the health of workers: the Council was connected with and owed its existence to a powerful character who saw workers as mere cogs in a machine.

Among the hygienists who wrote in the *Annales d'hygiène publique et de médicine légale* before the 1840s, the body/machine relationship was addressed extremely superficially. To protect workers from industrial hazards, they essentially recommended protective systems or appliances with safety devices that prevented any real debate about the onslaught of mechanisation in the productive sphere. For example, in 1836 they recommended enclosing the cylinder of the machine to strip white lead (a white pigment in paint which is a harmful lead carbonate) in a wooden casing in order to contain the dust produced. The same year, they presented similar safety bars around knife-sharpening machines to stop dangerous projections.[15] Claiming to want to reduce unsanitary conditions in workshops, Darcet imagined a device for use in large soap-making factories to prevent workers from falling into the boiling soap kettles over which they had to balance when mixing ingredients. This device hitched workers to a rope which could slide along a rail fixed to the wall.[16] For Darcet and his Health Council colleagues, the aim was to protect workers during handling operations, not to call for a ban on all risky production methods. While these recommendations undeniably helped avoid some accidents, they did nothing to challenge the free reign of mechanisation. In fact, members of the Health Council admired industry mechanisation, thereby lending weight to the arguments of economists and scientists such as Say, Droz, Arago and even the first socialists.[17] In 1834, Chevallier, one of the Council members most interested in work-related diseases, wrote a 40-page report on printers' illnesses, but in a single sentence he deferred the issue of machines – whose introduction was largely contested by the printers themselves – to hypothetical future research.[18] The council was dominated by unanimous agreement about the benefits of machines; this reached its apex in 1822–3, when the presence of steam engines in towns and cities was called into question due to the potential risk of explosion. The Council then put all of its energy into championing a reasoned lack of risk. Its arguments were based on its admiration of slick machinery, whose soft rhythmic noise was much more pleasant than the hoof-stamping and whinnying of the horses it replaced, or the sighs, shouts and grunts of working men helping and encouraging each other.[19]

It would be misleading to include all French hygienists in this attitude; indeed, some were horrified by the brutal progress of mechanisation, but their indignation only led to their marginalisation and exclusion from the canon of official hygienist discourse. The best example is that of Dr François-Emmanuel Fodéré from Marseilles, who was the only person to really challenge the relationship between machines and workers' bodies before 1830. At the beginning of the nineteenth century, Fodéré was a renowned doctor who, in 1798, had written the first French book on public hygiene (republished in 1813 in six volumes). His book openly criticised industrial pollution and urged the police to take action against business owners. In 1825, as Professor of Hygiene at the Strasburg School of Health, he published a critical book on the destructive effects of industrialisation on society, *L'essai sur la pauvreté des nations* (Essay on the Poverty of Nations), in which he regretted that hygienists had come down with 'machinitis' (by which he meant infatuation with new technical objects). In a chapter entitled 'On the advantages and disadvantages of dead forces', he weighed the positive aspects (replacing men for laborious work, better ventilated workspaces) against the negative aspects, including accidents, which he perceived as most serious: 'As I gave due praise to the inventors and masters of these devices, I asked myself how many different trades, how many workers had been dismembered by this simplicity [...] and by the substitution of a relatively large number of live forces by dead ones?'[20] Fodéré was particularly astounded by the numerous disabilities caused by machines. His book even suggested establishing industrial arts and trades councils in each administrative *département* to determine whether it was necessary or superfluous for machines to be introduced in industry; he noted that the decision should take into account the potential health hazards for workers. In the same decade, engineers also became concerned about the increased number of accidents in coalmines and, from 1833 onwards, statistics began to be compiled (albeit with some difficulty).[21]

Alongside Fodéré, hygienists from Troyes were also alarmed by the number of accidents in factories caused by machines. Troyes was a large textile town at the time. In 1833, its brand-new Health Council wrote a telling report on mechanical accidents in the town's factories, describing the injuries suffered by workers: fingers, legs and arms cut off, hair pulled out, and so on. Some workers were caught in the wheels and belts of machinery and were crushed to death. The Council was further surprised that in Paris, where a Health Council had existed for more than 30 years, this issue had not been addressed: 'Given that the accidents that have occurred in Troyes must also have been observed in all industrial towns, how is it possible that no one has spoken out to bring these to the attention of the highest authorities or even to local authorities, and that nothing has yet been published about this in public health treaties?' The report concluded by calling for urgent legislation on the issue.[22] The *Annales d'hygiène publique*, where the report was published, exceptionally included a reply from the editorial team which is particularly instructive. While acknowledging the work of the doctors involved, the editorial team expressed some reservations and requested statistical proof to back up the observations and recommended regulation: 'We cannot help but regret that the authors were not able to attach two important documents to their report: a copy of the hospital's records and statistics on mutilated workers currently in the town's factories. [...] [Preventive regulation] will be granted only if it is requested alongside proof of its usefulnesss.'[23] Thus a veritable rift appeared between several non-Parisian doctors who had witnessed accidents and the members of the Paris Health Council, who were the hygienists with the most influence on the government and who were in the majority on the editorial board of the *Annales d'hygiène publique*. With their questioning of the body/machine relationship, the former could have laid the foundations for an occupational-medicine policy, but they were *de facto* marginalised because of their criticism of the impact of mechanisation. Located primarily in Paris, the latter based their observations on statistics, going as far as to challenge the obvious by confounding occupational causality with a plethora of external factors.

The growing influence of the Paris hygienists resulted in a denial of the harmful influence of activities in the crafts and industrial sectors. As early as 1822, Darcet made addressing the illnesses of white-lead workers subordinate to the business imperatives and interests of French industrialists, and his recommendations were adopted by the government at first.[24] A few years later, with his Health Council colleague, Parent-Duchâtelet, Darcet used statistics to refute the harmfulness of work-related tasks in his study on workers employed in tobacco factories.[25] The article was published in the first volume of *Les Annales d'hygiène publique* in 1829 and was seminal for hygienist thinking. By extending their approach to any industry, the hygienists even challenged the connection between industrial activity and worker illness. Benoiston de Châteauneuf, Dr Lombard and the pharmacist Chevallier all followed the trail blazed by Darcet and Parent-Duchâtelet.[26] In so doing, they refused to acknowledge the new problem posed by the mechanisation of production processes. Darcet played a central role in this great hygienist legitimisation of industrial society. The true leader of the Paris Health Council, he also dominated the Academy of Sciences committee responsible for awarding the Montyon prize for insalubrious arts until his death in 1843. Created in 1782, suspended in 1791 and truly reinstated in 1825, this prize was awarded to a person who found the means 'to make a useful art less unhealthy'.[27] Between 1825 and 1843, when Darcet was a member of the academy committee almost without interruption, only 12 of the 35 award winners had examined industrial health and only one had investigated the body/machine relationship. The only prize winner with a proposal related to the body/machine interface was Robinet, a worker from the Baccarat crystal works (1832) who had designed a pump for blowing glass which helped glassblowers avoid putting their mouths in contact with the blowpipes, a vector of syphilis.[28] We cannot blame Darcet and his Academy friends for the lack of theses and action to promote worker health; we may however wonder why 60% of prizes were awarded for public-hygiene subjects completely unrelated to crafts and industry, and why nothing was done to encourage thinking about unhealthy trades and, more particularly, the body/machine relationship. With this prize, Fodéré and the Troyes hygienists might have found an answer to their concerns; it is quite telling that their concerns were not reflected in the prize, whose spirit was in large part diverted from its original purpose. Darcet was the main culprit in this great enterprise to erase workers' bodies:[29] in 1837 when, exceptionally (and for the second year running), Darcet was not appointed to the Montyon prize committee, the committee spokesman, Dumas, reminded its members that 'the prizes we are dealing with were created in the interest of improving the health and lives of workers whose jobs are detrimental to their health or capable of putting their lives at risk: let us not forget that.'[30] With Darcet, a political agenda emerged that aimed to justify industrialisation. While denying the existence of work-related illnesses[31], this agenda turned the worker into a component in the relentless industrial machine. It was as such that at the Mulhouse Industrial Society, Dr Weber stated in 1839 that 'industry left free to compete without any restrictions whatsoever turns every man it employs into a cog in the wheel of its complex machinery until it gradually reaches its goal.'[32] It is significant that this statement is quoted by Villermé as it fits in perfectly with his general conception of the relationship between humans and machines which he compiled starting in 1840, drawing largely on previous work by the Paris Health Council.

The mechanical credo and its limits (1840–70)

Paradoxically, English historiography is more familiar with Villermé's work than French historiography, where even his biography remains very basic.[33] Villermé was another doctor on the Paris Health Council who had made a name for himself by the 1830s with his statistical research on unequal mortality amongst Paris residents. With the rise of the 'social question', the Academy of Moral and Political Sciences commissioned Villermé, an Academy member, to write a report on the condition of workers in textile mills in 1834. After a lengthy investigation, he published his report: *Tableau de l'état physique et moral des ouvriers employés dans les manufactures de coton, de laine et de soie* (A Description of the Physical and Moral State of Workers Employed in Cotton, Wool and Silk Mills). Using statistical methods that took into account all factors explaining workers' health, he concluded that their health depended primarily on their housing, standard of living and lifestyle. Further, a short chapter ('The Influence of Modern Machines and the Current Organisation of Industry on the Fate of Workers') was specifically devoted to machines. Villermé found that they had many disadvantages and analysed these: longer working hours; the increase of child and women's labour; an end to the traditional bond between employers and their workers; short-term unemployment; a concentration of workers in a single factory; and, finally, accidents. Amongst the advantages, he noted that less physical effort was necessary and that some unhealthy tasks could be avoided. After comparing the advantages and disadvantages he concluded in favour of using industrial machines, but his reasoning was based on fatalistic economic policy above all other considerations. 'Neighbouring countries all use machines and we cannot compete with them if we don't use machines as well. [...] Woe betide the nation who should reject them: it would thus relinquish all benefit to its neighbours [...] Regardless of the issues raised by the introduction of machines in industry and regardless of the means employed to resolve them, their introduction is now stronger than anything that could be done to stop it. There is no option but to submit; we cannot fight against this fact.'[34] Thus, Villermé positioned himself greatly in favour of mechanisation; in his two-volume, 600-page book and after four years of research, he did not describe a single accident caused by a machine in a textile mill and he alluded only briefly and with scepticism to physical distortion. For Villermé, accidents were rare and caused by a lack of caution or attention on the part of manufacturers and workers; they were not intrinsically linked to mechanisation.[35] He also produced a synthesis advocating reform-minded social hygiene based on industrial development.[36]

In the *Annales d'hygiène publique* of the following decade, machines were only mentioned as being favourable to workers' health and enabling physical relief. In 1847, Dr Thouvenin used the same arguments as Villermé and extended this reasoning to include the beneficial impact of industry on hygiene in society. The following year, the journal published a report by Gérardin addressed to the Academy of Medicine in which he admitted that accidents caused by steam engines mostly occurred at night due to negligence or worker distraction.[37] And yet, with increasing numbers of industrial accidents, cracks began to appear in the quasi-unanimous hygienist front. In 1850, a report by the Lille Health Council on machine accidents appeared in the *Annales d'hygiène*, distantly echoing the 1833 Troyes report. The Lille investigation committee shared the conclusions and requests for legislation and safety rules with its counterpart in Troyes. It condemned 'the mechanical powers of the mills [that] have taken a heavy toll in surgical injuries from the working class' and the 'modern engines so aptly named peace canons [that], like those of war, produce victims and invalids' who unfairly remain unacknowledged.[38] Even Villermé could not remain indifferent to these facts, which he described as 'certain'; he reproduced the report with almost no changes in the *Journal des Economistes*. The Lille hygienists based their arguments on the example of Britain where legislation on occupational accidents already seemed to have reduced the number of accidents.[39] The columns of the *Annales* were opened to foreign doctors for the first international public-hygiene convention. During this event, held in Brussels in 1852, Villermé and his Belgian and British counterparts, Visschers and Ebrington, discussed the effectiveness of the British Factory Acts and, in particular, the law of 8 June 1847 on work hazards which was said to have improved worker alertness by reducing the length of the working day.[40] They took this occasion to underscore the benefits of machines. For Ebrington: 'The more we perfect machines, the less we require human strength; the more we use human intelligence, the more we need healthy attentive workers. With efficient, dare I say, automated machines with which men have little to do, excessive work yields less than moderate work.' Villermé could not have agreed more with this statement: 'I had asked to speak partly to bring to your attention what the Honourable Lord Ebrington has just expressed. I shall add that in our factories, in our large workshops, perfecting machinery and trades has greatly benefited the health of workers. I shall mention as an example the cotton-spinning mills that used to be so harmful to workers because of the large amounts of dust inhaled. Today, thanks to the devices introduced, this drawback has to a large extent disappeared.'[41]

For hygienists, industry was thus capable of curing the harm it produced and machines could alleviate workers' pain. During the central decades of the century, this vision turned into a veritable credo. Mechanical inventions, even those simply designed to increase productivity, were often presented as a means of improving workers' health. The case of white lead is particularly striking in this respect. In 1838, Chevallier requested that mechanical devices be used to strip oxidised lead in order to prevent workers from inhaling dust; two years later, his colleague Demesmay also stated that 'as far as possible, dry grinding and screening should be entrusted to an engine rather than a man.' This industry sector was mechanised by Théodore Lefebvre, a manufacturer from Lille. After a few unsuccessful attempts in 1837, he perfected a machine to strip oxidised lead sheets and grind the stripped parts into a powder in 1842.[42] Triumphant declarations about the benefits of machines were actually made in many sectors. Gaultier de Claubry, a member of the Paris Health Council, thought desirable in 1839 to substitute men with machines for mechanically kneading dough; they were introduced at least as early as 1847 in the Paris green (arsenic) industry and were called for in 1845 and 1848 in tobacco and mercuric fulminate manufacturing.[43] There was a long list of machines that were expected to greatly improve workers' health.[44] Despite not being comprehensive, Vernois' *Traité pratique d'hygiène industrielle* (Practical Treaty on Industrial Hygiene) (1860) listed several industry sectors in which mechanisation might have been beneficial to workers' health, for example, thread and wool picking, metal hammering, hemp or flax scutching and textile stripping.[45] Two machines were mentioned frequently: one invented by Caumont (or Chaumont) for softening the fur on animal hides, which prevented inhaling mercury dust, and another invented by Dannery for cotton and wool picking in the textile industry. Both inventors were awarded the Montyon prize for unhealthy arts respectively in 1857 and 1859.[46]

If a comprehensive list of these inventions were ever to be drawn up, however, it would no doubt reveal that many were unsuccessful. In the white-lead industry, for example, the machines presented as the cure to workers' ills in the 1840s were increasingly criticised and then abandoned after 1867. The workers dubbed the stripping machine the 'devil' because of the huge amount of dust it produced despite its protective casings: its rapid movements scattered the dust about even more. It could take up to 24 hours for the dust to fully settle, which led to frequent work stoppages. In the end, manufacturers reverted to manual stripping, even when efficient machines had been patented.[47] Similarly, in hide-softening operations, 'the methods that, allegedly, should have protected [the fur cutters] against the serious risks to which they were exposed because of the ancient method of using mercury nitrate [...] were successively and rapidly abandoned in the industry.'[48] More generally, machines designed only to relieve occupational fatigue or to avoid illnesses and accidents were not an integral part of the logic of industrial profit. Some were expensive, others ineffective, while others still slowed down operations; they needed maintenance, or were not comfortable or practical, and so on. Although they raised great hopes initially, they often disappointed further down the line. Such machines were first used to adapt to hazardous trades under the pretence that unhealthy tasks would disappear in the future, which meant that they served to justify mechanisation in the same way that pollution control was used as a justification for technological innovation in the same period.[49]

The concept of improving health through machines was in fact used deceptively to promote an industrialist ethos. Used as a pretence for improving health, it often concealed more important issues relating to the political economy, the organisation of labour and increasing productivity. Moreover, what was most important was not to adapt machines to the needs of the human body, but rather to prepare people's bodies for the needs of new machines. Dr Guérard illustrated this perfectly in 1843 when he referred to an '*adjustment* [that] could not have been effected without a relatively prolonged fight, sometimes lasting several months, which in some cases resulted in constitutional changes' in carders and pickers in cotton-spinning mills.[50] It was up to the workers to adapt or not to industry: 'Nowadays workers complain bitterly about the position that befalls them; everywhere there is help to improve their lot; but their fate also depends on their own attitude; they must live courageously by the motto of men of heart who want to depend first and foremost on their own efforts: *Help yourself and God will help you*!' concluded Dr Beaugrand in his study of tanners in 1862.[51] This reversal of logic in the precedence of control appeared constantly in hygienist arguments, as did the idea of fatality, the minimisation of risks, the naming and shaming of worker negligence and their assumed acceptance of risk.[52]

Hygienism did not challenge industrialisation's new mechanised system and all calls to remove machines were motivated by moral reasons. Between 1866 and 1870 debate arose amongst medical authorities over sewing machines after some doctors observed sexual arousal caused by workers' constant leg movements and more generally over the risk of sterility that this work might cause. In 1866, Dr Guibout called his colleagues' attention to the 'disadvantages of a machine that unfortunately was dangerous for two reasons because not only did it require muscular activity beyond the strength of women and, therefore, went against the equilibrium and harmony of their physiological functions, but it also in some cases promoted practices most harmful to their health. In most of the patients I have just referred to, you will have observed the damage produced by the involuntary onanism caused by the movement of the machine.' This was a fight against 'moral corruption' and the judgement of the medical profession contributed to the sexual control of work, as Michelle Perrot and Monique Peyrière have so aptly analysed.[53] It is also linked to the debate on the harmful effects of masturbation on health.[54]

If machines burst into hygienist discourse following Villermé's research, the problems they engendered were still far from investigated in depth. Thus, whereas the *Annales* were full of studies in forensic medicine (knife and gunshot wounds, household accidents, domestic poisoning and suffocation), injury and death resulting from work-related accidents due to machines were never clinically described in the journal prior to 1860. Similarly, there were no national statistical surveys on injuries or mortality related to mechanisation. Safety recommendations also remained very basic. For instance, in 1861, Dr Duchesne described several ways in which to protect cast-iron enamellers against lead poisoning: 'hygienic' masks, enamel-grinding machines surrounded by wooden structures, workshop ventilation systems; these were all devices already known at the end of the *ancien régime* (colour grinder by Chevallier in 1778; mask by Gosse, winner of the Montyon prize in the 1780s; the work of Gosse Jr and Darcet from 1815–20).[55]

Around 1860, optimism about machines began to wane, likely due to the stark increase in the number of accidents. Following a series of 'accidents occurring in mills and factories', the government conducted an initial survey, which resulted in the directive of 30 June 1860, which prescribed how to best avoid accidents.[56] This government foray into the field of industrial health was an isolated event. Yet it was nonetheless the reflection of a more understanding attitude towards the suffering of workers caused by mechanisation. In 1861, a study by Perron, a doctor from Besançon, was published in the *Annales*; it openly criticised the statistical methods introduced by the Paris Health Council and Villermé and systematised by Chevallier. 'Personally, I do not pay much heed to such surveys,' he wrote in an article rehabilitating clinical observation.[57] The following year, Maxime Vernois, a doctor from the Seine Public Hygiene Council and author of a major *Traité d'hygiène industrielle* (Treaty on Industrial Hygiene) published in 1860, wrote an article in which he described the 'marks' on workers' bodies, especially on their hands and feet. While he shared his colleagues' optimism about the future progress tied to the substitution of men by machines as well as legislation, workers' bodies had at last drawn attention. For example, weavers' hands were described as follows:

> Left hand: callus in the middle of the palm; right hand: small calluses on protruding parts of the palm when flexing to grip; feet: forced habitual extension of the toes; sacrum: two very brown and circular calluses or patches of rough skin, about an inch in diameter situated in front of the ischial tuberosities (pathognomonic nature). Causes: handling of the loom beam, feet pressing down on the bottom part controlling the beam's movement; workers' permanent seated position on a hard, inclined surface; forced position in which workers may only extend their arms by the width necessary to do their job and operate the loom.

The study was illustrated with several sheets showing various organs distorted by work.[58] Several other contributions during the 1860s regularly mentioned accidents. Some injured workers even dared to institute proceedings against their employers; the cases examined during these trials resulted in the recognition of employer responsibility for accidents after 1867.[59] This period coincided with engineers and doctors becoming distinct figures in the field of industrial health, with engineers playing a more dominant role. In response to accidents, the technical expertise necessary for preventative action to deal with mechanical risk indeed became more important than research in toxicology or epidemiology. Mechanical engineers from Rouen and Mulhouse, who witnessed daily accidents, sent reports to the government to suggest safety regulations. The mechanical engineers Drapier and Ovière in particular repeatedly alerted the Prefect of Rouen and the city's Society of Emulation, the press and the Minister about such accidents and suggested appropriate action to reduce their frequency.[60] In 1867, the Mulhouse Industrial Society formed the Association to Prevent Accidents Caused by Machines; its results were impressive after only one year of work and contrasted notably with hygienist activity over several decades.[61] Engineering practitioners probably understood the dangers of the body/ machine relationship much better and faster than the hygienists who followed after Villermé.

To understand completely this failure of hygienists to define a safe environment in the workplace, we have to think about their faith in progress during the age of industry and about their support of the liberal way of tackling the problem of pollution. Indeed, more generally, hygienists feared restrictions on the freedom of industry even for public-health reasons, believing that wealth was essential to health. They faced the new industrial world and found that it was good, despite its several and notorious flaws. Society had to accept them as an inescapable cost of industrialisation. The factory system could not be refused and to accept it, industrial nuisances had to be legitimate. For example, in agreement with the owners of the factories and workshops, hygienists often denied that the fumes were noxious or deleterious to the health of the neighbourhood, and even they and the workers and emphasised that the plants were giving large numbers of workers' employment and producing valuable products. During the first half of the century, support for the industry became the dominant motive of the hygienists, believing they could solve all the problems by technical means including safety measures in machinery. By 1830 onwards and for quite a while, industry had become an established feature of urban life, never mind its environmental impact. As was seen in Britain during the first half of the century,[62] machinery was assimilated to progress by French hygienists. This had been made possible by their reassuring discourse and their belief in the safety of the industry.[63] In some way, this support of industry can be related to the rhetorical vindication of industrialisation which occurred at the same time in Britain.[64]

The hygienists' ambiguous attitude towards work-related illnesses in some respects assisted and encouraged the industrialisation of society. Confidence in the benefits of machines slowly began to wane, however, due to regular accidents and warnings by critical doctors, engineers and mechanical-industry practitioners. A synthesis was found under the Third Republic between the hygienist movement of the middle of the century with its trust in industry and new emerging concerns about machines. It was also the time of scientific measuring of the concept of fatigue at work.[65] Between 1870 and 1898, a process to regulate health conditions at work led to the foundation of the Health and Safety Executive in 1874, followed by the adoption of health and safety regulations in 1892, and the Act on accidents at work passed in 1898. Although its interpretation was still being debated, the Act established a system to indemnify injured workers. It established the principle of lump-sum compensation for victims of workplace accidents but equally removed the right of workers and their families to pursue further claims for damages in a court of law.[66] It was a measure intended to build consensus in society and strengthen the Republican regime. In other words, in a context of escalating social tension, industrial hygienism created favourable conditions for reconciliation between social classes. It nonetheless took a century for government to officially recognise some of the harmful effects of mechanisation. Before 1870, the aim was rather to emphasise industrial progress and connect the advancement of mechanisation with improved working conditions. Ultimately, if the aim of French hygienists was to improve workers' health, as they said, we can consider it a failure. Conversely, if their goal was rather and implicitly to enable industrial society, then it was without any doubt a resounding success.

Notes

1. Corbin, Vigarello and Courtine, *Histoire du corps*, vol. 2 of *De la révolution à la Grande Guerre*; Rice and Sappol, *A Cultural History of the Human Body*.
2. For a previous but still stimulating overview of the literature in the United States, McEvoy, "Working Environments: An Ecological Approach to Industrial Health and Safety." For Britain, especially Bronstein, *Caught in the Machinery*; Bartrip and Burman, *The Wounded Soldiers of Industry*.
3. Rosental, ed., special issue of *Journal of Modern European History* 7 (2009): "Health and Safety at Work. A Transnational History"; Bartrip, *The Home Office and the Dangerous Trades*; Johnston and McIvor, "Dangerous Work, Hard Men and Broken Bodies"; Malone, *Women's Bodies and Dangerous Trades in England, 1880–1914*.
4. Van Manen, *The Climbing Boy Campaigns in Britain, c. 1770–1840*; Kirby, *Child Workers and Industrial Health, 1780–1850*.
5. "Les maladies professionnelles: genèse d'une question sociale (XIXᵉ-XXᵉ s.)," special issue, *Revue d'Histoire Moderne et Contemporaine* 1, no. 56 (2009); Guignard, Raggi, and Thévenin, *Corps et machines à l'âge industriel*; Moriceau, *Les douleurs de l'industrie*. See also Cottereau, "L'usure au travail: interrogations et refoulements," 3–9.
6. On hygienists as a community, Bourdelais, *Les hygiénistes. Enjeux, modèles et pratiques*. For a synthesis in Britain, Wohl, *Endangered Lives: Public Health in Victorian Britain*, chap. 10.
7. La Berge, *Mission and Method*; Jorland, "L'hygiène professionnelle en France au XIXᵉ siècle."
8. Hamlin, *"Public Health and Social Justice in the Age of Chadwick"*; Bluma and Uhl, *Kontrollierte Arbeit – Disziplinierte Körper*; Long, *The Rise and Fall of the Healthy Factory*, 191–60.
9. Corbin, *The Foul and the Fragrant*; Le Roux, *Pollutions et nuisances industrielles*; Jarrige, *Au temps des "tueuses de bras."*

10. 10 Schaffer, "Enlightened Automata," 126–65; Foucault, *Surveiller et punir*; Ashworth, "England and the Machinery of Reason, 1780 to 1830," 39–66; Lochard, "Le corps machinisé."
11. Chaptal, *De l'industrie française*.
12. Chaptal, *Essai sur le perfectionnement des arts chimiques en France*, 9–10.
13. For this whole paragraph, see Thomas Le Roux, *Le laboratoire des pollutions industrielles*, chaps 5 and 6.
14. Foucault, *Histoire de la sexualité. T. 1, La volonté de savoir*.
15. *Annales d'Hygiène Publique et de Médecine Légale* (hereafter *AHPML*) 15 (1836): 5–67 and 243–64. See also Rainhorn, Judith, "The banning of white lead: French and American experiences in a comparative perspective (early twentieth century)." *European Review of History—Revue européenne d'histoire* 20, no. 2 (2013): 197–216.
16. *AHPML* 21 (1839): 123–6.
17. Jarrige, *Au temps des "tueuses de bras,"* chap. 10.
18. *AHPML* 13 (1835): 304–44, especially 337.
19. Archives de la Préfecture de police, Rapport du Conseil de salubrité (15 November 1822).
20. Fodéré, *Essai historique sur la pauvreté des nations*, 270–92 and 257 for the quote.
21. Conus and Escudier, "Les transformations d'une mesure. La statistique des accidents dans les mines de charbon en France, 1833-1988." See also Bluma, Lars, "The hygienic movement and German mining 1890–1914." *European Review of History—Revue européenne d'histoire* 20, no. 2 (2013): 177–196.
22. *AHPML* 12 (1834): 5–25.
23. *AHPML* 12 (1834): 2530.
24. Le Roux, *Risques et maladies du travail*.
25. *AHPML* 1 (1829): 169–227; Lecuyer, "Les maladies professionnelles dans les *Annales d'hygiène publique et de médecine légale*."
26. *AHPML* (years 1830–40).
27. Maindron, *Les fondations de prix à l'Académie des sciences*, 95.
28. Académie des Sciences, *Procès-verbaux des séances de l'Académie des sciences, tenues depuis la fondation de l'Institut jusqu'au mois d'août 1835*; for the Robinet case, vol. 10, meeting of 12 November 1832, 149; for the years after 1835, Ibid., *Comptes rendus hebdomadaires des séances de l'Académie des Sciences*.
29. Le Roux, "L'effacement du corps de l'ouvrier."
30. Académie des Sciences, *Comptes rendus* (1838): 322–5.
31. Le Roux, "Risques et maladies du travail."
32. Quoted by Villermé, *Tableau de l'état physique et moral*, 543–4.
33. Coleman, *Death is a Social Disease*; Valentin, *Louis-René Villermé*.
34. Villermé, *Tableau de l'état physique et moral*, 531–46 for the chapter; 532 and 538 for the quote.
35. Ibid., 509.
36. Lecuyer, "Les maladies professionnelles dans les *Annales d'hygiène publique et de médecine légale*"; Viet, *Les voltigeurs de la République*; Démier, "Le *Tableau* de Villermé et les enquêtes ouvrières du premier XIXe siècle."
37. *AHPML* 37 (1847), on machines: 104–10; *AHPML* 39 (1848): 457.
38. *AHPML* 53 (1850): 261–89, especially 284 and 289 for the quotes.
39. *Journal des économistes* 115 (October 1850).
40. Unlike France, the history of work-related accidents and related regulations has been relatively well documented in Britain: Bronstein, *Caught in the Machinery;* Bartrip and Burman, *The Wounded Soldiers of Industry*.
41. *AHPML* 49 (1853): 204–45, 219–20 for the quotations.
42. *AHPML* 19 (1838): 5–38; *AHPML* 24 (1840): 189–91; Lestel, "La production de céruse en France au XIXe siècle."
43. Jarrige, "Le travail de la routine"; *AHPML* 21 (1839): 5–88; *AHPML* 38 (1847): 56–78; *AHPML* 40 (1848): 333–41; Mêlier, *De la santé des ouvriers employés dans les manufactures de tabac*.
44. For glass manufacturing, see for example Moriceau, "Hygiène et santé des verriers à l'heure de la mécanisation."
45. Vernois, *Traité pratique d'hygiène industrielle et administrative*.

46. Ibid., vol. 1, 539; Académie des Sciences, *Comptes rendus* 48 (1859): 507–9.
47. Lestel, "La production de céruse en France au XIXe siècle."
48. *AHPML* 36 (1896): 248.
49. Le Roux, *Le Laboratoire des pollutions industrielles*, chap. 7.
50. *AHPML* 30 (1843): 112–19.
51. *AHPML* 18 (1862): 280.
52. Moriceau, *Les douleurs de l'industrie*.
53. Perrot, "Femmes et machines au XIXe siècle"; Peyrière, "Femmes au travail, machines en chaleur: l'emprise de la machine à coudre"; Dr Guibout, "De l'influence des machines à coudre à pédales sur la santé et la moralité des ouvrières," report read to the hospital medical society, *Union médicale* (12 June 1866); see also *AHPML* 34 (1870): 105–17 and 327–42.
54. Corbin, *L'Harmonie des plaisirs*.
55. *AHPML* 16 (1861): 298–326.
56. Quote taken from Directive (Circulaire) 424 of 5 April 1880 by the Agriculture and Trade Ministry addressed to Prefects, mentioned by Hesse, "Les statistiques d'accidents du travail en Loire-Inférieure (1880-1894)."
57. *AHPML* 16 (1861): 70–104, 79 for the quote.
58. *AHPML* 17 (1862): 104–96, 149 for the quote.
59. *AHPML* 27 (1867): 362–85; (1869): 104–20; on this topic more generally, see François Ewald, *L'Etat-Providence*.
60. Drapier, *Mécanique industrielle. Méthodes et formules*; Oviève, *Accidents causés par les machines*.
61. Moriceau, *Les douleurs de l'industrie*, 190.
62. Berg, *The Machinery Question*.
63. Fressoz and Le Roux, "Protecting Industry and Commodifying the Environment: the Great Transformation of French Pollution Regulation, 1700–1840."
64. Bizup, *Manufacturing Culture*.
65. Rabinbach, *The Human Motor*.
66. Viet, *Les voltigeurs de la République*; Cottereau, "Droit et bon droit." See also the workshop on the 1898 law held in Paris on 15th May 2012 ("The 1898 Law on Workplace Accidents and the Pricing of Bodies in Europe", EHESS) and the main proceedings of this workshop in a volume of the journal *Histoire et Mesure* (forthcoming 2013).

Bibliography

Annales d'Hygiène Publique et de Médecine Légale, annual. 1829-1870.
Archives de la Préfecture de police, Rapport du Conseil de salubrité, 15 November 1822.
Académie des Sciences. *Procès-verbaux des séances de l'Académie des sciences, tenues depuis la fondation de l'Institut jusqu'au mois d'août 1835*, 10 vols. Paris: Hendaye, 1910-1922.
Académie des Sciences. (annual, 1835-1870) *Comptes rendus hebdomadaires des séances de l'Académie des Sciences*. Paris: Bachelier.
Ashworth, William J. "England and the Machinery of Reason, 1780 to 1830." In *Bodies/Machines*, edited by Iwan R. Morus, 39–66. Oxford – New York: Berg, 2002.

Bartrip, Peter. *The Home Office and the Dangerous Trades, Regulating Occupation Disease in Victorian and Edwardian Britain*. Amsterdam: Rodopi, 2002.

Bartrip, Peter, and Burman Sandra. *The Wounded Soldiers of Industry. Industrial Compensation Policy, 1833-1897*. Oxford: Clarendon Press, 1983.

Berg, Maxine. *The Machinery Question and the Making of political economy, 1815-1848*. Cambridge: Cambridge University Press, 1980.

Bizup, Joseph. *Manufacturing Culture: Vindications of Early Victorian Industry*. Charlottesville: University of Virginia Press, 2003.

Bluma, Lars. "The Hygienic Movement and German Mining 1890–1914." *European Review of History—Revue européenne d'histoire* 20, no. 2 (2013): 177–196.

Bluma, Lars, and Uhl Karsten, eds. *Kontrollierte Arbeit - Disziplinierte Körper? Zur Sozial- und Kulturgeschichte der Industriearbeit im 19. und 20. Jahrundert / Disciplined Bodies? A Social and Cultural History of Industrial Labor in Nineteenth and Twentieth Centuries*. Bielefeld: Transcript Verlag, 2012.

Bourdelais, Patrice, ed. *Les hygiénistes. Enjeux, modèles et pratiques*. Paris: Belin, 2001.

Bronstein, Jamie L. *Caught in the Machinery: Workplace Accidents and Injured Workers in Nineteenth-Century Britain*. Stanford: Stanford University Press, 2008.

Chaptal, Jean-Antoine. *De l'industrie française*. Paris: Imprimerie nationale (with an introduction by Louis Bergeron), 1993, [1st publication 1819].

Chaptal, Jean-Antoine. *Essai sur le perfectionnement des arts chimiques en France*. Paris: Déterville, 1799.

Coleman, William. *Death is a Social Disease. Public Health and Political Economy in Early Industrial France*. Wisconsin. The University of Wisconsin Press, 1982.

Conus, Marie-France, and Jean-Louis Escudier. "Les transformations d'une mesure. La statistique des accidents dans les mines de charbon en France, 1833-1988." *Histoire et Mesure* 12, no. 1/2 (1997): 37–68.

Corbin, Alain. *The Foul and the Fragrant: Odour and the Social Imagination*. Leamington Spa: Berg, 1986.

Corbin, Alain, Jean-Jacques Courtine, and Georges Vigarello, eds. *Histoire du corps*, vol. 2 of *De la révolution à la Grande Guerre*. Paris: Le Seuil, 2005.

Corbin, Alain. *L'Harmonie des plaisirs. Les manières de jouir du siècle des Lumières à l'avènement de la sexologie*. Paris: Perrin, 2007.

Cottereau, Alain. "L'usure au travail: interrogations et refoulements." *Le Mouvement social* 124 (1983): 3–9.

Cottereau, Alain. "Droit et bon droit. Un droit des ouvriers instauré puis évincé par le droit du travail (France, XIXe siècle)." *Annales HSS* 6 (2002): 1521–1557.

Démier, Francis. "Le *Tableau* de Villermé et les enquêtes ouvrières du premier XIXe siècle." [first publication, 1840] *Louis René Villermé, Tableau de l'état physique et moral des ouvriers employés dans les manufactures de coton, de laine et de soie*, 31–75. Paris: Etudes et documentations internationales, 1989.

Drapier, D., *Mécanique industrielle. Méthodes et formules*. Rouen: l'auteur, 1854.

Ewald, François. *L'Etat-Providence*. Paris: Grasset, 1986.

Fodéré, François-Emmanuel. *Essai historique sur la pauvreté des nations*. Paris: Mme Huzard, 1825.

Foucault, Michel. *Surveiller et punir. Naissance de la prison*. Paris: Gallimard, 1975.

Foucault, Michel. *Histoire de la sexualité. T.1, La volonté de savoir*. Paris: Gallimard, 1976.

Fressoz, Jean-Baptiste and Thomas Le Roux. "Protecting Industry and Commodifying the Environment: the Great Transformation of French Pollution Regulation, 1700-1840." In *Common Ground. Integrating the Social and Environmental in History*, edited by Geneviève Massard-Guilbaud, Stephen Mosley, 340–366. Newcastle: Cambridge Scholars Publishing, 2011.

Guibout Dr. "De l'influence des machines à coudre à pédales sur la santé et la moralité des ouvrières." *Union médicale* (12 June 1866).

Guignard, Laurence, Pascal Raggi, and Etienne Thévenin, eds. *Corps et machines à l'âge industriel*. Rennes: Presses Universitaires de Rennes, 2011.

Hamlin, Christopher. *Public health and social justice in the age of Chadwick: Britain, 1800-1854*. Cambridge: Cambridge University Press, 1998.

Hesse, Philippe-Jean. "Les statistiques d'accidents du travail en Loire-Inférieure (1880-1894)." *Histoire des accidents du travail* 5, Nantes: Centre de recherches d'histoire économique et sociale (1978): 3–54.

Jarrige, François. *Au temps des "tueuses de bras". Les bris de machines à l'aube de l'ère industrielle*. Rennes: PUR, 2009.

Jarrige, François. "Le travail de la routine: autour d'une controverse socio-technique dans la boulangerie du XIXe siècle." *Annales HSS* 65, no. 3 (2010): 645–677.

Johnston, Ronnie and Arthur J. McIvor. "Dangerous Work, Hard Men and Broken Bodies: Masculinity in the Clydeside Heavy Industries, C. 1930- 1970s." *Labour History Review* 69 (2004): 135–151.

Jorland, Gérard. "L'hygiène professionnelle en France au XIXe siècle." *Le Mouvement Social* 213 (2005): 71–90.

Journal des économistes, 115 (October 1850).

Kirby, Peter. *Child Workers and Industrial Health, 1780-1850*. Manchester: Manchester University Press, forthcoming 2013.

La Berge, Ann F. *Mission and Method. The Early-Nineteenth-Century French Public Health Movement*. Cambridge: Cambridge University Press, 2002.

Lecuyer, Bernard-Pierre. "Les maladies professionnelles dans les Annales d'hygiène publique et de médecine légale, ou une première approche de l'usure au travail." *Le Mouvement social* 124 (1983): 46–69.

Le Roux, Thomas. *Le laboratoire des pollutions industrielles. Paris, 1770-1830*. Paris: Albin Michel, 2011.

Le Roux, Thomas. "L'effacement du corps de l'ouvrier. La santé au travail lors de la première industrialisation de Paris (1770-1840)." *Le Mouvement social* 234 (2011): 103–119.

Le Roux, Thomas. "Risques et maladies du travail: le Conseil de salubrité de Paris aux sources de l'ambiguïté hygiéniste au XIXe siècle." In *La santé au travail, entre savoirs et pouvoirs (19e-20e siècles)*, edited by Anne-Sophie Bruno, Eric Gerkens, Nicolas Hatzfeld, and Catherine Omnès, 45–63. Rennes: Presses Universitaires de Rennes, 2011.

Lestel, Laurence. "La production de céruse en France au XIXe siècle: évolution d'une industrie dangereuse." *Technique & Culture* 38 (2002): 35–66.

"Les maladies professionnelles: genèse d'une question sociale (XIXe-XXe s.)." *Special issue, Revue d'Histoire Moderne et Contemporaine* 1, no. 56 (2009).

Lochard, Jacques. "Le corps machinisé. Réflexions sur les avatars de la pathologie industrielle." *Culture technique* 11 (1983): 235–241.

Long, Vicky. *The Rise and Fall of the Healthy Factory: The Politics of Industrial Health in Britain, 1914-60*. Basingstoke: Palgrave Macmillan, 2010.

Maindron, Ernest. *Les fondations de prix à l'Académie des sciences. Les Lauréats de l'Académie, 1714-1880*. Paris: Gauthier-Villars, 1881.

Malone, Carolyn. *Women's Bodies and Dangerous Trades in England, 1880- 1914*. Woodbridge: Boydell Press, 2003.

Mc Evoy, Arthur F. "Working Environments: An Ecological Approach to Industrial Health and Safety." *Technology and Culture* 36 (1995): S145–S172.

Mêlier, François. *De la santé des ouvriers employés dans les manufactures de tabac*. Paris: J.-B. Baillière, 1845.

Moriceau, Caroline. *Les douleurs de l'industrie. L'hygiénisme industriel en France, 1860-1914*. Paris: Editions de l'EHESS, 2009.

Moriceau, Caroline. "Hygiène et santé des verriers à l'heure de la mécanisation." In *Claude Boucher. Les cent ans d'une révolution: une histoire des industries verrières à Cognac*, edited by Pierre Bour, 44–53. Cognac: Musée de Cognac, 1998.

Oviève, Louis. *Accidents causés par les machines*. Rouen: Impr. de E. Cagniard, 1884.

Peyrière, Monique. "Femmes au travail, machines en chaleur: l'emprise de la machine à coudre." *Communications* 81 (2007): 71–84.

Rabinbach, Anson. *The human motor: energy, fatigue, and the origins of modernity*. New York: BasicBooks, 1990.

Rainhorn, Judith. "The banning of white lead: French and American experiences in a comparative perspective (early twentieth century)." *European Review of History—Revue européenne d'histoire* 20, no. 2 (2013): 197–216.

Rice, Stephen P., and Michael Sappol, eds. *A Cultural History of the Human Body: in the Age of Empire*. Oxford: Berg, 2010.

Rosental, Paul-André, ed. special issue of *Journal of Modern European History* 7 (2009), Health and Safety at Work. A Transnational History.

Schaffer, Simon. "Enlightened Automata". In *The Sciences in Enlightened Europe*, edited by William Clark, Jan Golinski, and Simon Schaffer, 126–165. Chicago: University of Chicago Press, 1999.

Valentin, Michel. *Louis-René Villermé*. Paris: Docis, 1993.

Viet, Vincent. *Les voltigeurs de la République: l'inspection du travail en France jusqu'en 1914*. Paris: CNRS, 1994.

Vernois, Maxime. *Traité pratique d'hygiène industrielle et administrative*. Paris: J.-B. Baillière et fils, 1860.

Perrot, Michèle. "Femmes et machines au XIXe siècle." *Romantisme* 41 (1983): 5–18.

van Manen, Niels. *The Climbing Boy Campaigns in Britain, c. 1770-1840: Cultures of Reform, Languages of Health and Experiences of Childhood*, PhD dissertation, University of York, 2010.

Villermé, Louis René. *Tableau de l'état physique et moral des ouvriers employés dans les manufactures de coton, de laine et de soie*. Paris: Etudes et documentations internationales, 1989, [first publication, 1840] .

Wohl, Anthony S. *Endangered lives: public health in Victorian Britain*. London: Dent & Sons, 1983.

The factory as environment: social engineering and the ecology of industrial workplaces in inter-war Germany

Timo Luks

Institut für Europäische Geschichte, Technische Universität Chemnitz

This article examines evidence from industrial sociology, welfare work, factory architecture and production engineering to analyse how industrial and social experts gained momentum in determining the perception and handling of industrial factories. As a consequence, the factory no longer appeared as a pure unit of production but as a spatial and social 'environment'. Sociologists and engineers faced the challenge of determining workers' behaviour, attitudes and morale by designing their surroundings. The article analyses the relationship between modernity, social engineering and the factory in inter-war Germany and emphasises the importance of social ecology within discourses on industrial work.

Introduction

There are many different answers to the question what a factory actually 'is'. On the one hand, historians are looking for a *heuristic* concept and try to construe a convincing ideal type of the modern industrial factory. According to their considerations, the factory must be analysed as an arena of economic contradictions, social conflict, political struggle and class formation or a socio-technical setting of production. On the other hand, historians are analysing discourses regulating different *historical* concepts, that is, the social and cultural construction of the factory. Historians 'may have to recognize', as Kenneth Lipartito referring to business history suggests, 'that firms are really "imagined communities", whose existence rests on the continued articulation of certain fundamental values and ideas that maintain key links of power and status within the firm hierarchy.'[1] I will follow this line to some extent, and analyse what Michel Foucault once called 'modes of problematisation'. Problematisation 'is the totality of discursive and non-discursive practices that brings something into the play of truth and falsehood and sets it up as an object for the mind'.[2]

The following article is not about the 'reality' of factory life as such but the ways of *governing* the factory. My argument draws on evidence from industrial sociology, welfare work[3], factory architecture and production engineering. It is not as much a history of any of these subjects but rather a history of *social engineering*. Social engineering is not identical with industrial sociology, welfare work, factory architecture or production engineering. Social engineering problematised the factory as an 'environment' or a 'milieu' and, by doing so, relied on ideas from different sources.

Recent studies on social engineering[4] argue that this particular way of dealing with modern societies gained momentum in the 1880s, won hegemony after the First World

War and even exceeded the Second World War (including, in Germany, the Nazi period). Social engineering, these studies argue, slowly faded away not before the late 1950s. The origins of social engineering can be traced back to the beginning of so-called high modernity. Hence, my analysis is part of an on-going debate about the questions of how to find a lasting periodisation of modern history and how to characterise modernity.[5] (High) Modernity, Ulrich Herbert writes, 'is not an ensemble of fixed principles but rather an open process of transformative dynamism, triggered and driven by all the extensive changes in science, technology, culture and society in the course of the advance of industrialism in the decades around 1900'.[6] It was marked by the hegemony of industrialism, the dominance of the semi-skilled and non-skilled mass worker. 'Cultural orientations were characterized by the contradictions springing from two aspects: on the one hand the dominance of mass society, orientation to the principles of progress, the dynamics of changes in ways of life and norms – and on the other the counter-reactions: orientation to tradition, the critique of modernity, the formation of radical counter-models and blueprints for living on the left and right.'[7] From the 1880s onwards, alternative and conflicting concepts of social order emerged, each reflecting and fostering structural change. James C. Scott coined the phrase 'seeing like a state' to describe this particular setting.[8] Thus, any study on social engineering must consider the rise of high-modernist techniques to impose a certain social order.

Social engineering became one of the most import instruments to rebuild social order after the First World War. Of course, its origins date back further and social engineering also exceeded the inter-war period, but I will limit my analysis to the inter-war years for two reasons. First, the structure, implications and effects of social engineering were most visible during the years of its hegemony. Second, in recent years there has been a renewed interest in the inter-war period. A study on social engineering can provide an essential contribution to these discussions.

In his influential study Detlev Peukert argues that Weimar Germany should be situated within a larger context of crisis-ridden modernity and modernisation. Peukert puts forward a long-term perspective on Weimar Germany that stresses, in particular, the implementation of industrial high modernity since the 1890s, its breakthrough after the First World War and its immediate crisis following the Great Depression. Weimar Germany was, thus, marked by a simultaneous experience of modernity and its crisis. In order to cope with this, the contemporaries relied on a profound belief in the feasibility of social order, a possibility and necessity of social reform and an interventionist spirit. Peukert identifies – without specifying the term – some kind of 'social engineering' at the core of political, scientific, cultural and industrial practices in Weimar Germany. 'Problem perceptions and problem solutions', he writes, 'were determined by utilitarian and technically motivated schemes.'[9] Gunther Mai's study on inter-war Europe confirms and broadens Peukert's argument in many ways. The war's legacy, Mai writes, was a broken and barely recognisable world in comparison to pre-war societies. Mai identifies a loss of normative commitment and obligation as much as a fevered search for stable ground and lasting liabilities in political, social and cultural respect. In the course of this search, holistic ideologies and radical politics gained momentum. The inter-war period was marked by efforts to implement 'rational' drafts of a fundamentalist world order by 'irrational' means, notably by violence, but also by a wide variety of other interventionist practices.[10]

Many historians regard an experience of ambivalence and crisis, a search for social order, efforts in rational, scientific planning, a rise of fundamentalist, radical and extremist ideologies,[11] reformist and utopian thinking,[12] violence and consumption[13] as essential issues to understand Weimar and inter-war Germany. When focusing on these topics, key events of political history become less important.[14] The following paragraphs will examine social engineering as one key issue of inter-war Germany that was marked by an astonishing stability and discursive continuity despite a turbulent political history. Therefore, I will firstly discuss the concept of social engineering. Secondly, I will analyse the rise of industrial experts and of social-ecologist discourses. Finally, I will answer the question of how social engineering fostered the idea of factories as socio-spatial settings.

The concept of social engineering

From the 1880s onwards, rapid urbanisation and industrialisation led to profound changes in social relations and social order. Contemporary observers interpreted these developments in the terms of 'crisis'.[15] The crisis trope generated the new practice of social engineering, providing sociologists, architects, welfare workers and engineers with scientific tools to tackle social problems in a 'rational' manner. Social engineering can be defined as a mode of rethinking and reworking modernity in order to overthrow what seemed to be a seriously threatening process of social disintegration and fragmentation. Social engineers tried to restore an integrated social order by focusing on middle-range social formations (for example, industrial work and the factory, traffic and transportation, urban planning and architecture, population and social policy).

The concept of social engineering has been introduced by Zygmunt Bauman to highlight specific features of modernity in order to situate the Holocaust within modernity.[16] 'I suggest', Bauman argues, 'that the bureaucratic culture which prompts us to view society as an object of administration, as a collection of so many "problems" to be solved, as "nature" to be "controlled", "mastered" and "improved" or "remade", as a legitimate target for "social engineering", and in general a garden to be designed and kept in the planned shape by force (the gardening posture divides vegetation into "cultured plants" to be taken care of, and weeds to be exterminated), was the very atmosphere in which the idea of the Holocaust could be conceived, slowly yet consistently developed, and brought to its conclusion.'[17] 'Problem solving' depended on scientific expertise, empirical research and social analysis. Applied (social) sciences became one of the most important instruments to design social relations and social order. This process paved the way for a permanent presence of experts within administrations, parliaments, political parties, pressure groups, industrial factories and so on.[18] Starting in the 1880s, one can witness the rise of a professional society. As Harold Perkin put it: 'In all its manifestations, liberal, conservative or socialist, the professional social ideal consistently applied the tests of justification by service to society and, in one form or another, of the greatest happiness of the greatest number, to the analysis and criticism of contemporary society. Down to about 1880, however, such criticisms were a disconnected series of individual correctives to the excessive materialism of the capitalist system while in no way threatening its continued existence. From the 1880s by contrast, concomitantly with the accelerated growth of professional occupations of all kinds, it began to take shape in a form that appeared to many landowners and business men to be an organised threat to the rights if not indeed to the security of private property and so the foundations of capitalist society.'[19] In my view, professional society and social engineering did not necessarily threaten private property and 'the foundations of capitalist society', as Perkin argues. It was rather that it marked a profound change within industrial and capitalist society. On the one hand, industrial production became the centre of society as a whole. The term 'industrialism' increasingly replaced 'capitalism' within this discourse. On the other hand, 'rational planning' and 'efficiency' became the hallmark of social order. Industrial experts took a fair share in these developments.

Industrial experts and social ecology

Between the 1880s and 1920s, Taylorist ideas dominated discourses on industrial work and factories.[20] Taylorism's main feature – at least the element discussed most intensively – was its decomposing, atomistic and disciplinary approach. Taylorism focused on individual bodies and reduced workers to an aggregation of bodily functions and movements.[21] 'The Taylorite tactic is to try and break the power of the work teams and work groups by pressure, and by appeal to individual ambition: to atomize the workforce. This is the dynamic reality behind "technological integration".'[22] In a second step, Taylorism fostered the re-integration of movements and operations into an 'efficient system', but what 'efficiency', 'system' or 'organisation' (an increasingly fashionable term then) meant, was still defined by mechanical engineers.[23] Beyond Taylorism, the early science of labour and its forerunners were part of a pre-social engineering mode of problematising industrial work, too. The science of labour, in a way, established a connection between work, modernity and physics. 'Social modernity, the project of superseding class conflict and social disorganization through the rationalization of the body, emerged at the intersection of two broad developments: the thermodynamic "model" of nature as labor power, and the concentration of human labor power and technology of the second industrial revolution. The metaphor of the human motor united these developments in the single idea that the working body is a productive force capable of transforming universal natural energy into mechanical work and integrating the human organism into highly specialized and technical work progress.'[24]

Social engineering was different from Taylorism and the science of labour. The latter focused both on technical and mechanical dimensions of work; the former emphasised the social dimensions. Instead of regulating individual bodies, social engineering focused on socio-spatial arrangements. Of course, Taylorism and ideas like the human motor did not suddenly disappear after the First World War. On the contrary, the 1920s and 1930s can be considered as the boom years of rationalisation, and the heyday of public discussions on Taylor and his principles of scientific management. However, all these developments were marked by a silent and careful shift in emphasis. What slowly became hegemonic was the special attention on human and social qualities of the workplace. Europeans, Charles Maier argues, were not that much interested in Taylor's achievements in mechanical engineering but in Taylorism's promise to restore social order and to supersede social conflict.[25] After the First World War, German managers, engineers and scientists of labour were especially interested in the human factor in the workplace. Although sceptical towards (US) mass production, they were keen to know more about cultivating human resources or building up long-term employment relationships. Recent research, notably by Karsten Uhl, has shown that this effort 'started long before 1933, but was intensified in the Third Reich, on the level of both political discourse and practical achievements'.[26]

The new mode of problematisation can be characterised as social, rather than technical or mechanical. Concepts like 'home', 'milieu' or 'environment' were mobilised against Taylorism's alleged shortcomings.[27] There were two sources of social engineering that have to be addressed individually: industrial sociology and welfare work, because their characteristics help to understand the clear rupture between social engineering and earlier modes of problematisation.

Welfare work – a combination of social service and labour management – was not just a prosecution of industrial paternalism with slightly different instruments. Although paternalism sometimes was less traditional than one might think, its focus was limited. Paternalism could be an efficient management style to maintain hierarchy and authority, but this usually was confined to smaller production units.[28] The development of large industrial factories fostered a quest for new ways to reconcile advanced production technology and the social demands of an ever-larger workforce as well as the social demands of production. Since the 1870s welfare work became an important tool for management and production engineering. Its unique feature was a combination of business administration and economic logic with entrepreneurial strategies and ideological concepts.[29] After the First World War, welfare departments were established within most of the larger industrial companies, but, at the same time, industrial welfare programmes came under attack. On the one hand, the rising welfare state claimed sole responsibility for workers' wellbeing and social security. On the other hand, trade-union supporters attacked welfare work for being an employers' attempt to strengthen control over the labour process and workers' lives.[30] Welfare work paved the way toward a more professional personnel management. Industrial paternalism focused on *ad hoc* measures and personal authority; welfare work focused on systematisation and increasingly became part of a much broader strategy of social rationalisation.[31] Christian Kleinschmidt argues that a significant sea change occurred in welfare work after the First World War. Post-war welfare work focused on modernisation of production processes, social integration of the labour force and reassurance of managerial prerogative as well. 'Technical and organisational rationalisation had been accompanied and extended by "social rationalisation" to cope with political, social, economic and technical change.'[32] For that reason, welfare work became one important source of social engineering.

Since the turn of the century, especially after the First World War, German sociology in general developed what can be called an interventionist paradigm ('Soziologie der Tat'). Sociologists defined it as their primary task not only to understand and explain social relations and social order but to design and maintain both. Within sociology as a whole many sub-disciplines were on the rise. '*Betriebssoziologie*' was one of them. This concept, which is not exactly the same as industrial sociology, industrial relations, personnel management or *sociologie du travail*, is a German peculiarity. Hans-Michael Rummler argues that the development of '*Betriebssoziologie*' reflected an earlier controversy about the social question. At the end of the nineteenth century, the social question had been aligned along topics of industrial work. Public discussions linked social problems to working hours, wages, output and efficiency. Therefore, industrial work became one of the most important and urgent topics that had to be addressed by scientific methods. The emergence of '*Betriebssoziologie*' signifies a new attention on human and social dimensions of industrial work and the factory as a distinguished social system. '*Betriebssoziologie*' began its career around 1900 when large industrial corporations caught public attention as a battleground for potential class warfare. This stimulated sociological efforts to explore the origins of the workers' alienation. Sociologists asked time and again if class conflict was industry's destiny or whether it could be solved by rational means.[33] After the First World War and along the lines of the new interventionist paradigm, sociologists discovered industrial workplaces as an urgent field of intervention. They started to re-define economic and technical questions as social questions. Beyond social policy and the workers' attitudes and morale, the factory itself became a new centre of sociological imagination.[34] An overtly interventionist '*Betriebssoziologie*' replaced Taylorist scientific management in delivering guidelines for the design and maintenance of industrial workplaces. Sociology not only became a preferred means to stabilise factory order but also raised awareness of the factory as a distinguished social unit in its own right.[35] Referring to the broader context of rationalisation, Mary Nolan argues that in Germany a combination of industrial sociology and welfare work fostered an all-embracing practice of 'engineering the new worker'. Sociologists and welfare workers tried to achieve this by transforming the factory – once a place of alienation, conflict, fragmentation and individualisation – into a harmonious and reconciling 'home'.[36]

Thus, welfare work and '*Betriebssoziologie*' can be identified as important sources and parts of a new mode of problematisation. This mode, in particular, was marked by stressing human and social qualities of workplaces, addressing factories as a socio-spatial arrangement designated to become some kind of home and environment. This ecologist discourse on the factory was part of a larger ecological discourse. High modernity, Raul Rabinow argues in his inspiring study *French Modern*, was characterised by a plethora of attempts to allocate population and the new factories within a certain territory. Attempts to impose order on modern society went along with influential discourses on the importance of what came to be known as the *milieu*. Sociologists and geographers advanced the idea that individual behaviour did not reflect moral character but (social) environment. Discourses on modern society were, in Paul Rabinow's catchy phrase, marked by a 'socio-spatial turn', beginning in the late nineteenth century. There was a discursive shift from 'Man as Worker' to 'Man as Habitant' that lasted at least until the 1950s.[37] Social engineers, who tried to re-establish social order by arranging the factory, took an active part in these developments. Social ecologism could, in their perspective, easily be adapted to other areas. The ecological paradigm offered a promising way of restoring a well-ordered society via reworking the organisational, technological, spatial and social order of the factory. Social engineering not only related the order of the factory to the order of society, but also modelled it as an all-embracing social and spatial environment. Social engineers were concerned with factory architecture and the organisational, technical and spatial layout of production – in order to determine social relations and motions within the factory. By doing so, industrial sociologists, welfare workers and production engineers reworked the concept of environment. The factory as a milieu or an environment incorporated physical, social and psychological dimensions. Designing environmental conditions became a new and urgent task for many experts concerned with industrial relations.

The factory as a socio-spatial setting

Factory architecture repeatedly became the subject of historical studies. Historians of architecture usually stress its importance in relation to modernist style. On the one hand, factory buildings became a laboratory of modernist architecture. Designing factory buildings was considered as an important and urgent task by some architects due to the undeniable importance of industrial work for modern societies.[38] Mauro F. Guillén tagged modernist architecture as the 'child of industry and engineering'.[39] On the other hand, industrialists, Roland Marchand argues, were aware of architecture's value in public relations.[40] Beyond this, according to Lindy Biggs, factory design became part of the production itself. From the end of the nineteenth century, engineers interpreted the buildings no longer as a merely passive shell but as an integrated and active factor of production processes. Buildings became something like a 'master machine'. Architects and production engineers tried to implement their ideal of a 'rational factory'.[41]

Over the course of the nineteenth century, the typical shape of factory buildings evolved everywhere in modern industrialised countries. Soon there was a shared idea about what a factory should look like. Orthogonal outlines or the notorious saw-tooth roof became highly visible signs of industrial production: signs for efficiency and rational order. The guiding principles of industrial architecture were clarity, distinctiveness, cleanliness and efficiency. Factory design sometimes was considered as a model and a symbol of modernity. German industrial architect Rudolf Lodders, who in 1934 designed Borgward's car factory buildings[42], stated in 1946:

> We know now that workplace and dwelling place are two different things, governed by different laws and different requirements. But it would be fine if we could carry the explicit principles of industrial design forward to the design of the dwelling place; that we could achieve the same edificial organisms within residential building as we do in industrial building. Industrial building today captures the style of our century, which is the century of technology.[43]

Beyond its model character in rather abstract terms, factory buildings were designed to meet the requirements of production and to push production processes. The famous Ford Highland Park plant – the result of co-operation between production engineers and architect Albert Kahn[44] – marked a new way to structure social relations within the factory via spatial arrangements in 1910. 'By virtue of improved design and layout, the buildings themselves would aid in the organisation and control of production. Space continued to be a constant concern to the growing enterprise, but movement soon became the overwhelming priority in designing the New Shop.'[45] Ford completed these developments between 1919 and 1935 when the famous River Rouge factory complex was built. River Rouge embodied the new principles of factory architecture at its best. 'By the time Kahn Associates helped build the Rouge plant, their philosophy regarding industrial architecture was fully developed: production engineers should lay out the work of the factory, and the architect "should be able to plan a factory around the scheme of production". [. . .] As building continued at the Rouge, individual buildings, and the plant as a whole, reflected new thinking about how to achieve rational manufacturing.'[46]

Ford became a model for many European production engineers and industrial architects. Among German efforts to adopt Ford's lessons in industrial engineering, some friction between Ford's idea of a factory as 'rational master machine' and the German tradition of 'organic' architecture and social order emerged. But, in the end, this friction was solved. Even in Nazi Germany, production engineers and architects favoured the idea of planning and composing factory buildings around the production process on the drawing board. In 1936 Opel opened its factory Werk Brandenburg. The official journal *Opel-Kamerad* on that occasion compared Werk Brandenburg with the older main factory in Rüsselsheim:

> Rüsselsheim once was small. It has been expanded. Work floors have been built and enlarged. Its growth was inevitable and followed an organic course. Werk Brandenburg, in contrast, took its actual shape from the beginning. It looked the same on the architect's drawing board as it looks now. It is a factory of a piece ['*aus einem Guß*'].[47]

Production within the factory and the look of the buildings were expected to mirror each other. Both followed the same aesthetic principles. Such ideas structured the planning and building of the Volkswagenwerk from the beginning: this plant should become some kind of German River Rouge.[48] In terms of production capacity and appearance the plant was supposed to be able to compete with River Rouge, but it should also embody German peculiarities. Therefore, the Volkswagenwerk – just like Opel's Werk Brandenburg – incorporated elements of fortification to highlight Germany's '*Wehrhaftigkeit*' and to accentuate the important part of industrial production within the all-embracing warfare logic. Fortress-like plants suggested that work and production were most valuable and had to be defended.

Beyond this, the *dynamic* character of any production *process* had to be captured and supported by architecture. 'Flow' became an important feature. Production was interpreted as a setting of continuous movements. Dynamics and vitality of the production had to be echoed by the buildings and the layout of production inside the factory.[49] The introduction of the flow line induced an intensive discussion about the principles of social and spatial order. Of course, technological and organisational questions were far from being neglected. But these questions had been relocated into a much broader framework. One can witness the emergence of an elaborated paradigm reconciling dynamics and stable order. Movements, therefore, had to be channelled by architecture and production layout.[50] German trade unionist Friedrich Alt expressed a clear sense of these links in 1926. The regrouping of machines according to the principles of flow production, he wrote, changed the 'position and standing of the machine within production, but also the relation between machine and man'.[51] In a similar way, the Metal Workers' Union argued that factories must be treated as a 'more or less organic entity composed of space and utilisation'.[52] To achieve efficient production and proper working conditions, the trade union argued, there had to be systematic studies concerning the realms of space *and* technical equipment within the factory. The changes in the very nature of social and spatial relations required new modes of control and communication to guarantee smooth and frictionless operation. Absence of friction became one of the most important ideals of order incorporating a wide range of social, technological and organisational problems of industrial workplaces:

> 'Flow line production', it was stated in 1926, 'implies the term of frictionless activity. But no human or mechanical activity is that perfect and without occasional friction. Therefore, inspecting all the activities on the line is a necessity without flow line production is impossible.'[53]

In addition to flow-line production, some engineers focused on group production. Both had the same implications. Both opened opportunities to rationalise production and stabilise social order on the shop floor. Daimler introduced group production in 1919. It was meant to be some kind of middle ground between traditional workshops and flow-line production. Group production was one way to restructure the factory by breaking down the traditional departments, workshops and social bonds. '[Y]et the emerging new arrangement at Daimler nonetheless marked a clear break with the previous organization of the workplace and set the stage for the thoroughgoing industrial transformation of the late 1920s and 1930s. Moreover, in the context of labor's new militancy, which was well entrenched in many Daimler departments, the company's reorganization of parts of the labor processes was fraught with political overtones.'[54] To a lesser extent Opel experimented with new modes of production as well.[55] The main purpose was to merge different activities, different machines and different workers into one consistent unit. Every tool, every single component and every worker required to assemble, for example, a rear axle, were allocated and concentrated on one straightforward shop floor. Daimler production engineer Richard Lang, who was responsible for the introduction of group production, tried to capture its main features. He argued that group production could foster 'human qualities' of the workplace and the attachment of every single workman to his work group and his task. Lang believed that it was possible to avoid the workmen 'losing touch' with their work or being degraded to the state of machines.[56] German sociologist Willy Hellpach, a close observer of Daimler's experiments, argued in 1922 that group production could be considered as a means to prevent social fragmentation and isolation:

> [Group production] is pointing the way to a kind of differentiation and specialisation that does not necessarily result in physical and human atomisation of the workman and his work. It is generating the fact of organic bonds between the workmen.[57]

Flow-line and group production combined the arrangement of machines and the allocation of workmen. Industrial sociologists, welfare workers and production engineers, my argument goes, followed an approach best characterised as ecology of work and workplaces. This approach inspired their search for production methods, organisational schemes and the design of buildings and workrooms. Addressing the factory as an environment is one important feature of social engineering. It is the hallmark of a passage from organisational or technological problems to those of a social kind. But 'social' in this case meant the interaction of workers with their environment: with the factory buildings, the shop floor, the arrangement and allocation of machines and co-workers. This implied some enlargement of the environment concept, which now included physical, psychological and social factors. In a partly metaphorical way the factory became a natural habitat of workmen. German sociologist Theodor Geiger, being an outsider at this time, criticised such ideas as early as 1929, calling it the newest ideological and political fashion to reconcile class warfare without talking about capitalism's contradictions.[58]

Many of Geiger's contemporaries interpreted the factory as 'most impressive model of human habitat ["*Lebensraum*"]'.[59] Goetz Briefs, one of the most influential industrial sociologists in Weimar Germany, argued in 1931 that it is particularly the factory that is a spatial entity, incorporating social, cultural and sanitary conditions.[60] Briefs and others promoted an ecological view on factories and workplaces. Industrial sociologists stressed the strong influence of the spatial and social habitat on workers' attitudes, morale and behaviour:

> The entanglement of every individual within a factory is eminently close and strong because individuals are not only linked spatially but also because everyone depends in his work on each other. Everyone who enters a factory is entering a very special environment.[61]

Of course, this 'very special environment' required adoption and adjustment. 'Every employee', Heinrich Lechtape wrote in 1929, 'has to adjust to the social environment of the factory, to the social demands and standards of the factory.'[62]

Statements like these were common within the discourse on industry in the first half of the twentieth century. Industrial sociologists, welfare workers and production engineers took their own route to govern the factory and the workers. This route was quite different from Taylorism and the earlier science of labour because it gave attention to a holistic social and spatial order and by doing so overthrew segregating approaches. Obviously, there is a difference between regulating single operations and shaping an environment. The environmental conditions had to be shaped in a particular way to avoid fragmentation or isolation. Attempts were driven by a notorious fear of the 'masses' and the dissolution of a well-ordered space – the imminent transformation of '*Lebensraum*' (human habitat) into '*Zweckraum*' (functional space):

> That is to say the factory is at first a spatial entity. Co-operation of several men [. . .] requires a spatial dimension. [. . .] But the factory space also depends on social, cultural and hygienic conditions, which are subject to change during history. A question of sociological importance is furthermore whether the workplace is pure functional space or not.[63]

The task of welfare work was to fight these threats by fostering the 'human qualities' of the workmen's environment. Most important was the effort to create adequate and proper environmental conditions at work and beyond. The factory, just like clothing or housing, many welfare workers argued, must protect the workmen against 'a great number of dangerous enemies and attacks'.[64] The factory, the argument went, should be at least in part a '*Lebensraum*' – becoming something like a workman's 'home'. Workmen should obtain, Gerhard Albrecht stated in 1928, some of kind of entitlement to be at home in the factory ['*eine Art Heimatsberechtigung am Betriebe*'].[65] At this point, the factory undeniably had become much more than a production unit. It had become a place to live in, a home and a human habitat.

Conclusion

The environmentalist or ecologist discourse analysed in the previous sections fostered a very special perception and handling of industrial workplaces. Social engineering designed spatial and social surroundings in order to structure behaviour and movements of workers in an indirect way. It preferred instruments to build a holistic environment, and it wanted this environment to predetermine every single movement and the placement of every worker. Inter-war discourses on industrial workplaces championed socio-spatial arguments over those of a technical nature, integrative approaches over those of anatomising. Social engineering replaced mechanical engineering or, at least, the hierarchies and dependencies of both had been reversed. The human-motor metaphor lost its persuasive power to emerging ecologist metaphors. The discourse on the factory as an environment was not only a discourse on industry and production but rather on modernity and social order as such. It was driven by the fear of dissolution and by the confidence in the abilities of professionals to prevent dissolution. It was a discourse on situating the factory, industrial work and workplaces within modern societies.

Notes

1. Lipartito, "Practice of Business History," 35. For different concepts of industrial history see Welskopp, "Betrieb"; Zeitlin, "Labour History."
2. Quoted in Castel, "Problematization," 237–8.
3. The today unfashionable term "welfare work" is a translation of the German concepts "*betriebliche Sozialpolitik*" and "*soziale Betriebspolitik*". It has been chosen because "welfare work" was widely used in Britain to describe a distinctive managerial task from the end of the nineteenth century until at least the 1950s that reassembled most elements of the German concepts. "More recently," industrial sociologist J. Henry Richardson wrote in 1954, "investigation and experience have shown that there is an intimate relation between working conditions and the workers' efficiency, and many progressive employers now recognise that welfare work, widely interpreted, is an essential part of business management. Its scope has, therefore, been greatly enlarged and it is now sometimes defined as so to be almost synonymous with labour management. [...] Industrial welfare in its widest sense is considered in Great Britain to include any arrangement of working conditions, organisation of social and sports clubs, and establishment of funds by a firm, which contribute to the workers' health and safety, comfort, efficiency, economic security, education and recreation." (Richardson, *Study of Industrial Relations*, 171–2).
4. See Etzemüller, *Ordnung der Moderne*; Etzemüller, *Romantik der Rationalität*; Kuchenbuch, *Geordnete Gemeinschaft*; Luks, *Betrieb*; Schlimm, *Ordnungen des Verkehrs*.
5. See Dipper, "Moderne"; Doering-Manteuffel, "Konturen von Ordnung." For a detailed discussion of social engineering and different concepts of modernity see Luks, "Moderne."
6. Herbert, "Europe in High Modernity," 11.
7. Ibid., 19; cf. Raphael, "Ordnungsmuster der Hochmoderne."
8. See Scott, *Seeing Like A State*.

9. Peukert, *Krisenjahre der klassischen Moderne*, 137–43.
10. Mai, *Europa 1918–1939*.
11. See Bolz, *Auszug aus der entzauberten Welt*.
12. See Hardtwig, *Utopie und politische Herrschaft*.
13. Volker Berghahn's interpretation focuses on "a confrontation of war and consumption that started in Europe in 1914 and ended in 1945 with the breakthrough of the latter". Man of violence and man of consumption, Berghahn argues, mark two fundamentally different modes of organising industrial high modernity (Berghahn, *Europa*, 15).
14. For a broader discussion see Hardtwig, *Politische Kulturgeschichte*.
15. The significance of the crisis trope is discussed by Föllmer and Graf, "Krise"; Graf, *Zukunft*; Hardtwig, *Ordnungen in der Krise*.
16. See Luks, "Moderne."
17. Bauman, *Modernity and the Holocaust*, 18.
18. See Raphael, "Verwissenschaftlichung des Sozialen"; Szöllösi-Janze, "Wissensgesellschaft in Deutschland."
19. Perkin, *Rise of Professional Society*, 123.
20. See Banta, *Taylored Lives*; Guillén, *Taylorized Beauty*; Homburg, "Anfänge des Taylorsystems"; Haber, *Efficiency and Uplift*; Littler, "Understanding Taylorism"; Nelson, "Taylorism versus Welfare Work."
21. See Yanorella, "Repoliticizing the Body-Machine Complex."
22. Littler, "Understanding Taylorism," 195–6.
23. See Guillén, *Models of Management*; Shenhav, *Manufacturing Rationality*.
24. Rabinbach, *Human Motor*, 289.
25. See Maier, "Taylorism and Technocracy."
26. Uhl, "Scientific Management," 525.
27. See Burchardt, "Technischer Fortschritt"; Maier, "Taylorism and Technocracy."
28. See Berghoff, "Unternehmenskultur und Herrschaftstechnik."
29. See Fiedler, "Betriebliche Sozialpolitik," 373f.
30. See Schulz, "Betriebliche Sozialpolitik"; Welskopp, "Betriebliche Sozialpolitik."
31. See Fiedler, "Betriebliche Sozialpolitik," 367–73.
32. Kleinschmidt, "Betriebliche Sozialpolitik," 40.
33. See Rummler, *Entstehungsgeschichte der Betriebssoziologie*.
34. See Schuster, *Industrie und Sozialwissenschaften*, 110–24.
35. Ibid., 327–86.
36. See Nolan, *Visions of Modernity*, 183–91.
37. Rabinow, *French Modern*, 4.
38. See Banham, *Concrete Atlantis*.
39. Guillén, *Taylorized Beauty*, 1.
40. See Marchand, *Creating the Corporate Soul*, 28–32, 255–62.
41. See Biggs, *Rational Factory*.
42. See Mende, "Kunst der Technik."
43. Lodders, "Industriebau und Architektur," 53.
44. See Banham, *Concrete Atlantis*, 56–60; Hildebrand, *Designing for Industry*.
45. Biggs, *Rational Factory*, 119.
46. Ibid., 143–4.
47. "Wie bauen unsere Brandenburger den Blitz?", 216.
48. See Grieger, "River Rouge am Mittellandkanal"; Mommsen and Grieger, *Volkswagenwerk*, 250–68.
49. See Bönig, *Einführung von Fließbandarbeit*; Fridenson, "Coming of the Assembly Line"; Kugler, "Von der Werkstatt zum Fließband."
50. See Luks, "Kanalisierte Dynamik."
51. Alt, "Maschine und Maschinengruppe," 65.
52. Deutscher Metallarbeiter-Verband, *Jahr- und Handbuch 1928*, 85–6.
53. Kienzle, "Revision in der Fliessarbeit," 197.
54. Bellon, *Mercedes in Peace and War*, 161; cf. Kugler, "Von der Werkstatt zum Fließband," 329–32; Stahlmann, *Die erste Revolution in der Autoindustrie*, 117–43.
55. See Kugler, *Arbeitsorganisation und Produktionstechnologie*; Idem., "Von der Werkstatt zum Fließband," 333–8; Stahlmann, *Die erste Revolution in der Autoindustrie*, 67–88.

56. Lang, "Gruppenfabrikation," 4–5.
57. Hellpach, *Gruppenfabrikation*, 92. On Hellpach's evaluation of Daimler's group production see Campbell, *Joy in Work*; Hinrichs, *Seele des Arbeiters*; Pfanzer, *Begründung der Arbeitswissenschaft*.
58. Geiger, "Zur Soziologie der Industriearbeit," 775.
59. Hellpach, *Gruppenfabrikation*, 8–9, 11.
60. Briefs, "Betriebssoziologie," 32. Briefs was the leading figure of the emerging industrial sociology in Weimar Germany. His articles and books led the way to a coherent body of knowledge on industrial workplaces and set the agenda for further research. Briefs also founded the "Berliner Institut für Betriebssoziologie und soziale Betriebslehre" [Berlin Institut for industrial sociology and welfare work]. See Klein-Zirbes, *Der Beitrag von Goetz Briefs*; Wilke, "Goetz Briefs und das Institut für Betriebssoziologie."
61. Fischer, "Der Betrieb als geistige Gemeinschaft," 302.
62. Lechtape, "Soziale Probleme," 297.
63. Briefs, "Betriebssoziologie," 32.
64. Neubert, "Körperpflege," 5, cf. Hanauer, "Hygiene der Fabrikbauten," 204.
65. Albrecht, "Arbeitsgemeinschaft," 536–7.

Bibliography

Albrecht, Gerhard. "Arbeitsgemeinschaft, Betriebsgemeinschaft, Werksgemeinschaft." *Jahrbücher für Nationalökonomie und Statistik* 128 (1928): 530–62.
Alt, Friedrich. "Maschine und Maschinengruppe. Ein durch Fließarbeit verändertes Verhältnis." *Metallarbeiter-Zeitung* 44 (1926): 65–71.
Banham, Reyner. *A Concrete Atlantis. US Industrial Building and European Modern Architecture.* Cambridge/MA: MIT Press, 1989.
Banta, Martha. *Taylored Lives. Narrative Productions in the Age of Taylor, Veblen, and Ford.* Chicago and London: University of Chicago Press, 1993.
Bauman, Zygmunt. *Modernity and the Holocaust.* Ithaca/NY: Cornell University Press, 1989.
Bellon, Bernard P. *Mercedes in Peace and War. German Automobile Workers 1903–1945.* New York: Columbia University Press, 1990.
Berghahn, Volker. *Europa im Zeitalter der Weltkriege. Die Entfesselung und Entgrenzung der Gewalt.* Frankfurt/Main: Fischer, 2002.
Berghoff, Hartmut. "Unternehmenskultur und Herrschaftstechnik. Industrieller Paternalismus: Hohner von 1857 bis 1918." *Geschichte und Gesellschaft* 23 (1997): 167–204.
Biggs, Lindy. *The Rational Factory. Architecture, Technology, and Work in America's Age of Mass Production.* Baltimore: Johns Hopkins University Press, 1996.
Bönig, Jürgen. *Die Einführung von Fließbandarbeit in Deutschland bis 1933. Zur Geschichte einer Sozialinnovation.* Münster and Hamburg: LIT, 1993.
Bolz, Norbert. *Auszug aus der entzauberten Welt. Philosophischer Extremismus zwischen den Weltkriegen.* Munich: Fink, 1989.
Briefs, Goetz. "Betriebssoziologie." In *Handwörterbuch der Soziologie*, edited by Alfred Vierkandt, 31–53. Stuttgart: Enke, 1931.
Burchardt, Lothar. "Technischer Fortschritt und sozialer Wandel. Das Beispiel der Taylorismus-Rezeption." In *Deutsche Technikgeschichte*, edited by Wilhelm Treue, 52–98. Göttingen: Vandenhoeck & Ruprecht, 1977.
Campbell, Joan. *Joy in Work, German Work. The National Debate 1800–1945.* Princeton: Princeton/NJ University Press, 1989.
Castel, Robert. "'Problematization' as a Mode of Reading History." In *Foucault and the Writing of History*, edited by Jan Goldstein, 237–52. Oxford and Cambridge/MA: Blackwell, 1994.
Metallarbeiter-Verband, Deutscher. *Jahr- und Handbuch 1928.* Berlin: DMV, 1929.
Dipper, Christof. "Moderne, Version: 1.0." *Docupedia-Zeitgeschichte*, 25.08.2010: http://docupedia.de/zg/Moderne

Doering-Manteuffel, Anselm. "Konturen von Ordnung in den Zeitschichten des 20. Jahrhunderts." In *Die Ordnung der Moderne. Social Engineering im 20. Jahrhundert*, edited by Thomas Etzemüller, 41–66. Bielefeld: transcript, 2009.

Etzemüller, Thomas, ed. *Die Ordnung der Moderne. Social Engineering im 20. Jahrhundert*. Bielefeld: transcript, 2009.

Etzemüller, Thomas. *Die Romantik der Rationalität. Alva & Gunnar Myrdal – Social Engineering in Schweden*. Bielefeld: transcript, 2010.

Fiedler, Martin. "Betriebliche Sozialpolitik in der Zwischenkriegszeit. Wege der Interpretation und Probleme der Forschung im deutsch-französischen Vergleich." *Geschichte und Gesellschaft* 22 (1996): 350–75.

Fischer, Ludwig. "Der Betrieb als geistige Gemeinschaft." In *Die sozialen Probleme des Betriebes*, edited by Heinz Potthoff, 300–9. Berlin: Spaeth & Linde, 1925.

Föllmer, Moritz, and Rüdiger Graf, eds. *Die "Krise" der Weimarer Republik. Zur Kritik eines Deutungsmusters*. Frankfurt and New York: Campus, 2005.

Fridenson, Patrick. "The Coming of the Assembly Line to Europe." *The Dynamics of Science and Technology*, edited by Wolfgang Krohn, et al., 159–75. Dordrecht: Springer, 1978.

Geiger, Theodor. "Zur Soziologie der Industriearbeit und des Betriebs." *Die Arbeit* 6 (1929): 673–689, 766–781.

Graf, Rüdiger. *Die Zukunft der Weimarer Republik. Krisen und Zukunftsaneignungen in Deutschland 1918–1933*. Munich: Oldenbourg, 2008.

Grieger, Manfred. "River Rouge am Mittellandkanal. Das Volkswagenwerk während des Nationalsozialismus." *Zukunft aus Amerika. Fordismus in der Zwischenkriegszeit: Siedlung – Stadt – Raum*, 163–73. Dessau: Stiftung Bauhaus, 1995.

Guillén, Mauro F. *Models of Management, Work, Authority, and Organization in a Comparative Perspective*. Chicago and London: Chicago University Press, 1994.

Guillén, Mauro F. *The Taylorized Beauty of the Mechanical. Scientific Management and the Rise of Modernist Architecture*. Princeton/NJ: Princeton University Press, 2006.

Haber, Samuel. *Efficiency and Uplift. Scientific Management in the Progressive Era 1890–1920*. Chicago and London: Chicago University Press, 1964.

Hanauer, W. "Die Hygiene der Fabrikbauten." *Betriebsräte-Zeitschrift* 9 (1928): 204–8.

Hardtwig, Wolfgang, ed. *Utopie und politische Herrschaft im Europa der Zwischenkriegszeit*. Munich: Oldenbourg, 2003.

Hardtwig, Wolfgang, ed. *Politische Kulturgeschichte der Zwischenkriegszeit 1918–1939*. Göttingen: Vandenhoeck & Ruprecht, 2005.

Hardtwig, Wolfgang, ed. *Ordnungen in der Krise. Zur politischen Kulturgeschichte Deutschlands 1900–1933*. Munich: Oldenbourg, 2007.

Hellpach, Willy. *Gruppenfabrikation*. Berlin: Springer, 1922.

Herbert, Ulrich. "Europe in High Modernity. Reflections on a Theory of the 20th Century." *Journal of Modern European History* 5 (2007): 5–21.

Hildebrand, Grant. *Designing for Industry. The Architecture of Albert Kahn*. Cambridge/Main, MA: MIT Press, 1974.

Hinrichs, Peter. *Um die Seele des Arbeiters. Arbeitspsychologie, Industrie- und Betriebssoziologie in Deutschland*. Cologne: Pahl Rugenstein, 1981.

Homburg, Heidrun. "Anfänge des Taylorsystems in Deutschland vor dem Ersten Weltkrieg." *Geschichte und Gesellschaft* 4 (1978): 170–94.

Kienzle, Otto. "Die Revision in der Fliessarbeit." In *Fliessarbeit. Beiträge zu ihrer Einführung*, edited by Frank Mäckbach and Otto Kienzle, 197–206. Berlin: VDI, 1926.

Klein-Zirbes, Arnd. *Der Beitrag von Goetz Briefs zur Grundlegung der Sozialen Marktwirtschaft*. Frankfurt: Peter Lang, 2004.

Kleinschmidt, Christian. "Betriebliche Sozialpolitik als Soziale Betriebspolitik. Reaktionen der Eisen- und Stahlindustrie auf den Weimarer Interventionsstaat." In *Unternehmen zwischen Markt und Macht. Aspekte deutscher Unternehmens- und Industriegeschichte im 20. Jahrhundert*, edited by S. Werner Plumpe, 29–41. Essen: Klartext, 1992.

Kuchenbuch, David. *Geordnete Gemeinschaft. Architekten als Sozialingenieure – Deutschland und Schweden im 20. Jahrhundert*. Bielefeld: transcript, 2010.

Kugler, Anita. *Arbeitsorganisation und Produktionstechnologie der Adam Opel Werke von 1900–1929*. Berlin: WZB, 1985.

Kugler, Anita. "Von der Werkstatt zum Fließband. Etappen der frühen Automobilproduktion in Deutschland." *Geschichte und Gesellschaft* 13 (1987): 304–39.

Lang, Richard. "Gruppenfabrikation." *Daimler Werkzeitung* 1 (1919): 4–5.

Lechtape, Heinrich. "Soziale Probleme im industriellen Betrieb." *Kölner Vierteljahrshefte für Soziologie* 8 (1929): 293–301.

Lipartito, Kenneth. "Culture and the Practice of Business History." *Business and Economic History* 24 (1995): 1–41.

Littler, Craig R. "Understanding Taylorism." *British Journal of Sociology* 29 (1978): 18–202.

Lodders, Rudolf. "Industriebau und Architektur und ihre gegenseitige Beeinflussung." In *Rudolf Lodders. Schriften zum Wiederaufbau 1946–1971*, edited by Olaf Bartels, 45–55. Hamburg: Christians, 1989.

Luks, Timo. *Der Betrieb als Ort der Moderne. Zur Geschichte von Industriearbeit, Ordnungsdenken und Social Engineering im 20. Jahrhundert.* Bielefeld: transcript, 2010.

Luks, Timo. "Kanalisierte Dynamik, angeordnete Körper. Bewegungsmetaphern, Gesellschaftsordnung und der Industriebetrieb (1920–1960)." In *Kontrollierte Arbeit – Disziplinierte Körper? Zur Sozial- und Kulturgeschichte der Industriearbeit im 19. und 20. Jahrhundert*, edited by Lars Bluma and Karsten Uhl, 253–83. Bielefeld: transcript, 2012.

Luks, Timo. "Eine Moderne im Normalzustand. Ordnungsdenken und Social Engineering in der ersten Hälfte des 20. Jahrhunderts." *Österreichische Zeitschrift für Geschichtswissenschaften* 23 (2012): 15–38.

Mai, Gunther. *Europa 1918–1939. Mentalitäten, Lebensweisen, Politik zwischen den Weltkriegen.* Stuttgart: Kohlhammer, 2001.

Maier, Charles S. "Between Taylorism and Technocracy. European Ideologies and the Vision of Industrial Productivity in the 1920s." *Journal of Contemporary History* 5 (1970): 27–61.

Marchand, Roland. *Creating the Corporate Soul. The Rise of Public Relations and Corporate Imagery in American Big Business.* Berkeley and Los Angeles: University of California Press, 1998.

Mende, Michael. "'Kunst der Technik oder die Technik der Kunst'. Carl F.W. Borgward und sein Architekt Rudolf Lodders." *Technische Intelligenz und "Kulturfaktor Technik". Kulturvorstellungen von Technikern und Ingenieuren zwischen Kaiserreich und früher Bundesrepublik Deutschland*, edited by Burkhard Dietz, et al., 221–50. Münster: LIT, 1996.

Mommsen, Hans, and Manfred Grieger. *Das Volkswagenwerk und seine Arbeiter im Dritten Reich.* Düsseldorf: Econ, 1996.

Nelson, Daniel. "Taylorism versus Welfare Work in American Industry. H.L. Gantt and the Bancrofts." *Business History Review* 46 (1972): 1–16.

Neubert, R. "Was gehört zur Körperpflege?" *Opelgeist* 2 (1931): 5–6.

Nolan, Mary. *Visions of Modernity. American Business and the Modernization of Germany.* Oxford: Oxford University Press, 1994.

Perkin, Harold. *The Rise of Professional Society. England since 1880.* London: Routledge, 1989.

Peukert, Detlev J. K. *Die Weimarer Republik. Krisenjahre der Klassischen Moderne.* Frankfurt/Main: Suhrkamp, 1987.

Pfanzer, Thomas. *Die Begründung der Arbeitswissenschaft in der Soziologie von Willy Hellpach*, Ph. D. diss., University of Würzburg 1995.

Rabinbach, Anson. *The Human Motor. Energy, Fatigue, and the Origins of Modernity.* Berkeley and Los Angeles: University of California Press, 1992.

Rabinow, Paul. *French Modern. Norms and Forms of the Social Environment.* Chicago and London: Chicago University Press, 1989.

Raphael, Lutz. "Die Verwissenschaftlichung des Sozialen als methodische und konzeptionelle Herausforderung für eine Sozialgeschichte des 20. Jahrhunderts." *Geschichte und Gesellschaft* 22 (1996): 165–93.

Raphael, Lutz. "Ordnungsmuster der Hochmoderne? Die Theorie der Moderne und die Geschichte der europäischen Gesellschaften im 20. Jahrhundert." In *Dimensionen der Moderne. Festschrift für Christof Dipper*, edited by Ute Schneider and Lutz Raphael, 73–91. Frankfurt/Main: Peter Lang, 2008.

Richardson, J. Henry. *An Introduction to the Study of Industrial Relations.* London: Routledge, 1954.

Rummler, Hans-Michael. *Die Entstehungsgeschichte der Betriebssoziologie in Deutschland. Eine wissenschaftshistorische Studie.* Frankfurt/Main: Peter Lang, 1984.

Schlimm, Anette. *Ordnungen des Verkehrs. Arbeit an der Moderne – deutsche und britische Verkehrsexpertise im 20. Jahrhundert*. Bielefeld: transcript, 2011.

Schulz, Günther. "Betriebliche Sozialpolitik in Deutschland seit 1850." In *Staatliche, städtische, betriebliche und kirchliche Sozialpolitik vom Mittelalter bis zur Gegenwart*, edited by Hans Pohl, 137–76. Stuttgart: Steiner, 1991.

Schuster, Helmuth. *Industrie und Sozialwissenschaften. Eine Praxisgeschichte der Arbeits- und Industrieforschung*. Opladen: Westdeutscher Verlag, 1987.

Scott, James C. *Seeing like a State. How Certain Schemes to Improve the Human Condition have Failed*. New Haven: Yale University Press, 1998.

Shenhav, Yehouda A. *Manufacturing Rationality. The Engineering Foundations of the Managerial Revolution*. Oxford: Oxford University Press, 1999.

Stahlmann, Michael. *Die erste Revolution in der Autoindustrie. Management und Arbeitspolitik von 1900–1940*. Frankfurt/Main and New York: Campus, 1993.

Szöllösi-Janze, Margit. "Wissensgesellschaft in Deutschland: Überlegungen zur Neubestimmung der deutschen Zeitgeschichte über Verwissenschaftlichungsprozesse." *Geschichte und Gesellschaft* 30 (2004): 277–313.

Uhl, Karsten. "Giving Scientific Management a Human Face. The Engine Factory Deutz and a German Path to Efficiency, 1910–1945." *Labor History* 52 (2011): 511–33.

Welskopp, Thomas. "Betriebliche Sozialpolitik im 19. und frühen 20. Jahrhundert. Eine Diskussion neuerer Forschungen und Konzepte und eine Branchenanalyse der deutschen und amerikanischen Eisen- und Stahlindustrie von den 1870er bis zu den 1930er Jahren." *Archiv für Sozialgeschichte* 34 (1994): 333–74.

Welskopp, Thomas. "Der Betrieb als soziales Handlungsfeld. Neuere Forschungsansätze in der Industrie- und Arbeitergeschichte." *Geschichte und Gesellschaft* 22 (1996): 118–42.

"Wie bauen unsere Brandenburger den 'Blitz'?" *Opel-Kamerad* 7 (1936): 213–7.

Wilke, Manfred. "Goetz Briefs und das Institut für Betriebssoziologie an der Technischen Hochschule Berlin." In *Wissenschaft und Gesellschaft. Beiträge zur Geschichte der Technischen Universität Berlin 1879–1979*, edited by Reinhard Rürup, 335–51. Berlin: Springer, 1979.

Yanorella, Ernest J. "From Trained Gorilla to Humanware. Repoliticizing the Body-Machine Complex between Fordism and Post-Fordism." In *The Social and Political Body*, edited by Theodore Schatzki and Wolfgang Natter, 181–219. New York: Guilford Press, 1996.

Zeitlin, Jonathan. "From Labour History to the History of Industrial Relations." *Economic History Review* 40 (1987): 159–84.

The ideal of *Lebensraum* and the spatial order of power at German factories, 1900–45

Department of History, Darmstadt University of Technology, Darmstadt, Germany

Industrial experts, engineers and architects in the early twentieth century faced the so-called 'factory problem'. It had two important components that were interrelated: on the one hand, the plant's spatial order; on the other, the quest for more effective ways of exercising power at the workplace. Both were centred on a new interest in the human factor of production. Workers were no longer regarded as mere objects of discipline but rather as individuals whose individuality was to be utilised. In this context a new discourse on work environment began. Some of the most important German architects and engineers were determined to beautify the factory and to create a human habitat (*Lebensraum*) inside, not least because of the increasing number of female labourers. Accordingly, notions of efficiency were combined with the new concept of beautification: rationalisation was 'humanised'. The problem experts faced was how to create an atmosphere of trust which would promote the efficient usage of workers' abilities. In this context, external discipline had to be more and more replenished by chosen workers' self-discipline. It had been most important to humanise the workplace, respect the worker as subject of production and create conditions which increased working morale.

Introduction

'Are our industrial buildings not human workplaces? Should it not to be our aim to turn these workplaces into places of joyous work? Should architecture not express this notion?'[1] The eminent modernist architect Hans Poelzig, who had been the president of the German Werkbund between 1919 and 1921, posed these rhetorical questions in an article on 'The Architectural Development of Factory Construction' published in 1930. However, according to Poelzig, the most important figure in the history of industrial architecture in the early twentieth century had not been the architect, but the engineer. The engineer had demonstrated a solution to the problem of factory construction. Until 1930, however, architects had improved: most of them had lost their old-fashioned romantic approach, as they had realised that plant construction required more skill of the architect than just adding a few formalistic contents to the engineer's draft. Poelzig concluded: 'The architect had learned to think like an engineer.'[2] Now, the architect realised that he had to deliberate the whole complex and every detail of the building to produce an architectural unity. Everything had to be prearranged: construction, choice of material, colouring.[3] Poelzig did not just draw this conclusion retrospectively. In 1911, he had already called for the architect to think as an 'artist' and thus to emulate and even exceed the engineer's deep deliberation of the construction's basic principles. It was this credo that consequently functioned as the foundation for Poelzig's architectural work.[4]

The management historian Mauro Guillén portrayed modernist architecture as being deeply influenced by Frederick W. Taylor and scientific management.[5] Guillén's argument is convincing, but I would like to suggest examining it within a wider context: modernist architects did not only consider Taylor's scientific management as an ideal; rather the engineer became the architects' role model. This article will take a deeper look at the engineers, the architects and the history of modern factory building in the first part of the twentieth century. At the end of the nineteenth century an increased interest in factory building and in concepts to integrate it into the production process arose as workflow was rationalised and new machines were integrated into the process of production. I will investigate how the engineering ideal enriched industrial architects' scope. How did this new (virtual) collaboration between architects and engineers come to exist? Moreover, when and why did this new interest in factory building, a task long neglected by architects, start?

David Kuchenbuch's study on architects as social engineers in Germany and Sweden showed that debates on housing were based on similar ideas.[6] Therefore, my article on industrial architecture does not merely cover a special-interest history. It corresponds to wider issues especially the reformist social movements of the Weimar Republic. Moreover, I would like to argue that the spatial factor played a major role in reformist debates. In this regard, Bruce Kaufman's convincing research on *The Early Years of Human Resource Management* needs a certain completion. Kaufman claims that after the First World War a new type of personnel management arose based on 'a more enlightened and forward-looking form of employer self-interest'.[7] Naming the origins of human-resource management he lists among other things scientific management, the industrial-safety movement and industrial-welfare work.[8] As this article will show, Kaufman misses one crucial point: the debate on the working space, especially as articulated by some of the most important modern architects.

In the US context, as historian Lindy Biggs has shown, the factory ceased its function as a 'passive shell simply to house machines, tools, and workers', but 'became part of production technology, helping to solve problems that stood in the way of efficient mass production'.[9] At the same time factory-welfare work came to the fore. Biggs tells the history of factory-welfare work starting with a problem managers and engineers faced: how to transform the employee into a better, more reliable worker. It was no longer sufficient to regard the worker in a simple mechanistic way: as a human machine. The problem therefore was: what would encourage employees to work harder? One way to apparently solve this problem was in appealing to workers' concerns through factory-welfare policy. Biggs pointed out that this meant more than 'age-old paternalism'. Instead the factory-welfare work was related to the progressive movement and integrated the concern for worker issues into the industrial bureaucracy.[10]

In Germany company welfare policy (*Fabrikwohlfahrtspflege*) had a long tradition starting in the late nineteenth century. As business historian Susanne Hilger has demonstrated, employers' motivation was rather based on business and less on philanthropic endeavours. Binding workers to the company and establishing a higher discipline was their main concern.[11] In this regard, humanisation of work and scientific management followed the same logic and had the same aims. In this context, both in the United States and in Germany, a new discourse on work environment began. Mainly, it was about improvements in lighting, heating and cooling and about rearrangement of workstations. This is where the interests of engineers and architects met: architects joined and broadened the discourse by focusing on the factory building as a whole and its aesthetic qualities.

Given these developments in US industry, I would like to investigate how these processes went in an economy featuring important pecularities like Germany. The 'varieties of capitalism' approach argues that even today, the differences between 'liberal market economies' (like the United States and Great Britain) and 'co-ordinated market economies' (like Germany) seem crucial. Analysing the varieties of capitalism, Peter A. Hall and David Soskice point out that firms' production strategies in co-ordinated market economies usually rely on a 'highly skilled labour force given substantial work autonomy'.[12] Therefore, it can be expected that in early twentieth-century Germany, the interest in the human factor of production was higher than in the United States or Britain. Otherwise, architects and factory experts already took part in international debates. That means there obviously was no singular German development, but merely a special accent to the transnational debate. To explore the differences between the countries, this article will start with a closer look at similarities and contrasts in industrial architectural discourse between the British and US 'liberal market economies' and the German 'co-ordinated market economy'.

The mutual efforts of engineers and industrial architects were part of manifold approaches to face the so-called 'factory problem'. What exactly was seen to constitute the factory problem in the early twentieth century? It had at least two important components which were interrelated: on the one hand the plant's spatial order, and on the other the sought-for more effective ways of exercising power inside the plant. Both were centred on a new interest in the human factor of production. To analyse this process we can use Michel Foucault's concept of governmentality. Workers were no longer regarded as mere objects of discipline but rather as individuals whose individuality was to be utilised.[13] Traditional discipline and surveillance by foremen became less important in comparison to the exercise of the new governmental power on workers.[14] We have to deal with a complex that combines two techniques of power, or as Foucault puts it: 'techniques of domination and techniques of the self'. In this sense power is exercised in a form that Foucault calls 'government'. He argues that the 'contact point, where the individuals are driven by others is tied to the way they conduct themselves'.[15]

Exploring the example of the Ford company in the first part of the twentieth century, Richard Coopey and Alan McKinlay demonstrated that a Foucauldian approach can be helpful in analysing historical developments in factory regimes. They conclude that the inter-war River Rouge plant had been characterised by a 'system of terror', while after the war Ford shifted to a 'disciplinary regime'.[16] However, I would like to suggest that the authoritarian Ford approach of industrial relations does not provide a good example for the general development of twentieth-century factories. Therefore, we should not one-sidedly focus on 'discipline', but rather look for those more flexible forms of power called 'government' by Foucault.

Foucault's theory is especially useful for my approach because it conceives of the connection between power and space. According to Foucault, 'discipline is, above all, analysis of space'.[17] Accordingly, disciplinary power is exercised by the spatial distribution of bodies, which thus allows 'judging them, measuring or evaluating them and placing them so they can be utilized to the maximum'.[18] This process can be understood as discipline forming the basis for the subsequent 'government' of the individuals. I will focus on the process, which Foucault calls the creation of 'a useful space' by distributing individuals in space. Most notable is the process of 'individualizing partitioning'; that means 'each individual has his own place; and each place its individual.'[19] Foucault described how the distribution of individuals was invented in the eighteenth-century military and in schools, but a detailed analysis of these processes in factories still has to be done.[20] Foucault states that this operation was especially complex in factories because the 'production machinery [...] had its own requirements': 'The distribution of bodies, the spatial arrangement of production machinery and the different forms of activity in the distribution of "posts" had to be linked together.'[21] First of all, I will follow Foucault's idea of a dual spatial order: 'mixed spaces' are as real as they are ideal.[22] On the one hand, workers and machines are arranged. On the other hand, classifications and hierarchies are simultaneously constituted. Thus, spatial arrangement is where discourse and practices interact.

Therefore, the generation of atmospheres in spaces deserves special attention. The sociologist Martina Löw defines atmospheres as the potentiality of spaces 'which can influence feelings'.[23] Atmospheres obscure the very practice of positioning[24]; that means, the act of exercising power by giving each individual its own place vanishes out of consciousness. The sociologist is interested in the 'simultaneity of effect and perception'; therefore she wants to show how atmospheres 'arise through the perception of interactions between people'.[25] However, this article's main focus is on the way atmospheres were 'deliberately deployed' by arrangements of space. The engineers and architects who planned these spatial orderings partly anticipated the sociological insight that the 'workings of atmospheres are not [...] perceived in the same way by everyone'.[26] They recognised perception being class and gender specific and tried to arrange the factory as a special habitat for working-class people, and, later, even as a human habitat which considered different requirements for men and women. The gender issue deserves closer attention: it fostered the efforts to 'humanise' the factory because many experts were convinced that women workers particularly needed a homely environment.

Firstly, I will investigate early-twentieth-century concepts of architects and industrial engineers on the factory's spatial order. I would like to argue that in order to understand the German discourse on factory design, it will be crucial to focus on the attempts to rearrange modern factories in a way which would restore a crucial quality they had lost in industrialisation: *Lebensraum* (human habitat). In the second part I will analyse another group of actors: social scientists sharpened the debate on the plant as a human habitat beginning in the 1920s. In the last part of the article, I will explore the discourse on the aesthetics of production, which was virulent during the Third Reich under the catchphrase 'Beauty of Labour'. It will be evident that there was an on-going debate on the aesthetics of industrial workplaces, which was characterised by a strong line of continuity.

First, it is important to show that the German discourse on plant environment was part of an international debate. Indeed, the humanisation of workspaces was not a unique German path to Fordism, but it had special features. In contrast to Britain and the United States, efficiency seemed to be more closely bound to the idea of humanisation: taking care of the human factor at once meant enforcing efficiency. In other words, the idea was to humanise scientific management. In the second part of this article, it will be important to work out the line of continuity between the German Empire, the Weimar Republic and the Nazi regime. The Nazis took advantage of already existing debates and did not invent them. Moreover, it is important to emphasise that plans to create a human habitat at work were not determined to lead to Nazi political connotations. They turned out to be quite flexible: they could be integrated as well into the progressive social reform of the Weimar Republic accepting unions and workers councils, as into the repressive Nazi labour policy.

Industrial architecture and plant environment

Betsy Hunter Bradley showed in her work on the history of *The Industrial Architecture of the United States* that 'industrial engineers promoted themselves as uniquely qualified to provide efficient plans for the works.' The plant had to be arranged in the most effective way to allow the greatest efficiency in production. Besides the comfort of workers, that meant good lighting, sufficient heat, adequate space and convenient rest rooms were seriously considered.[27] A manual for 'Industrial Engineering and Factory Management' in 1928 claimed that 'the typical architect' had not been trained to consider the 'human factor', which, however, was of utmost importance for production. According to the manual, architects had too little knowledge of the requirements of the production processes and factory management. Most of all, they neglected the potential reactions of workers to the facilities which were to be designed.[28] Nevertheless, the manual acknowledged that on the one hand some architects improved their skills and were capable of planning industrial buildings while on the other, a lot of engineers lacked the training and practice needed for plant design.[29]

The architectural historian Hyungmin Pai argues that architects were unqualified for factory construction because they ignored commercial needs and the 'human factor'.[30] In fact, in the United States as well as in Germany, architects just began to play a role in factory construction in the second decade of the twentieth century.[31] The First World War forced architects to deal with industrial architecture, which they had previously neglected and left to engineers. During the war, however, factories and workers' housing remained the only building projects.[32] Just as their German counterparts did, US architects turned to efficiency experts after the war as role models for the new tasks at hand.[33] I would like to suggest that German architects succeeded in promoting their expertise for factory construction because unlike their US colleagues, they showed a deep interest in *both* concerns: they wanted to combine efficiency with the 'human factor'.

Management historian Mauro Guillén considers this the big difference between US, British and Continental European architects. Whereas the US architects remained marginal figures in industrial architecture, and the British architects looked for alternatives to the machine age, the Continental European architects understood themselves as advocates of social reform.[34] The architectural historian Mark Peach even states that 'much of German architectural modernism seemed devoted to the encouragement of work and higher productivity.' The workers' healthiness and happiness – that means the 'human factor' – was of particular interest to the architects because it promised increased production.[35] How did this idea develop?

Until the end of the nineteenth century most German factories were planned and built by master craftsmen. Later on, mechanical engineers assumed the major role in industrial architecture.[36] Only after the turn of the century did academically trained architects concern themselves with factory projects. The first manual on industrial architecture written by a German architect was published in 1923[37]; all former manuals had been written by engineers. Then, architects began to deal with the technical and organisational needs of the factory buildings. This was quite similar to the developments Lindy Biggs describes for US industrial engineers planning the rational factory as the 'master machine'.[38]

In Britain, industrial architecture evolved analogue. Like in Germany, architects replaced builders and engineers as designers of factories, at least concerning the most prestigious projects.[39] Architects still closely collaborated with engineers to deal with the intricate requirements of plant construction.[40] Moreover they envisioned themselves as having a great societal task because of the widespread belief that environment formed one's character.[41] Therefore, they believed the construction of factories would have direct impact on a worker's life and consequently considered good factory building a possible solution to the social question. After the First World War, the beautification of the factory became a common request in Britain.

Nevertheless, the debate on industrial architecture can only be understood in the context of transnational history. An important voice in the British discussion was the US architect Moritz Kahn. He was a brother of Albert Kahn, famous for his work for the Ford Company at their Highland Park plant. Moritz was sent to Britain to establish a branch of the family's Trussed Concrete Steel Company. In his book on *The Design and Construction of Industrial Buildings* published in 1917, Moritz Kahn described factory construction as a way to improve workers' attitudes towards work, as a way to affect their mentality.[42] Kahn's idea of factory construction was to combine 'the greatest possible efficiency of output [...] with the greatest possible convenience and comfort for the workers'.[43] Thus according to Kahn, welfare work itself was directly in the 'interests of industrial efficiency'.[44] It provided the opportunity to attract and keep the best workers and fight the 'danger of industrial unrest'.[45] The factory of the future would be a 'really efficient factory' because it would take care of its workers by establishing a gymnasium, reading rooms, playground and the like. Therefore, the new factory would be an institution with a 'soul'.[46]

Another strong impetus for the betterment of the work environment in the United States and Britain originated from the rising numbers of female workers. Managers and engineers wanted to extend the 'woman's sphere' beyond the home; therefore they established among other things rest rooms and included decorative features into the layout of the workplace.[47] Similar regards about gender played an important role in German discourse about the factory as a human habitat (*Lebensraum*), which will be portrayed below.

This development in construction concepts corresponded with the new managerial style that established itself in the early decades of the twentieth century. The historians Mauro Guillén and Matthew Jefferies have shown how modernist architecture was inspired by the ideas of Frederick Taylor and *scientific management*. Above all, the idea of order reigned supreme. Modernist architects deemed themselves technocrats, as organisers, as social engineers.[48] The concept of the 'quality workplace' especially was very virulent in Germany; that meant that the function and hygiene of the factory building became more important than 'fancy historicist facades', which had been favoured by the traditional school of architects.[49]

In Germany, the collaboration between engineers and architects concerning factory construction also gave ground to new reflections on the building's social meaning. In 1911, Werkbund and later Bauhaus member Walter Gropius designed the Fagus shoe factory, 'generally taken to be the seminal building of the modern movement in architecture'.[50] Construction started in the same year. About this time, Gropius presented his concept of industrial architecture in several articles and a lecture at the Hagen Folkwang Museum. He understood industrial architecture as a part of the efficiency movement and believed in a universal sense of beauty shared by workers. Therefore, it was crucial that the factory resembled 'well-proportioned rooms' rather than 'ugly industrial barracks'.[51] Gropius continued:

> A worker will find that a room well thought out by an artist, which responds to the innate sense of beauty we all possess, will relieve the monotony of the daily task and he will be more

willing to join in the common enterprise. If the worker is happy, he will take more pleasure in his duties, and the productivity of the firm will increase.[52]

Hence, Gropius called for the establishment of factory-'palaces', thereby breaking with the architectural tradition. Consequently, his 'palaces' were not to be created by merely adding some decorative elements to beautify the factory, but the whole concept was based on a new form of functional aesthetic: 'Work must be established in palaces that give the workman, now a slave to industrial labour, not only light, air, and hygiene, but also an indication of the great common idea that drives everything. Only then can the individual submit to the impersonal without losing the joy of working together for that common good previously unattainable by a single individual.'[53] Gropius hoped that awaking workers' 'awareness' of a new work spirit could prevent a 'social catastrophe'.[54] This example confirms historian Guillén's argument that architects as well as scientific managers considered themselves technocratic experts who solved social problems through 'technical improvements and social engineering'.[55]

Art historian Frederick Schwartz raises the well-informed objection that Gropius and his Werkbund fellows reduced the labour problem to the sphere of culture. According to Schwartz, the social question and the problem of alienation could not have been ignored by the Werkbund members unless they chose to lose their status as significant political and cultural voices. However, they curtailed the labour aspect of any claims for social change. Instead, Gropius had turned the worker 'into a consumer of his own site of production'.[56] I would like to argue that Gropius' notion of the labour problem was significant for the beginning of a new discourse on factory labour. As Reyner Banham has shown, Gropius' ideas did not differ significantly from US attempts to improve industrial relations.[57] Moreover, I will demonstrate that on the one hand his approach to the encounters of aesthetics and productivity relied heavily on previous concepts of industrial architecture; on the other, Gropius' revision created discursive space for a whole school of social experts who were later to solve the labour problem by 'human relations'. Thereby, they neglected any claims for material change in the realm of production.

To some degree, modern architects merely followed the path engineer-builders had shaped before. For instance, in 1907 the engineer Ludwig Utz formulated three goals for the further development of industrial architecture in his manual of factory construction, which combined efficiency and 'humanisation' in a similar fashion. First priority was to be on an 'economic and rational operation'. The second concern was on accident avoidance and the third on 'welfare facilities'; that meant rest rooms, canteens and the like.[58] Thus, the designer of a factory not only had to consider efficiency issues but also the human factor of production.

New to modernist architecture was the combination of aesthetics and productivity, which started with the Werkbund. For example, architect Franz Mannheimer published an article in 1910 about the 'art of factories' drawing a connection between a higher sense of beauty and improved competitiveness. According to Mannheimer, bright and large rooms and well-proportioned machines helped workers to do their work joyously and therefore proficiently.[59] Architects inspired by Taylor's scientific management went even further than Taylor himself. While Frederick Taylor neglected workers' psyches some of his followers combined notions of efficiency with the psychological needs of the 'human factor'. Modernist architects were especially interested in these topics. Hence, they belonged to the early predecessors of Elton Mayo's Human Relation approach; he had not been the first by far to raise the question of 'the human problem in industry', even though he tried to promote himself as the inventor.[60]

For the utilitarian school of architecture it was only consequential to show a deep concern for the human factor: they even regarded the building as an organism. Peter Behrens, inspiration to and teacher of some of the most important modernist architects,[61] described his concept in an inauguration speech for the Mannesmann administration building he designed in 1912. First of all, the architect had to observe the planned building's 'organism'. He had to study its 'nervous system' to create a viable body for this 'complex being'. According to Behrens, whose famous AEG turbine factory of 1908/09 served as a (partly criticised) role model for the Fagus factory,[62] the 'organism's' living conditions consisted of maximum brightness, unobstructed communication between rooms, flexible resizable rooms, and maximum utilisation of space.[63] This concept of architecture using organic metaphors implied the need to consider also the 'human factor' and its psychological and social needs. Moreover, the imagination of the building as a living being created discursive space, which was later filled by the discourse on the factory as a human habitat (*Lebensraum*).

Even after architects who had learned from engineers about industrial architecture entered the field of factory construction, engineers still played an important role; in most aspects both groups, who still collaborated in construction practice, shared the same concepts. Engineer Robert Hauer's manual on *Modern Principles of Factory Building* published in 1922 pointed to social and aesthetic requirements of factories, which had been denied for a long time but were largely accepted by then. Generally, it was accepted that workers' psychological and physical wellbeing had an impact on the company's output. The pivotal point was to convince workers that productivity had to be increased. Therefore, all had to be done to create a feeling of 'joy in work'. Proper means for this cause were, according to Hauer, on the one hand an overall aesthetic design of the plant; on the other the establishment of staff rooms like canteens[64], sanitary rooms and the like. Although Hauer, in contrast to Gropius, did not believe in workers' aesthetic sensibility, he was sure that even 'the simple worker' realised that his workplace had been created in a pleasant and appealing way. He was certain that work conducted in beautiful rooms had the most positive effects on workers' performance.[65]

To which extent were such theoretical concepts applied to actual factories? In the US context, Robert Lewis argues that the 'rational factory' was a generally accepted ideal, although architects rarely implemented it to its full extent. Usually, pragmatism prevailed: architects, engineers and managers selected those elements of the 'rational factory' concept that seemed to offer the best ratio between building costs and expected increase in efficiency. Furthermore, different people had different ideas about what would prove to be 'efficient'. Consequently, there was no single model which dominated the scene, but selective adaptation chosen by actual factory designers.[66]

In Germany, it was common practice since the late nineteenth century for companies to rent factory buildings, which meant it was rarely possible to adapt the factory space to production needs[67]: engineers had to deal with the space management rented. In addition, in most rented factories sanitary rooms were of poor quality – sometimes even missing completely. For instance, as late as 1928 a textile worker reported that her factory – rented by her employer – did not even provide a changing room.[68] Nevertheless, there are examples of actual factory constructions or redesigns which combined rationalising aspects with 'humanising' factors. For instance, the Cologne-based engine factory Deutz reconstructed its plant in 1911 after general director Fritz Wolfensberger had visited modern factories in the United States a year before. Such study trips to the United States became common for German engineers and managers in the following years, especially during the Weimar period, as historian Mary Nolan has shown.[69] Wolfensberger was one of the early adaptors of Americanisation; his concept clearly resembles the ideas Biggs described as the plan of the 'rational factory'. The constructional changes he put forward were part of the factory's total rationalisation: technological changes went hand in hand with the installation of a new production process and rebuilding measures. In detail, after his return to Cologne, Wolfensberger asked the management board to integrate the isolated factory rooms under a master plan.[70] As he explained in another memorandum to the board, the workshop's 'systematic rearrangement' implied restructuring the work process to avoid all interim transportation and backward movements of products. Associated with the efficiency of the new spatial order was furthermore the hygienic aspect. Wolfensberger demanded the 'improvement of the sanitary conditions' of several of the company's shops because he believed that such measures would consequently increase the general output.[71]

Hence, the discourse on modern industrial architecture merged concerns about productivity and efficiency with matters of health and aesthetics: the 'rational factory' at once became the 'human factory' because around 1900 US experts started to acknowledge the 'human factor' as the single most important element in industrial production.[72] Similar debates took place one decade later in Germany, cumulating in a 'movement for "human rationalization"'.[73] Wolfensberger had been an early exponent of this cause. Architects and engineers concerned with factory construction shared the belief in the importance of the human factor of production.

Even the German labour movement supported rationalisation. Of course, in contrast to the employers, who mainly hoped for more profit, the unions had a different vision. They considered rationalisation as a means towards shorter working time, increased wages, and better working conditions.[74] However, neither the unions nor the workers' councils showed much interest in the improvement of working conditions and the work environment. For obvious reasons, their main interest was in wages and working hours.[75] Nevertheless, there is some evidence that factory workers themselves were dissatisfied with the work environment and longed for betterment. In 1930, the textile-workers' union published an edited volume containing 150 short reports of women workers on their everyday life. Numerous women complained about poor working conditions and miserable staff rooms, but the editors' afterword neglected those complaints. Instead, the textile-workers' union had two main requests to improve female workers' living conditions: higher wages and public housing.[76] Of course, these were the most important issues for improving workers' living conditions.

Lebensraum: the factory as a human habitat

While architects and engineers were articulating a social problem and sought a practical solution in factory construction, sociologists simultaneously dealt with similar issues. Starting in the early 1920s, the idea of creating joy in work through the design of the plant environment sparked a new discourse on the factory as a human habitat: the *Lebensraum*. As Woodruff Smith has shown, the term Lebensraum, which was first used by the geographer Friedrich Ratzel in the 1890s, has not only been popular in the widely known imperialist sense of Nazi politics. The term was very flexible, allowing it to be applied in different political and social settings.[77] In the following, I would like to point out that the Lebensraum concept had a wider pre-history before being used by the Nazis. Perhaps the most important starting point of the discourse on Lebensraum at the factory was the work of the social scientist and liberal politician Willy Hellpach. His study *Team Production* (Gruppenfabrikation) published in 1922 stated that the workplace's spatial order had not been acknowledged as a crucial part of the factory problem at that time.[78] According to

Hellpach, the factory problem itself had to be understood as a part of the human habitat problem (the *Lebensraumproblem*).[79] Hellpach pointed out that the problem of overflow within the factory buildings, which was regularly addressed in temporary debates, was not the only matter of concern. He argued that another key factor of modern industrial production had been of no lesser impact, but neglected so far: the individuals were isolated and there ceased to be any human connection between workers at the rationalised workplace. According to Hellpach, the issue was at the heart of the modern factory problem.[80]

I would like to argue that Hellpach's point of view, which soon found followers in industrial psychology and sociology, marked an important change: it was not possible to solve the problems of industrial production through discipline alone. Yet, until the start of the twentieth century, the main focus remained the disciplining of the workers as a proper means to increase output. Discipline was used to limit the workers' horseplay and chitchat during working time.[81] Hellpach realised that the combination of discipline at the workplace and the changes brought upon by modern work organisation were responsible for the elimination of any personal bonds between the worker, his work and the work environment.[82] However, as Hellpach made clear while giving a lecture at the German *Werkbund* meeting in 1924, he was not one of 'those romantics' longing for an idealised version of medieval handicraft. He accepted the modern division of labour, but looked for ways to humanise work. Meaning and moral had to be restored to the highly fragmented production process in order to reintegrate the worker's human side with his job.[83] According to Hellpach, who served as Minister of Education in the state of Baden 1922–5, the institution of vocational apprenticeship promised one way to partly solve this problem by educating young workers for the practicalities of the modern manufacturing process.[84]

Eugen Rosenstock's study, *The Industrial Workers' Lebensraum*, published in 1922 demonstrated why it was important to create a human habitat at the factories. Usually the worker gave merely his labour, but it was important to get all capacities incorporated in his whole personality[85]; that meant to catch the whole human being, not only the worker. According to Rosenstock, the first step towards this aim was to give the relevant things new names. The 'worker' should rather be called 'staff member' (*Betriebsangehöriger*); the 'work rules' imposed by the director should become a 'factory agreement' between employers and employees. Under these changed conditions, the working space would change and inevitably acquire the quality of a human habitat (*Lebensraum*). The new spatial order at the factories and the new interest in a beautification of workplaces seemingly had to go hand in hand with a new rhetoric to be effective.

Both Hellpach and Rosenstock tried to implement their ideas at the shop-floor level at the *Daimler Motors Corporation*. Rosenstock established Daimler's company magazine in 1919. This might have been an early effort to change workers' mentalities, which he later postulated. In 1919, first and foremost Daimler management worried about workers radicalised through war and revolution. Institutionalising a kind of corporate community seemed to be an adequate antidote to this menace.[86] Hellpach's co-author, Richard Lang, implemented teamwork (*Gruppenfabrikation*) at the Deutz plant, although without any long-term success.[87] Nevertheless, some managers acknowledged the sociological concept of *Lebensraum*. In his last book published in Nazi Germany before his emigration to the United States in 1934, industrial sociologist Götz Briefs argued that the factory ceased to be merely an objectified space, and started to regain the quality of a human habitat. According to Briefs, managers realised that absolute objectification of the workshop was opposed to the concept of the rational factory. Therefore, unpleasant workplaces had to be overcome.[88]

Moreover, there was a gender component to the *Lebensraum* discourse. In a study on juvenile female factory workers published in 1929, the sociologist Hildegard Jüngst emphatically postulated: 'Establish *Lebensraum* at the factory!' With a focus on women and girls, it became especially important to create a home-like feeling at work. This had to be achieved by redesigning the work environment and staff rooms, and moreover by providing the opportunity to exercise after the lunch-break.[89] Like Hellpach, Jüngst accepted the changes industrialisation caused, but sought ways to conserve or reactivate the pre-industrial atmosphere in a modern environment: 'Human habitat and working place are separated and it is not possible to reunite them.' Nevertheless, it was of utmost importance to partly transfer a homely atmosphere to the work place, and therefore to finally 'establish *Lebensraum* at the factory'. According to Jüngst, this aim could be reached by providing at least a recreation room, 'a room at the plant where the girl feels at home, a plain, but tasteful canteen that is designed in a way to appeals to the girl's fantasy'.[90]

In the same year Elisabeth Krüger published an article in the German *Journal for Industrial Hygiene and Accident Prevention* about the challenges a female workforce posed to factory inspectors. Krüger asked for an innovation in factory construction: factory inspectors trained as physicians should take part in construction planning because according to Krüger, hygiene started with the drawing of the footprint. Once again, the concepts of efficiency and 'humanisation' merged. A hygienic plant improved the workers' 'atmosphere of living' as well as their 'productive efficiency', therefore increasing the company's profit potential.[91] Dealing with the problem of female labour, both Jüngst and Krüger focused on humanisation to improve the factory as a human habitat. Hence, the gender issue gave a strong impetus to this discourse because women appeared to be in special need of an appropriate environment. The imperative of special care for women workers also played in a catalytic role in the 'Beauty of Labour' programme.

The 'Beauty of Labour'

Architectural historian Mark Peach characterises the devotion of Weimar architects to working-condition issues as a 'pre-Nazi form of "Strength through Joy".'[92] Maybe Peach overrates the similarities, but nonetheless he points to an important line of continuity. After the Nazi seizure of power the 'Beauty of Labour' programme (Schönheit der Arbeit) gave a specific answer to the problems of modern industrial production. The Beauty of Labour Bureau (Amt 'Schönheit der Arbeit'), led by Albert Speer, was founded in late 1933 as a branch of the Nazi leisure organisation Strength through Joy (Kraft durch Freude), itself part of the German Labour Front (Deutsche Arbeitsfront), the Nazi organisation that replaced the free trade unions of the Weimar Republic.[93] The bureau became widely known for its campaigns to improve plant facilities, such as 'Good Light – good Work', 'Clean People in Clean Plants' or 'Good Ventilation at the Workplace'.[94]

In a broad sense, Beauty of Labour followed the debates about aesthetic and healthy factories, which started even before the First World War. Still, the main idea was to combine aesthetics with factory-welfare work to finally increase productivity. However, the Nazis tried to clarify that Beauty of Labour had nothing to do with 'soppy aestheticism', but rather demonstrated the strong and fierce National Socialistic worldview.[95] In contrast to the Weimar Republic, the Third Reich tended to replace former welfare policies with the idea of joy in work.[96] The Nazis did not abolish social policy, but mostly considered it an agent for increased productivity.[97] Consequently, the popular propaganda book *Beauty of Labour: the Paperback Volume* (Das Taschenbuch 'Schönheit der Arbeit') quoted a slogan by the leader of the German Labour Front, Robert Ley as a preface: 'The best social policy is also the best economic policy.'[98] In general, Beauty of Labour followed the path of the Weimar movement for human rationalisation. As Mary Nolan has shown, this movement's most prominent protagonist, the German Institute for Technical Labour Training (Deutsches Institut für technische Arbeitsschulung – Dinta), aimed at creating a new type of worker 'committed to achievement and productivity'.[99] Hence, Dinta could easily be integrated into the Nazi state: in 1933 it joined the Labour Front and became the Office for Vocational Education and Firm Leadership.[100]

The fusion of humanising and rationalising work still appeared as a solution to the industrial problem; however, the Nazis did not care about actual social change for the workers, as reformers like the architect Gropius or the social scientist Hellpach had done. Rather, the Nazis regarded beautiful workplaces and joy in work as sufficient. Wiltraut Best's 1935 doctoral dissertation on *The Overcoming of Rationalisation's Disadvantages by the Bureau of Beauty of Labour* (Die Überwindung nachteiliger Folgen der Rationalisierung durch das Amt Schönheit der Arbeit) gives an account on this concept. Implicitly Best relied on Rosenstock's idea concerning the *Lebensraum* problem: healthy and beautiful workplaces, according to Best, could offer the opportunity to motivate workers to participate in their daily tasks with their souls. Therefore, work would become their purpose in life again.[101] In the end, Beauty of Labour would be in favour of increased profitability, and additionally, solve the social question.[102]

Hence, Beauty of Labour did not contain many original ideas. Mainly, the Nazis interpreted the existing debates in their own political sense and rejected any traditions of democratic social policy. Even the actors remained partly the same. Some members of the German Werkbund, before 1933 opponents to the Nazi movement, worked at the Beauty of Labour Bureau after the Nazi seizure of power. For example, Wilhelm Lotz, former editor of the Werkbund journal *Form*, became co-editor of the journal *Beauty of Labour*.[103] Sometimes, the *Lebensraum* debate was explicitly resumed: a series on German model plants stressed that factories were more than mere production facilities. Furthermore, they had to become a 'human habitat' (*Lebensraum*) to be in accordance with the idea of 'Beauty of Labour'.[104]

In a Foucauldian perspective, Beauty of Labour oscillated between discipline and government. For instance, under the label of 'Beauty of Labour', the clockmakers Thiel demanded strict hygiene. The workers had to wear white cloaks so that stains could be spotted. Furthermore, they initiated a contest for the most beautiful workplace. Of course, the management tended toward peer pressure: the honoured workstation served as a good example urging the co-workers to catch up. Moreover, management wanted the workers to internalise the hygiene standard of taking the opportunity to beautify their workplace in an individual fashion.[105] Therefore, it was no longer sufficient to discipline the workers regarding this concern anymore; instead they had to become useful individuals, as Foucault has described it. To a certain extent they were given the freedom to act subjectively because this gave them opportunity to harness their whole human potential, not only their labour. In the process, flowers at the workplace played a special role. According to managers' belief, giving workers the permission to decorate their workstation with flowers allowed them to create a closer bond with their work: workers cared for the workplace and wanted to beautify it, thereby providing a good example to their colleagues.[106]

The Labour Front's position concerning women's work was ambivalent. Within the first months after their seizure of power, the Nazis intended to displace women from the labour market, for instance by campaigning against double-income couples. However, the industry was not willing to abandon female workers.[107] Moreover, after achieving full employment, Germany – heading for war – needed to increase its workforce for the build-up of arms. In this context, Beauty of Labour was perceived as an important factor for integrating women into the industrial workforce. In 1939 the economist Angela Meister published a study on the female German industrial worker. Meister suggested that the layout of the industrial workplace in Nazi Germany was especially adapted for women. Allegedly in contrast to the terrible working conditions in early Manchester capitalism – where workshops had been 'humble, dark, wet and dirty holes', workspaces in Nazi Germany had been 'large, bright, clean and airy'.[108] This and the possibility of giving their workplace a personal touch had been a means to take care of 'psychological and aesthetic female needs'.[109] Industrial psychologist Martha Moers, who often disagreed with Meister, shared this opinion. According to Moers, Beauty of Labour was of utmost importance for women: 'bright, airy, clean and beautiful rooms' related to natural female affection because women depended to a high degree on the environment.[110]

The Beauty of Labour Bureau itself was also interested in questions of gender. Its propaganda brochures presented images of plants adapted for women: 'Flowers near the window, bright working rooms and order at the workplace. Therefore, women like to work here, too.'[111] To be awarded the designation 'model plant' by the German Labour Front, a company had, among other things, to take 'care of women'.[112] The establishment of day-care facilities for children was one of these measures also labelled as 'Beauty of Labour'.[113] I do not want to suggest that Beauty of Labour was all about gender. Instead, gender was one important factor in stressing the importance of beautifying factories.

However, historians agree that the bureau's actual measures were far exceeded by the amount of its propaganda. While Tim Mason has classified the bureau as 'a total failure',[114] Matthias Frese claims that even in Beauty of Labour's heyday in the first years after the Nazi seizure of power, there was scarcely more money spent for beautifying causes at the company level than during the Weimar period.[115] However, according to Frese, workers' reactions oscillated between indifference and gradual acceptance.[116] Alf Lüdtke even rates Beauty of Labour as a propagandistic success because workers gained the perception that the government was interested in their everyday problems for the first time.[117] Having said that, the debate on Beauty of Labour was part and parcel of the racist Nazi utopia where forced labourers had to do unqualified work while skilled male German workers had 'joy in work'.[118] During the war, the Nazis brutally tried to realise this utopia. Historical research on the Labour Front has demonstrated that the Second World War did not mean a watershed in Nazi social politics. Starting in 1933, social policy had always been a means to the end of armament.[119] The Labour Front even gained more influence: only after the start of the war did it take part in all-important decisions on working conditions.[120] Nonetheless, funding prompted some problems. The Beauty of Labour Bureau had to accept budget cuts and therefore nearly stopped its activities in building projects.[121]

Nevertheless, the main discourse on Beauty of Labour had no Nazi origins. On the one hand, as has been shown above, liberal reformers sought ways to beautify factory work during the Weimar Republic and even before. On the other hand, the idea of work aesthetics was international. Even Nazi scientists of work pointed to British or US model plants.[122] Historian Shelley Baranowski pointed out that even early French utopians like

Saint-Simon and Fourier or the British Garden City movement must be accounted as prototypes of Beauty of Labour.[123]

Conclusion

Historian Anson Rabinbach characterises Beauty of Labour as an 'effort to legitimize state regulation and the intensive rationalisation of industry'.[124] Rather, I would like to argue that it went far beyond: Beauty of Labour was understood as an integral part of completing the endeavour of rationalisation. It closely resembled the efforts of early twentieth-century architects and engineers who were determined to beautify the factory and to create *Lebensraum* inside. It was intended to make way for 'human rationalisation'.[125] Focus was on humanising the workplace, respecting the worker as subject of production and creating conditions to increase the workers' joy in work and will to work.

To some degree, Jeffrey Herf's conception of the Nazis as 'reactionary modernists' helps to explain certain similarities between the modern school of architecture and the Beauty of Labour Bureau. Both 'celebrated beauty and form as ethic ideals in themselves'.[126] Of course, major differences remained; this shared belief is only one of six themes Herf lists to define reactionary modernism. The respective political aims of the liberal reformers in the 1910s/20s on the one hand and the Nazis on the other totally differed. However, the problem they faced was the same: how to create an atmosphere of trust, which then should become the basis for efficiently utilising workers' abilities. External discipline had to be more and more replenished by chosen workers' self-discipline and the encouragement of proactive behaviour, although this does not imply that external discipline was neglected; 'beautiful' factories had to provide effective means for worker surveillance as well.

In this regard, labour history benefits from investigating architecture. At an early stage while scientific management was preoccupied with the concept of efficiency, architects like Gropius combined beautification with efficiency. Simultaneously, they chose a solution to the shortcomings inherent in scientific management, which did not implicate social change. They were concerned with 'human relations' *avant la lettre* providing a cultural solution to a social problem. The encounter of architects and engineers produced the two-fold result of changing both fields: industrial architecture and engineering. Industrial architects emulated the engineering ideal incorporating the notion of functionality and efficiency in their concepts. In turn, architecture gave impetus to industrial engineering expanding its focus: the human factor of production was no longer reduced to a problem of mechanised production. Rather, engineers and managers started to conceive of workers as human resources to be cultivated for the firm's benefit.[127]

Accordingly, architectural discourse on the work environment set the stage for the convergence of humanisation and rationalisation. Architects introduced atmospheres as an important factor of productivity. Therefore, spatial arrangements in regard to the workers' psyche were the first step towards a holistic approach to the industrial workplace as a human habitat. Afterwards, personnel departments complemented the architects' efforts by new approaches of leadership, which were concerned with means to increase working morale. The gender question thereby played an important role in two ways: first, several workplace designers and experts of work were considerate of female labour. They believed women workers needed a special habitat in order to work at a factory. Moreover, this engagement with the problems of the work environment fostered considerations regarding the whole labour force, men and women.

In contrast to the metaphor of the 'human motor', which Rabinbach described as being crucial for the establishment of the new science of work in the late nineteenth century,[128] the 'human resources' of the twentieth century were gendered. Whereas the early scientists of work reduced workers to a 'human motor' and were obsessed with the problem of fatigue, seeking ways to eliminate 'the stubborn resistance to perpetual work',[129] the architects, engineers and sociologists this article introduced stressed the humanity of the 'human factor'. Nevertheless, their main interest was the same: productivity. Their objects – the workers – were either male or female, and showed certain reactions to their environment as well as to the respective style of leadership. This marks an important shift: it was no longer regarded sufficient to overcome certain restrictions of the human motor. Rather, a human habitat had to be created at the factory to make the most out of the human resource.

Acknowledgements

I am grateful to Anna Rothfuss, Mikael Hård, Michael Löffelsender and Noyan Dinçkal who gave incisive reading to this article. My research project on 'Gender, Technology, and Workplace Engineering: Rationalising Factories in Germany, 1900–1970' was supported by the DFG (German Research Foundation).

Notes

1. Poelzig, "Architektonische Entwicklung des Fabrikbaus," 37–8.
2. Ibid., 34–5. On Poelzig's influence on industrial architecture see Bolz' doctoral dissertation, Bolz, "Hans Poelzig."
3. Cf. Poelzig, "Architektonische Entwicklung des Fabrikbaus," 34–5.
4. Poelzig, "Neuzeitliche Fabrikbau," 102.
5. Cf. Guillén, *Taylorized Beauty*. David Kuchenbuch investigated to which extent architects concerned with housing projects saw themselves as "social engineers": cf. Kuchenbuch, *Geordnete Gemeinschaft*.
6. Kuchenbuch, *Geordnete Gemeinschaft*.
7. Kaufman, *Managing the Human Factor*, 287.
8. Ibid., 301.
9. Biggs, *Rational Factory*, 2. Lindy Biggs gives a brilliant investigation of how the rational factory became the master machine of production in the United States.
10. Ibid., 75.
11. Hilger, "Welfare Policy," 51–2.
12. Hall and Soskice, "An Introduction to Varieties of Capitalism," 24.
13. See Michel Foucault's concept of governmentality: Foucault, *Security, Territory, Population*, 87–114.
14. However, this new strategy did not imply a neglect of accompanying factory discipline, cf. Uhl, "Giving Scientific Management."
15. Foucault, "Beginning of the Hermeneutics of the Self," 203.
16. Coopey and McKinlay, "Power without Knowledge," 120.
17. Foucault, "Incorporation of the Hospital," 147.
18. Ibid., 148.
19. Foucault, *Discipline and Punish*, 143–4.
20. Foucault, "Incorporation of the Hospital," 146–7.
21. Foucault, *Discipline and Punish*, 144–5.
22. Ibid., 148.
23. Löw, "Constitution of Space," 44.
24. Löw, *Raumsoziologie*, 272.
25. Löw, "Constitution of Space," 44.
26. Ibid., 46.
27. Bradley, *The Works*, 81.
28. Anderson, *Industrial Engineering*, 93.
29. Ibid., 94.
30. Cf. Pai, *Portfolio and the Diagram*, 87.

31. Cf. Bradley, *The Works*, 24.
32. Cf. Pai, *Portfolio and the Diagram*, 83.
33. Cf. Ibid., 84.
34. Cf. Guillén, *Taylorized Beauty*, 9.
35. Peach, "Wohnfords," 61.
36. Cf. Mislin, *Industriearchitektur*, 218; Ostermann, *Fabrikbau*, 39.
37. Franz, *Fabrikbauten*.
38. Cf. Mislin, *Industriearchitektur*, 174; Biggs, *Rational Factory*.
39. Cf. Loader and Skinner, "Management," 101.
40. Cf. Skinner, *Form and Fancy*, 28.
41. Cf. Ibid., 25.
42. Cf. Loader and Skinner, "Management," 85.
43. Kahn, *Design and Construction*, 63.
44. Ibid., 62.
45. Ibid., 54.
46. Ibid., 62 3.
47. Loader and Skinner, "Management," 85.
48. Guillén, *Taylorized Beauty*, 4, 21.
49. Jefferies, *Politics and Culture*, 185.
50. Jaeggi, *Fagus*, 6. Hildebrand argues that Fagus is to be seen as an "offspring of the American work", especially the Ford Highland Park plant, Hildebrand, "Beautiful Factories," 20. Art historian Reyner Banham points out that the Faguswerk owes a lot of its image as a milestone of the Modern Movement to "carefully chosen propaganda pictures" and Gropius' friendship to some important historians, Banham, *Theory and Design*, 79. Banham, *Concrete Atlantis*, 194.
51. Gropius, "Sind beim Bau," 6.
52. Ibid.(translation by Banham, *Concrete Atlantis*, 201).
53. Gropius, "Monumentale Kunst und Industriebau," 31 (translation by Banham, *Concrete Atlantis*, 198).
54. Gropius, "MonumentaleKunst und Industriebau," 31.
55. Guillén, *Taylorized Beauty*, 21.
56. Schwartz, *Werkbund*, 55–6.
57. Banham, *Concrete Atlantis*, 200.
58. Utz, Moderne *Fabrikanlagen*, 314.
59. Mannheimer, "Fabrikenkunst," 289. Such concepts of industrial architecture were similar to those ideas of "social engineering" housing projects were based on, which historian Kuchenbuch described. According to Kuchenbuch, "social engineers" tried to "humanise" modernity, cf. Kuchenbuch, *Geordnete Gesellschaft*, 25.
60. Cf. Bruce, "Human Relations Historiography," 177–8.
61. Cf. Anderson, *Peter Behrens*.
62. Jaeggi, *Fagus*, 6. According to Jaeggi, the "Fagus factory can be interpreted as an architectural revision of the Turbine factory," Ibid., 43.
63. Mannesmann Archive, file M 30.011. Booklet: *Zur Erinnerungan die Einweihung des Verwaltungsgebäudes der Mannesmannröhren-Werke in Düsseldorf, 10. Dezember 1912*, Berlin, no date, 70.
64. For the Swiss context, Jakob Tanner shows efforts to give the factory canteen an atmosphere of an "emotional filling station," Tanner, *Fabrikmahlzeit*, 369.
65. Hauer, *Fabrikbau nach neuzeitlichen Grundsätzen*, 7–8, 51, 54.
66. Cf. Lewis, "Redesigning the Workplace," 667–8, 684.
67. Cf. Schmitz, *Fabrikbauten*, 126
68. Cf. Deutscher Textilarbeiterverband, *Mein Arbeitstag, mein Wochenende*, 141.
69. Cf. Nolan, *Visions of Modernity*, 17–29.
70. Cf. Fritz Wolfensberger, "Memorandum to the Deutz management board," 19 July 1910. Rheinisch-WestfälischesWirtschaftsarchiv, file 107-VII/2-IX, 85.
71. Cf. Ibid., 87.
72. For the new general interest in the human factor in industry and the development of modern personnel management as a forerunner of human resource management, see Kaufman, *Managing the Human Factor*.

73. Nolan, *Visions of Modernity*, 180.
74. Cf. Winkler, *Schein der Normalität*, 467.
75. Cf. Plumpe, *Betriebliche Mitbestimmung*, 412–3.
76. Cf. Deutscher Textilarbeiterverband, *Mein Arbeitstag*, 221–3.
77. Smith, "Friedrich Ratzel," 52, 68.
78. Lang and Hellpach, *Gruppenfabrikation*, 20–1.
79. Ibid., 8.
80. Ibid., 22, 26.
81. Alf Lüdtke has shown that it was nearly impossible to totally stop expressions of worker's self-reliance (*Eigen-Sinn*) by shop discipline, cf. Lüdtke, "Organizational Order or Eigensinn."
82. Lang and Hellpach, *Gruppenfabrikation*, 26.
83. Hellpach, "Erziehung der Arbeit," 55.
84. Ibid., 61–2.
85. Rosenstock, *Werkstattaussiedlung*, 7–8.
86. Luks, *Betrieb*, 13–14.
87. Cf. Hinrichs, *Um die Seele*, 172, 187.
88. Briefs, *Betriebsführung*, 3, 25.
89. Jüngst, *Jugendliche Fabrikarbeiterin*, 112–3.
90. Ibid., 112.
91. Krüger, "Frauenarbeit und Gewerbeaufsicht," 17–8.
92. Peach, "Wohnfords," 61.
93. See Baranowski, *Strength Through Joy*.
94. On the history of Beauty of Labour, see Rabinbach, "*Aesthetics of Production*; Friemert, *Produktionsästhetikim Faschismus*.
95. Reichsamt Schönheit der Arbeit, *Schönheit der Arbeit*, no page.
96. Cf. Von Hübbenet, *Taschenbuch "Schönheit der Arbeit*," 232. On the history of the debate on "joy in work", see Campbell, *Joy in Work*.
97. Geyer, "Soziale Sicherheit," 393.
98. von Hübbenet, *Taschenbuch "Schönheit der Arbeit,"* 7.
99. Nolan, *Visions of Modernity*, 179.
100. Ibid., 234.
101. Best, *Überwindung*, 19.
102. Ibid., 18–19, 56.
103. Cf. Campbell, *German Werkbund*, 276.
104. Cf. Piorkowski, *Zellwollerzeugung*, 77.
105. Cf. Bauer, *Taschen- und Armbanduhren-Erzeugung*, 50, 52.
106. Cf. Ibid., 52.
107. Siegel, "Rationalisierung statt Klassenkampf," 119.
108. Meister, *Deutsche Industriearbeiterin*, 57–8.
109. Ibid., 59.
110. Moers, *Fraueneinsatz*, 30–1.
111. Lotz, *Schönheit der Arbeit*, 23.
112. Siegel, "Rationalisierung statt Klassenkampf," 119.
113. Burger, *Arbeitsplätze im Gau Köln-Aachen*, 40; cf. Rabinbach, "Aesthetics of Production," 196.
114. Mason, *Social Policy*, 164.
115. Cf. Frese, *Betriebspolitikim "Dritten Reich,"* 345.
116. Cf. Ibid., 349–50.
117. Cf. Lüdtke, *Eigen-Sinn*, 333.
118. Cf. Hachtmann, *Industriearbeit*, 84.
119. Linne, "Die innere Front," 16.
120. Siegel, "Welfare Capitalism," 95.
121. Rabinbach, "The Aesthetics of Production," 214.
122. Cf. Geck, *Soziale Betriebsführung*, 97; Geck, "Schönheit der Arbeit."
123. Cf. Baranowski, *Strength Through Joy*, 79.
124. Rabinbach, "Aesthetics of Production," 211.
125. See Nolan, *Visions of Modernity*, 179–80 and 203.

126. Herf, *Reactionary Modernists*.
127. For the history of early Human Resource Management, see Kaufman, *Managing the Human Factor*.
128. Cf. Rabinbach, *Human Motor*, 6.
129. Ibid., 2.

Bibliography

Anderson, Arthur G. *Industrial Engineering and Factory Management*. New York: Ronald Press, 1928.

Anderson, Stanford. *Peter Behrens and a New Architecture for the Twentieth Century*. Cambridge, MA: MIT Press, 2000.

Banham, Reyner. *Theory and Design in the First Machine Age*. 2nd ed. Cambridge, MA: MIT Press, 1982.

Banham, Reyner. *A concrete Atlantis. U.S. Industrial Building and European Modern Architecture, 1900–1925*. Cambridge, Mass: MIT Press, 1989.

Baranowski, Shelley. *Strength through Joy. Consumerism and Mass Tourism in the Third Reich*. Cambridge: Cambridge University Press, 2004.

Bauer, Friedrich. *Taschen- und Armbanduhren-Erzeugung und Sondermaschinen für den Werkzeugbau der Gebrüder Thiel GmbH Ruhla Thüringen*. Leipzig: Arnd, 1938.

Best, Wiltraut. *Die Überwindung nachteiliger Folgen der Rationalisierung durch das Amt Schönheit der Arbeit*. Großenhain: Weigel, 1935.

Biggs, Lindy. *The Rational Factory. Architecture, Technology, and Work in America's Age of Mass Production*. Baltimore: Johns Hopkins University Press, 1996.

Bolz, Hans-Stefan. "Hans Poelzig und der 'neuzeitliche Fabrikbau'. Industriebauten 1906–1934." PhD diss, University of Bonn, 2008. http://hss.ulb.uni-bonn.de/diss_online

Bradley, Betsy Hunter. *The Works. The Industrial Architecture of the United States*. New York: Oxford University Press, 1999.

Briefs, Götz. *Betriebsführung und Betriebsleben in der Industrie. Zur Soziologie und Sozialpsychologie des modernen Großbetriebs in der Industrie*. Stuttgart: Enke, 1934.

Bruce, Kyle. "Henry S. Dennion, Elton Mayo, and Human Relations Historiography." *Management & Organizational History* 1 (2006): 177–99.

Burger, Willy. *Arbeitsplätze im Gau Köln-Aachen. Einst und jetzt*. Cologne: Aufbruch, 1938.

Campbell, Joan. *The German Werkbund. The Politics of Reform in the Applied Arts*. Princeton: Princeton University Press, 1978.

Campbell, Joan. *Joy in Work, German Work. The National Debate, 1800–1945*. Princeton: Princeton University Press, 1989.

Coopey, Richard, and Alan McKinlay. "Power without Knowledge? Foucault and Fordism, c. 1900–50." *Labour History* 51 (2010): 107–25.

Deutscher Textilarbeiterverband, ed. *Mein Arbeitstag, mein Wochenende. 150 Berichte von Textilarbeiterinnen*. Berlin: Textilpraxis, 1930.

Foucault, Michel. *Discipline and Punish. The Birth of the Prison*. New York: Pantheon Books, 1977.

Foucault, Michel. "About the Beginning of the Hermeneutics of the Self. Two Lectures at Dartmouth." *Political Theory* 21 (1993): 198–227.

Foucault, Michel. *The Incorporation of the Hospital into Modern Technology Space, Knowledge and Power. Foucault and Geography*, edited by Jeremy W. Crampton and Stuart Elden, 141–51. Aldershot: Ashgate, 2007.

Foucault, Michel. *Security, Territory, Population. Lectures at the Collège de France 1977–1978*. Basingstoke and New York: Palgrave Macmillan, 2009.

Franz, Wilhelm. *Fabrikbauten*. Leipzig: J.M. Gebhardt, 1923.

Frese, Matthias. *Betriebspolitik im "Dritten Reich". Deutsche Arbeitsfront, Unternehmer und Staatsbürokratie in der westdeutschen Großindustrie*. Paderborn: Schöningh, 1991.

Friemert, Chup. *Produktionsästhetik im Faschismus. Das Amt "Schönheit der Arbeit" von 1933 bis 1939*. Munich: Damnitz, 1980.

Geck, Ludwig Heinrich Adolph. "Schönheit der Arbeit in England und Schottland." *SozialeArbeit* 44 (1935): 73–8.

Geck, Ludwig Heinrich Adolph. *Soziale Betriebsführung*. Munich: C.H. Beck, 1938.

Geyer, Martin H. "Soziale Sicherheit und wirtschaftlicher Fortschritt. Überlegungen zum Verhältnis von Arbeitsideologie und Sozialpolitik im 'Dritten Reich'." *Geschichte und Gesellschaft* 15 (1989): 382–406.

Gropius, Walter. "Sind beim Bau von Industriegebäuden künstlerische Gesichtspunkte mit praktischen und wirtschaftlichen vereinbar?" *Der Industriebau* 3 (1912): 5–6.

Gropius, Walter. "Monumentale Kunst und Industriebau. Vortrag gehalten am 10.4.1911 im Folkwang-Museum Hagen." In *Walter Gropius. Ausgewählte Schriften, Vol. 3*, edited by Hartmut Probst and Christian Schädlich, Berlin: Verlag für Bauwesen, 1988.

Guillén, Mauro. *The Taylorized Beauty of the Mechanical. Scientific Management and the Rise of Modernist Architecture*. Princeton: Princeton University Press, 2009 First published 2006.

Hachtmann, Rüdiger. *Industriearbeit im "Dritten Reich". Untersuchungen zu den Lohn- und Arbeitsbedingungen in Deutschland 1933–1945*. Göttingen: Vandenhoeck & Ruprecht, 1989.

Hall, Peter A., and David Soskice. "An Introduction to Varieties of Capitalism." In *Varieties of Capitalism. The Institutional Foundations of Comparative Advantage*, edited by Peter A. Hall and David Soskice, 1–68. New York: Oxford University Press, 2001.

Hauer, Robert. *Der Fabrikbau nach neuzeitlichen Grundsätzen*. Leipzig: Uhlands Technische Bibliothek, 1922.

Hellpach, Willy. "Die Erziehung der Arbeit." In *Das Problem der Industriearbeit. Zwei Vorträge gehalten auf der Sommertagung des Deutschen Werkbundes*, edited by Deutscher Werkbund, 39–70. Berlin: Julius Springer, 1925.

Herf, Jeffrey. *Reactionary Modernism. Technology, Culture, and Politics in Weimar and the Third Reich*. Cambridge: Cambridge University Press, 2003.

Hildebrand, Grant. "Beautiful Factories." In *Albert Kahn. Inspiration for the Modern*, edited by Brian Carter, 17–27. Ann Arbor: University of Michigan Museum of Art, 2001.

Hilger, Susanne. "Welfare Policy in German Big Business after the First World War: Vereinigte Stahlwerke AG, 1926–33." *Business History* 40 (1998): 50–76.

Hinrichs, Peter. *Um die Seele des Arbeiters. Arbeitspsychologie, Industrie- und Betriebssoziologie in Deutschland*. Cologne: Pahl-Rugenstein, 1981.

Jaeggi, Annemarie. *Fagus. Industrial Culture from Werkbund to Bauhaus*. New York: Princeton Architectural Press, 2000.

Jefferies, Matthew. *Politics and Culture in Wilhelmine Germany. The Case of Industrial Architecture*. Oxford: Berg, 1995.

Jüngst, Hildegard. *Die jugendliche Fabrikarbeiterin. Ein Beitrag zur Industriepädagogik*. Paderborn: Schöningh, 1929.

Kahn, Moritz. *The Design and Construction of Industrial Buildings*. London: Technical Journals, 1917.

Kaufman, Bruce E. *Managing the Human Factor. The Early Years of Human Resource Management in American Industry*. Ithaca: Cornell University Press, 2008.

Krüger, Elisabeth. "Frauenarbeit und Gewerbeaufsicht." *Zentralblatt für Gewerbehygiene und Unfallverhütung* special edition no. 13 (1929): 8–19.

Kuchenbuch, David. *Geordnete Gemeinschaft. Architekten als Sozialingenieure – Deutschland und Schweden im 20. Jahrhundert*. Bielefeld: transcript, 2010.

Lang, Richard, and Willy Hellpach. *Gruppenfabrikation*. Berlin: Julius Springer, 1922.

Lewis, Robert. "Redesigning the Workplace. The North American Factory in the Interwar Period." *Technology and Culture* 42 (2001): 665–84.

Linne, Karsten. "Die 'innere Front'." *Zeitschrift für Geschichtswissenschaft* 43 (1995): 15–26.

Loader, Robert, and Joan S. Skinner. "Management, Construction and Architecture. The Development of the Model Factory." *Construction History* 7 (1991): 83–103.

Lotz, Wilhelm. *Schönheit der Arbeit in Deutschland.* Berlin: Deutscher Verlag, 1940.

Löw, Martina. *Raumsoziologie.* Frankfurt: Suhrkamp, 2001.

Löw, Martina. "The Constitution of Space. The Structuration of Spaces Through the Simultaneity of Effect and Perception." *European Journal of Social Theory* 11 (2008): 25–49.

Lüdtke, Alf. "Organizational Order or Eigensinn? Workers' Privacy and Workers' Politics in Imperial Germany." In *Rites of power. Symbolism, ritual, and politics since the Middle Ages,* edited by Sean Wilentz, 303–33. Philadelphia: University of Pennsylvania Press, 1985.

Lüdtke, Alf. *Eigen-Sinn, Fabrikalltag, Arbeitererfahrungen und Politik vom Kaiserreich bis in den Faschismus.* Hamburg: Ergebnisse Verlag, 1993.

Luks, Timo. *Der Betrieb als Ort der Moderne. Zur Geschichte von Industriearbeit, Ordnungsdenken und Social Engineering im 20. Jahrhundert.* Bielefeld: transcript, 2010.

Mannheimer, Franz. "Fabrikenkunst." *Die Hilfe. Wochenschrift für Politik, Literatur und Kunst* 16 (1910): 289–90.

Mason, Timothy W. *Policy in the Third Reich. The Working Class and the "National Community".* Providence: Berg, 1993.

Meister, Angela. *Die deutsche Industriearbeiterin. Ein Beitrag zum Problem der Frauenerwerbsarbeit.* Jena: Fischer, 1939.

Mislin, Miron. *Industriearchitektur in Berlin 1840–1910.* Tübingen and Berlin: Ernst Wachsmuth, 2002.

Moers, Martha. *Der Fraueneinsatz in der Industrie. Eine psychologische Untersuchung.* Berlin: Duncker & Humblot, 1943.

Nolan, Mary. *Visions of Modernity. American Business and the Modernization of Germany.* New York: Oxford University Press, 1994.

Ostermann, Ingrid. *Fabrikbau und Moderne. Konzeptionen und Gestaltungsformen – dargestellt an Beispielen aus Deutschland und den Niederlanden des Interbellums des 20. Jahrhunderts.* Delft: IHAAU, 2006.

Pai, Hyungmin. *The Portfolio and the Diagram. Architecture, Discourse, and Modernity in America.* Cambridge, MA: MIT Press, 2002.

Peach, Mark. "Wohnfords, or German Modern Architecture and the Appeal of Americanism." *Utopian Studies* 8 (1997): 48–65.

Piorkowski, Curt. *Die Zellwollerzeugung der Thüringischen Zellwolle Aktiengesellschaft Schwarza/ Saale.* Leipzig: Verlag Übersee-Post, 1938.

Plumpe, Werner. *Betriebliche Mitbestimmung in der Weimarer Republik. Fallstudienzum Ruhrbergbau und zur Chemischen Industrie.* Munich: Oldenbourg, 1999.

Poelzig, Hans. "Der neuzeitliche Fabrikbau." *Der Industriebau* 2 (1911): 100–5.

Poelzig, Hans. "Die architektonische Entwicklung des Fabrikbaus." *Zentralblatt für Gewerbehygiene und Unfallverhütung* special edition no. 18 (1930): 31–40.

Rabinbach, Anson. "The Aesthetics of Production in the Third Reich." In *International Fascisms. New Thoughts and Approaches,* edited by George L. Mosse, 189–222. London: Sage, 1979.

Rabinbach, Anson. *The Human Motor. Energy, Fatigue, and the Origins of Modernity.* Berkeley: University of California Press, 1992.

Reichsamt Schönheit der Arbeit, ed. *Schönheit der Arbeit. Sozialismus der Tat.* Berlin: Verlag der Deutschen Arbeitsfront, 1936.

Rosenstock, Eugen. *Werkstattaussiedlung. Untersuchungen über den Lebensraum des Industriearbeiters.* Berlin: Julius Springer, 1922.

Schmitz, Britta. *Fabrikbauten in Remscheid, Solingen und Wuppertal. Eine Studie zur Entwicklung des Gebäudetyps.* Berlin: Progris, 1991.

Schwartz, Frederick J. *The Werkbund. Design Theory and Mass Culture before the First World War.* New Haven: Yale University Press, 1996.

Siegel, Tilla. "Rationalisierung statt Klassenkampf. Zur Rolle der Deutschen Arbeitsfront in der nationalsozialistischen Ordnung der Arbeit." In *Herrschaftsalltag im Dritten Reich. Studien und Texte,* edited by Ralph Angermund, Hans Mommsen, and Susanne Willems, 97–150. Düsseldorf: Schwann, 1988.

Siegel, Tilla. "Welfare Capitalism, Nazi Style. A Re-evalution of the German Labor Front." *International Journal of Political Economy* 18 (1988): 82–116.

Skinner, Joan S. *Form and Fancy. Factories and Factory Buildings by Wallis, Gilbert & Partners, 1916–1939.* Liverpool: Liverpool University Press, 1997.

Smith, Woodruff D. "Friedrich Ratzel and the Origins of Lebensraum." *German Studies Review* 3 (1980): 51–68.

Tanner, Jakob. *Fabrikmahlzeit. Ernährungswissenschaft, Industriearbeit und Volksernährung in der Schweiz 1890–1950*. Zurich: Chronos, 1999.

Uhl, Karsten. "Giving Scientific Management a 'Human' Face: The Engine Factory Deutz and a 'German' Path to Efficiency, 1910–1945." *Labor History* 52 (2011): 511–32.

Utz, Ludwig. *Moderne Fabrikanlagen*. Leipzig: Uhlands Technischer Verlag, 1907.

Von Hübbenet, Anatol. *Das Taschenbuch "Schönheit der Arbeit"*. Berlin: Verlag der Deutschen Arbeitsfront, 1938.

Winkler, Heinrich August. *Der Schein der Normalität. Arbeiter und Arbeiterbewegung in der Weimarer Republik 1924 bis 1930*. 2nd ed. Berlin and Boon: Dietz Nachfolger, 1988.

Index

For Product Safety Concerns and Information please contact our EU
representative GPSR@taylorandfrancis.com Taylor & Francis Verlag GmbH,
Kaufingerstraße 24, 80331 München, Germany

Printed and bound by CPI Group (UK) Ltd, Croydon, CR0 4YY
01/05/2025
01858414-0014